THE CAMBRIDGE COMPA
ELIZABETH GASKF

KU-406-755

In the past few decades, Elizabeth Gaskell has become a figure of growing importance in the field of Victorian literary studies. She produced work of great variety and scope in the course of a highly successful writing career that lasted for about twenty years from the mid-1840s to her unexpected death in 1865. The essays in this *Companion* draw on recent advances in biographical and bibliographical studies of Gaskell and cover the range of her impressive and varied output as a writer of novels, biography, short stories, and letters. The volume, which features well-known scholars in the field of Gaskell studies, focuses throughout on her narrative versatility and her literary responses to the social, cultural, and intellectual transformations of her time. This *Companion* will be invaluable for students and scholars of Victorian literature, and includes a chronology and guide to further reading.

JILL L. MATUS is Professor of English at the University of Toronto.

A complete list of books in the series is at the back of this book.

THE CAMBRIDGE
COMPANION TO
ELIZABETH GASKELL

EDITED BY
JILL L. MATUS

CAMBRIDGE
UNIVERSITY PRESS

CAMBRIDGE UNIVERSITY PRESS
Cambridge, New York, Melbourne, Madrid, Cape Town, Singapore, Sao Paulo, Delhi

Cambridge University Press
The Edinburgh Building, Cambridge CB2 8RU, UK

Published in the United States of America by Cambridge University Press, New York

www.cambridge.org
Information on this title: www.cambridge.org/9780521609265

First published 2007
Reprinted 2009

Printed in the United Kingdom at the University Press, Cambridge

A catalogue record for this publication is available from the British Library

Library of Congress Cataloging in Publication Data

The Cambridge companion to Elizabeth Gaskell / [edited by] Jill L. Matus.
p. cm. – (Cambridge companions to literature)
Includes bibliographical references and index.
ISBN 978-0-521-84676-9 (hardback)
ISBN 978-0-521-60926-5 (paperback)
1. Gaskell, Elizabeth Cleghorn, 1810–1865 – Criticism and interpretation – Handbooks,
manuals, etc. 2. Women and literature – England – History – 19th century. 1. Matus, Jill L.,
11. Title. 111. Series.
PR4711.c34 2007
823′.8–dc22

CONTENTS

NOTES ON CONTRIBUTORS

JOHN A. V. CHAPPLE is Emeritus Professor of English, University of Hull, and President of the Gaskell Society. He is the author of *Elizabeth Gaskell: A Portrait in Letters* (1980) and *Elizabeth Gaskell: The Early Years* (1997), and an editor of her letters (1966 and 2000). He has also published on John Dryden and Samuel Johnson, on the relations between history and literature 1880–1920, and on science and literature in the nineteenth century.

DEIRDRE D'ALBERTIS teaches English literature at Bard College, New York. She is the author of *Dissembling Fictions: Elizabeth Gaskell and the Victorian Social Text* (1997) and a volume editor (*Ruth*) for the new Pickering & Chatto edition of Gaskell's complete works. Her current research is on the idea of work in the writing of Hannah Cullwick, Eliza Lynn Linton, Margaret Oliphant, and Margaret Harkness.

SHIRLEY FOSTER is former Reader in English and American Literature at the University of Sheffield. Her research interests include nineteenth-century British fiction, especially by women; nineteenth-century American fiction; and travel writing, with particular reference to Anglo-American exchanges. She has published in all these areas; her most recent publication is *Elizabeth Gaskell: A Literary Life* (2002).

NANCY HENRY is Associate Professor of English at the State University of New York at Binghamton. She is the author of *George Eliot and the British Empire* and the editor of several Victorian texts, including *Ruth* and *Sylvia's Lovers*. She is currently writing a book about Victorian women and finance.

SUSAN HAMILTON is Associate Professor of English at the University of Alberta. She writes on Victorian feminism and Victorian antivivisectionism, and is most recently editor of the three-volume *Animal Welfare and Anti-Vivisection 1870–1910: Nineteenth-Century Women's Mission* (Routledge, 2004). Her book *Frances Power Cobbe and Victorian Feminism* is forthcoming with Palgrave Macmillan.

LINDA K. HUGHES is Addie Levy Professor of Literature at Texas Christian University in Fort Worth. She is co-author of *Victorian Publishing and Mrs. Gaskell's Work* (1999) and editor of volume IV, of the new Pickering & Chatto edition of Gaskell's complete works. Her biography *Graham R.: Rosamund Marriott Watson, Woman of Letters* appeared in 2005.

AUDREY JAFFE is the author of *Vanishing Points: Dickens, Narrative, and the Subject of Omniscience* (1991) and *Scenes of Sympathy: Identity and Representation in Victorian Fiction* (2000). She currently lives and works in Berkeley, California.

JILL L. MATUS, Professor of English at the University of Toronto, is the author of *Unstable Bodies: Victorian Representations of Sexuality and Maternity* (1995), *Toni Morrison* (1998), and many essays on Victorian authors such as Charles Dickens, George Eliot and the Brontës. She is currently working on a book on theories of the unconscious, emotion, and memory in Victorian fiction and psychology.

LINDA H. PETERSON is Niel Gray Jr. Professor of English at Yale University. She is the author of *Victorian Autobiography* (1986) and *Traditions of Victorian Women's Autobiography: The Poetics and Politics of Life Writing* (1999), and the editor of Elizabeth Gaskell's *Life of Charlotte Brontë* (2006) and Harriet Martineau's *Autobiography* (2006). She is currently at work on a study of nineteenth-century women of letters.

NATALIE ROSE wrote her doctoral dissertation at the University of Toronto on constructions of English masculinity in the mid-Victorian novel. Her research focuses on issues of bounded selfhood and hybridity. She has published essays on Charles Dickens and George Eliot.

MARION SHAW is an Emeritus Professor of English at Loughborough University. She has published on Victorian literature, particularly on Alfred, Lord Tennyson, and is the editor of *Sylvia's Lovers* for Pickering & Chatto (2006). She has also written *The Clear Steam* (1999), a biography of the Yorkshire novelist and reformer Winifred Holtby.

PATSY STONEMAN is an Emeritus Reader in English at the University of Hull. Her publications include *Elizabeth Gaskell* (shortly to be reissued in an augmented edition by Manchester University Press), *Brontë Transformations*, and other works on the Brontës. She has just completed an edition of eight Victorian stage versions of *Jane Eyre*.

NANCY S. WEYANT is Associate Professor/coordinator of reference services at Bloomsburg University in Bloomsburg, Pennsylvania. Her publications on Gaskell include *Elizabeth Gaskell: An Annotated Bibliography of English Language Sources 1976–1991* and *Elizabeth Gaskell: An Annotated Guide to English Language Sources, 1992–2001*. She posts annual bibliographic supplements on her webpage (http:\\library.bloomu.edu\weyant\).

ACKNOWLEDGMENTS

I would like first to thank the contributors to this volume, not only for their expertise but also for the considerable time and effort each has devoted to this project. It has been a pleasure to work with such well-organized and responsive colleagues. We are all indebted to the able and painstaking work of my research assistant at the University of Toronto, Natalie Rose, who brought our references into conformity and helped to prepare the "Guide to further reading." My thanks go also to our editors Linda Bree and Maartje Scheltens at Cambridge University Press. Linda's wisdom and professional experience in producing many excellent *Companions* have made her an invaluable resource at every stage of the project, not least its conception. I like to think of the beginning of this project as being our conversation entitled "What about Gaskell?" at the launch in Haworth of *The Cambridge Companion to the Brontës*. I would like, too, to thank the outside readers of the proposal, many of whose savvy suggestions have been incorporated. My gratitude goes finally to the friends and colleagues who read sections of the volume and offered advice and support along the way.

CHRONOLOGY

NANCY S. WEYANT

1797   December 1 William Stevenson (WS) marries Elizabeth Holland (EHS), daughter of Samuel and Mary Holland. The Holland family plays a significant role in the intellectual, cultural and social development of Elizabeth Cleghorn Stevenson (ECS).

1798   November 27 John Stevenson (JS), first child of WS and EHS, born.

1806   Founding of the Portico Library, a subscription library for which William Gaskell (WG) served as chairman from 1849 until his death in 1884. The Portico was an important resource for both WG and Elizabeth Gaskell.

1810   September 29 ECS born.

1811   October 29 (?) EHS dies, her sister Hannah Lumb (née Holland) in attendance.
         November 1 or 2 Marianne Lumb writes to her mother Hannah, proposing that ECS live with them.
         November (early) ECS taken to live with the Lumbs in Knutsford.

1812   March 31 Marianne Lumb dies at the age of twenty-one.

1814   April 11 WS remarries (Catherine Thompson).

1815   Corn Laws passed. A tariff on imported grains drives up prices with devastating consequences for the poor.

1816   March 19 JS writes the first extant letter to his sister before sailing for Bombay. Vividly describes activities in Berwick and his excitement about going to sea. Reports he will be sending her two books. Over the next eight years, JS is an attentive older brother, corresponding about his experiences in India, pleading for her to write with news from home, and generally encouraging his younger sister in her studies.

1821   September ECS begins formal studies at the Miss Byerlys' school at Barford House, later relocated to Avonbank, Stratford-upon Avon.

1824   Founding of the Mechanics' Institute in Manchester. WG would serve on its board and teach English literature at the Institute.
June 21 Repeal of the Combination Acts of 1799–1800 that outlawed trade unions and labour strikes.

1825   JS writes to ECS and Aunt Lumb, proposing that ECS keep a diary to provide her with material for letters to him.
June 15 Date on ECS's first "music book" in which she transcribes music, lyrics, and dance notes.

1826   June ECS leaves Avonbank, ending her formal education.
Winter ECS in London with WS and her stepmother. WS tutors her in Latin, Italian, and French.

1827   July 2 WS writes the only extant letter to his daughter in Knutsford, forwarding a letter from JS. Encourages her to write to her brother and to continue her studies, especially Latin and Italian. Suggests she keep a journal if she holidays with the Holland family in Wales.

1828   July 30 JS writes to ECS, complimenting her on her "rescue story" of Captain Barton, noting "it would almost make the foundation of a novel." This tale has not survived.
August 3 WG appointed assistant minister to John Gooch Robberds at Cross Street Chapel in Manchester.
August 15 JS writes to ECS, suggesting he may stay in India. Informs her that Smith, Elder rejected his manuscript and that his hopes of being an author are ended.
Autumn (?) JS is either lost at sea or disappears in India. Although ECS scarcely refers to her brother in her letters, the lost and/or returning male character motif is repeated in her fiction.

1829   March 20 WS has a stroke, dying two days later. ECS is with him when he dies.
Late autumn ECS visits William Turner and daughter Ann in Newcastle upon Tyne. While there, participates in the active social, cultural, and intellectual world of her relatives. Possible modeling of portrait bust of ECS by David Dunbar. Turner, a Unitarian minister who had married into the Holland family, is considered in part the source for the character of Thurston Benson in *Ruth*.

1830   Autumn ECS travels to Edinburgh with Ann Turner, staying through the early months of 1831.

1831   Ebenezer Elliott publishes *Corn Law Rhymes*, verses condemning the exorbitant tax on bread.
January 3 Thomas Ashton murdered, an event incorporated in Elizabeth Stone's *William Lanshawe, The Cotton Lord* and fictionalized in the death of Harry Carson in *Mary Barton* (*MB*).

June Earliest extant letter from ECS, written to Anne Burnett. ECS/ECG (Elizabeth Cleghorn Gaskell) was a prolific correspondent. In spite of large-scale destruction of her letters by her daughters, almost 950 survived to be published.

June 18, August 31, October 20 Series of three lengthy letters written by ECS to Harriet Carr that display the pattern of wit, humor, chatty gossip, and observational skills which characterize her correspondence. They include numerous references to authors she read, her awareness of current events, her early interest in popular music and her sensitivity to acquaintances in distress.

September–October ECS travels between Knutsford, Liverpool, Sandlebridge, and Manchester with Ann Turner, staying with Reverend and Mrs. Robberds in Manchester, where it is assumed that ECS meets WG.

1832 Cholera epidemic spreads dramatically.
Sir James Kay-Shuttleworth publishes *The Moral and Physical Condition of the Working Classes Employed in the Cotton Manufacture in Manchester.*
March Engagement of ECS to WG.
April Publication of Thomas Carlyle's essay on biography, quoted in *Mary Barton.*
June 4 First Reform Bill passed.
June ECS in Edinburgh, where W. J. Thompson paints her portrait in miniature.
August 30 Marriage of ECS (henceforward ECG) to WG at St. John's parish church, Knutsford. After a month of travel in Wales, the couple take up residence in Manchester.

1833 July ECG gives birth to a stillborn daughter (later eulogized in her sonnet "On Visiting the Grave of My Stillborn Little Girl").

1834 September 12 Marianne Gaskell born.

1835 March 10 ECG starts *My Diary*, documenting her daughter's development, her views of herself and WG as parents, the value she assigns to her role as a mother, her faith in God, and (later) the dynamics between Marianne and her sister, Margaret (Meta) Emily.

1836 ECG and WG co-author "Sketches among the Poor," published in *Blackwood's Magazine* (January 1837).

1837 February 5 Margaret (Meta) Emily Gaskell born.
March 8 Aunt Lumb has a stroke. ECG and daughters go to Knutsford to be with her. She dies on May 1.
June 20 Death of King William IV. Accession of Queen Victoria.

1838   May ECG first writes to William and Mary Howitt, lovingly describing the town in which she lived as a child.
September 23 Formation of Anti-Corn Law League.
November 15 WG's sister Elizabeth marries Charles Holland, further cementing a life-long close relationship between ECG and Elizabeth Gaskell Holland.

1839   WG anonymously publishes *Temperance Rhymes*.
June 14 Petition of the National Convention presented by working men's delegates to the House of Commons (portrayed in *MB*). Rejected one month later.
December 28 Carlyle's *Chartism* published.

1840   Economic recession results in high unemployment, debilitating poverty, and suffering in Manchester.
(Early) Publication of William Howitt's *Visits to Remarkable Places* containing a contribution on Clopton Hall by "a lady" (ECG).
April Publication of Howitt's *The Rural Life of England* with ECG's "Notes on Cheshire Customs."

1841   July ECG and WG travel to Belgium and Germany. Germany had a strong influence on ECG's short-story writing in both theme and structure. Makes important connections.

1842   May 2 Chartists present second petition to the House of Commons. Hearing denied.
August Labour unrest in Manchester, including strikes, mob gatherings and riots.
October 7 Florence (Flossy) Elizabeth Gaskell born.
December (late) Winkworth sisters meet the Gaskells.

1843   July Month-long Gaskell family holiday at Gibraltar Farm, Silverdale, Morecambe Bay. Includes visits with the Winkworths.

1844   October 23 William (Willie) Gaskell born.

1845   Friedrich Engels's *The Condition of the Working Class in England* published.
July–August Family holidays in Wales.
August 10 Willie Gaskell dies from scarlet fever.
November ECG begins writing *MB* with WG's encouragement.

1846   June 25 Repeal of the Corn Laws.
September 3 Julia Bradford Gaskell born.

1847   June 5, 12, 19 Publication dates of each "era" of "Libbie Marsh's Three Eras" in *Howitt's Journal* (*HJ*). ECG uses pseudonym Cotton Mather Mills, Esq.

September 4 "The Sexton's Hero" appears in *HJ* under same pseudonym.

October 16 Charlotte Brontë's (CB) *Jane Eyre* published.

1848   January 1 "Christmas Storms and Sunshine" published in *HJ*. Last use of pseudonym.

March–July Letters from ECG to Edward Chapman regarding *MB*, including ECG's wish to have the novel published anonymously.

October 18 *Mary Barton: A Tale of Manchester Life* published.

October 21–November 30 Positive reviews of *MB*, praising it for its truthful portrayal of the working class, its handling of dialect, its adherence to truths, and its sympathetic tone. Extensive speculation regarding author's identity.

November 11 ECG replies to a letter from Carlyle praising *MB*, acknowledging she is the author.

December 1 First American edition of *MB* published.

1849   April–May ECG "lionized" in London, meeting and socializing with Edward Chapman, her publisher, and a broad range of prominent people – Eliza (Tottie) Fox, the Dickenses, the Howitts, the Carlyles, etc.

July "The Last Generation in England" appears in *Sartain's Union Magazine of Literature and Art*.

July–December "Hand and Heart" published in four parts in *The Sunday School Penny Magazine*.

November (late) ECG asks Tottie Fox for help in identifying the author of *Jane Eyre* and *Shirley*.

1850   January 8 ECG solicits Charles Dickens's advice about assisting Pasley (a seduced girl whom she has been visiting in prison). Draws on Pasley for title character of *Ruth*.

February "Martha Preston" published in *Sartain's Union Magazine* (later reworked and published as "Half a Lifetime Ago" in *Household Words* [*HW*]).

February–March ECG and Dickens negotiate revisions to "Lizzie Leigh," the first part of which is published March 27 in the first issue of *HW*. Parts 2 and 3 follow on April 6 and April 13.

June Gaskell family moves to Plymouth Grove in Manchester. ECG meets Charles Eliot Norton, a Boston Unitarian. They later become close friends and regular correspondents.

August 29 ECG invited by Lady Kay-Shuttleworth to Briery Close to meet CB. Stays for three days.

September (late) ECG returns to Manchester after an absence of some four months with only intermittent returns home.

November–December "The Well of Pen-Morfa," "The Moorland Cottage," and "The Heart of John Middleton" published in parts in

HW, the last without revisions despite Dickens's attempts to persuade ECG to change the ending.

1851   February, March, April "Mr. Harrison's Confessions" published anonymously in three installments in *The Ladies' Companion and Monthly Magazine*.
February 6 George Richmond paints ECG's portrait.
June 7 "Disappearances" published in *HW*.
November ECG completes first volume of *Ruth* and writes first installment of *Cranford*.
December 13 "Our Society at Cranford" appears in *HW*. Subsequent installments appear January, 1852, and May, 1853.

1852   January–March Series of compassionate initiatives on behalf of an elderly impoverished Knutsford author and the ailing prison reformer Thomas Wright.
January–April "Bessy's Troubles at Home" published in *Sunday School Penny Magazine*.
October ECG writes "The Old Nurse's Story" for *HW*. Dickens, unhappy with ending, pushes for revisions, finally publishing it in the Christmas issue as submitted.

1853   January *Ruth* published by Chapman and Hall (first American edition follows one month later). Responses from first reviewers and friends generally favorable but some, offended by its heroine's "fallen" state, are highly critical. Controversy continues into late summer.
January 22 "Cumberland Sheep-Shearers" published in *HW*.
April 21–28 CB stays at Plymouth Grove.
May 13–23 ECG and WG visit Paris, spending significant time with Madame Mohl. Visit inspires several short stories ECG writes for *HW*.
May 26–mid-June ECG in London. Numerous dinner parties with influential individuals.
June 17 *Cranford* published in book form. First American edition published August 5.
September 19–23 ECG visits Brontës in Haworth.
October 27 F. D. Maurice's dismissal from King's College, Cambridge, for views on doctrine of eternal punishment triggers national debate that continues through year's end with ECG an active participant.
November–December "Morton Hall," "Traits and Stories of the Huguenots," "My French Master," and "The Squire's Story" published in *HW*. ECG seriously ill with influenza.

1854   ECG begins writing *North and South* (*NS*).
Mid-January ECG travels to Paris with Marianne.
March 27 Crimean War begins, lasting until February 28, 1856.
Mid-late April Series of letters from CB regarding her engagement to

Arthur Bell Nicholls and a May visit to Plymouth Grove.

April 1–August 12 Dickens's *Hard Times* published in *HW*.

May 1–4 CB at Plymouth Grove. Expresses reservations about impending marriage.

May 3 Fifth edition of *MB* issued with WG's lectures on the Lancashire dialect.

May 20 "Company Manners" published in *HW*.

June 1–13 ECG in London, staying with Emily (Winkworth) and William Shaen. Numerous dinner parties, visits to theater, and cultural events.

June 29 CB marries Arthur Bell Nicholls.

June–August Letters document conflicts between ECG and Dickens regarding *NS*: its title, her failure to make recommended cuts and revisions, length of sections, etc.

August (late) ECG meets Florence Nightingale.

August (late) – September 13 ECG in Isle of Man, focusing on her writing.

September 2 First installment of *NS* published in *HW*. Serialized version concludes in January, 1855.

September–December Reports from Crimea record military failures, significant casualties, and rampant disease.

Mid-to-late October ECG stays at Lea Hurst, the Nightingales' summer home, focusing on writing *NS*.

1855   ECG writes a series of letters addressing her dissatisfaction with the pace of *NS* and its rushed ending.

February 14 Harper's publishes two-volume version of *NS*.

Mid-February–April 4 ECG in Paris with Meta. Letters record social and cultural activities and document breadth of reading.

March 26 Revised and expanded *NS* published by Chapman and Hall.

March 31 CB dies.

April 3 ECG returns to England, devastated by her friend's death.

April-May Mixed reviews of *NS*. ECG begins gathering information about CB with hope of writing a memoir.

June 16 Patrick Brontë asks ECG to write a brief life of CB.

June–December ECG purposefully gathers information to write a truthful life of CB. Contacts John Greenwood, Ellen Nussey, Mary Taylor, makes multiple visits to Haworth, and travels to Glasgow with Marianne.

August 25 "An Accursed Race" appears in *HW*.

September *Lizzie Leigh and Other Tales* published by Chapman and Hall.

October 6, 13, and 20 "Half a Lifetime Ago" serialized in *HW*.

1856	ECG intensely researching and writing *The Life of Charlotte Brontë* (*LCB*).
	December 13, 20, 27 "The Poor Clare" serialized in *HW*.
1857	February 7 ECG completes *LCB*.
	February 13 ECG leaves for the Continent, stopping in Paris on the way to Rome with Marianne, Meta, and Catherine Winkworth. In Rome they stay with Americans Emelyn and William Story.
	February 24 ECG reconnects with Charles Eliot Norton and Harriet Beecher Stowe. Whirlwind of dinners, parties, touring, and visiting.
	March 25 *LCB* published in two volumes by Smith, Elder.
	April Reviews praise *LCB*, which appears in a second edition mid-month.
	May (early) Threats of libel levied by Lady Scott. Unrevised edition published in America.
	May (late)–August Publisher recalls *LCB* and William Shaen drafts a statement on the absent ECG's behalf, retracting statements regarding Lady Scott. Positive reviews continue.
	May 28 ECG returns to Plymouth Grove.
	July–August ECG works on revisions of *LCB*, fielding expressions of praise and attacks.
	September (early) "Revised and Corrected" third edition of *LCB* published.
1858	January, June "The Doom of the Griffiths" and "An Incident at Niagara Falls" published in *Harper's New Monthly Magazine*.
	June 19–September 25 *My Lady Ludlow* serialized in *HW*.
	October 1–December 6 ECG travels to Heidelberg with Meta and Flossy.
	October 14 *My Lady Ludlow* published by Harper's; not published in England until July 6, 1861.
	November 27 "The Sin of a Father" (later revised and published as "Right at Last") published in *HW*.
	December 7 "The Manchester Marriage" published in *HW*.
1859	February 1 *Adam Bede* published. ECG laudatory, recommending it to many.
	March 19 *Round the Sofa and Other Tales* published. In addition to previously published stories, it includes "The Half Brothers"; second edition published May 7.
	October 8, 15, 22 Serialization of *Lois the Witch* in *All the Year Round* (*ATYR*).
	November 2–12 ECG in Whitby with Meta and Julia, researching setting for *Sylvia's Lovers* (*SL*).
	December 30 "The Ghost in the Garden Room" (later "The Crooked Branch") published in *ATYR*.

1860 February "Curious If True" published in *Cornhill Magazine*.
April 8–January 1863 ECG writing *SL* while continuing background historical research.
July–mid-August ECG in Heidelberg with Flossy and Julia. They make trips to Cologne and Mannheim.

1861 January 5, 12, 19 "The Grey Woman" serialized in *ATYR*.
March 14 *Lois the Witch and Other Tales* published by Tauchnitz.
May 17–June 3 ECG travels to France, visiting sites associated with Madame de Sévigné.

1863 January 24–March 21 "A Dark Night's Work" published in nine parts in *ATYR*. Book version issued in America April 14 with English edition published April 24.
February 20 *SL* published. Second edition follows on April 1.
March (early) ECG in Paris with Julia. When joined by Meta and Flossy, they visit Versailles and Avignon before continuing to Italy for ten weeks, going to Rome, Assisi, Florence, and Venice.
Mid-March Flossy engaged to Charles Crompton.
March 17 First American edition of *SL* published with special dedication to Charles Eliot Norton and his wife.
August 29 ECG writes to Mrs. Sarah Gould Shaw, mother of Colonel Robert Gould Shaw who was killed leading a black regiment in American Civil War. Later writes a memorializing obituary for *Macmillan's Magazine*.
September 8 Flossy marries Charles Crompton.
November–February 1864 *Cousin Phillis* serialized in *Cornhill Magazine*.

1864 April–June "French Life" serialized in *Fraser's Magazine*.
June 11 Book version of *Cousin Phillis* published by Harper's.
August Monthly serialization of *Wives and Daughters* (*WD*) begins in *Cornhill Magazine*. ECG travels to Switzerland with daughters.
Autumn ECG ill for three months.
December ECG tells George Smith she is setting aside money to purchase a house.

1865 March 10 ECG travels to Paris, staying with Madame Mohl until April 20.
March 25–April 25 "A Column of Gossip from Paris" published in *Pall Mall Magazine* (*PMM*).
August 11–September 5 "A Parson's Holiday" serialized in five parts in *PMM*.
August 23 ECG tells George Smith about purchase of a house (The Lawn) and need for a tenant.

September ECG speculates on the relationship between her poor health and the drains in Plymouth Grove.

October ECG travels to Dieppe.

October 21 *The Grey Woman and Other Tales* published.

November 12 ECG dies suddenly and unexpectedly.

1866   February 2 First American edition of *WD* published with ending provided by Meta. First English edition follows ten days later.

ABBREVIATIONS

Except in the case of the following abbreviations, full details of works referred to are given after each chapter in the notes.

C   Elizabeth Gaskell, *Cranford* (1853), ed. Elizabeth Porges Watson, intro. and notes Charlotte Mitchell (Oxford: World's Classics, 1998).

CH   *Elizabeth Gaskell: The Critical Heritage*, ed. Angus Easson (London: Routledge, 1991).

CP   Elizabeth Gaskell, *Cousin Phillis* (1864). Elizabeth Gaskell, *Cranford/ Cousin Phillis*, ed., intro., and notes Peter Keating (Harmondsworth: Penguin, 1986).

FL   *Further Letters of Mrs Gaskell*, ed. John Chapple and Alan Shelston (Manchester: Manchester University Press, 2003).

L   *The Letters of Mrs Gaskell*, ed. J. A. V. Chapple and Arthur Pollard (1966) (Manchester: Mandolin, 1997).

LCB   Elizabeth Gaskell, *The Life of Charlotte Brontë* (1857), ed., intro., and notes Elizabeth Jay (Harmondsworth: Penguin, 1997).

MB   Elizabeth Gaskell, *Mary Barton* (1848), ed., intro., and notes Edgar Wright (Oxford: World's Classics, 1998).

MC   Elizabeth Gaskell, *The Moorland Cottage and Other Stories*, ed. Suzanne Lewis (Oxford: World's Classics, 1995).

NS   Elizabeth Gaskell, *North and South* (1855), ed. and notes Angus Easson, intro. Sally Shuttleworth (Oxford: World's Classics, 1998).

PV   *Private Voices: The Diaries of Elizabeth Gaskell and Sophia Holland*, ed. J. A. V. Chapple and Anita Wilson (Keele: Keele University Press, 1996).

R   Elizabeth Gaskell, *Ruth* (1853), ed., intro., and notes Alan Shelston (Oxford: World's Classics, 1998).

SL   Elizabeth Gaskell, *Sylvia's Lovers* (1863), ed., intro., and notes Andrew Sanders (Oxford: World's Classics, 1999).

W   *The Works of Mrs Gaskell*, 8 vols., ed. A. W. Ward (London: Smith, Elder, 1906) (Knutsford Edition).

WD   Elizabeth Gaskell, *Wives and Daughters* (1866), ed., intro., and notes Angus Easson (Oxford: World's Classics, 2000).

I

JILL L. MATUS

Introduction

In the past few decades, Elizabeth Gaskell has become a figure of growing importance in the field of Victorian literary studies. It is now widely recognized that she produced work of great variety and scope in the course of a highly successful writing career that lasted for about twenty years. A gifted storyteller, with a zest for anecdote, legend, and social observation, she was innovative and experimental in her use of genre, particularly in the realm of shorter fiction. She is significant also in the history of biography, where her controversial contribution, *The Life of Charlotte Brontë* (1857), was instrumental in changing conceptions of that genre. Nurtured by the rich social and religious context of nineteenth-century Unitarianism, Gaskell is typically open-minded in response to social transformation and change. This is evident in her early fiction in the treatment of the problems of working-class life and prostitution as well as in her last novel's magisterial representation of provincial life in the context of changing social structures and gender and class relations. Generations of readers have valued her for her geniality, sympathy, and imaginative expressiveness, but critics are increasingly coming to acknowledge that she is neither artless nor transparent. They are also granting growing recognition to her intellectuality, her familiarity with matters of scientific, economic, and theological inquiry, and her narrative sophistication.

Today, Gaskell commands a wide readership. She is not only a perennial on course lists within academic institutions, but also has a dedicated popular following of the kind that the Brontës and Jane Austen attract. Gaskell's canonical status today is a restoration rather than a continuity of her reputation in her own day. Indeed, Gaskell criticism has been very engaged with debating her rank among the great Victorian novelists, and finding reasons for the slump and subsequent rise in Gaskell's reputation during the twentieth century. In her lifetime she was a well-respected, even lionized author. Like so many women writers of the nineteenth century, however, she fell into relative obscurity after her death, though *Cranford* (1853) continued to sell extremely well and was reprinted on numerous occasions. When her name cropped up in Lord David Cecil's *Early Victorian Novelists* (1934), it was as a "minor novelist" with "slight talent." Damning her with faint and gendered praise, Cecil set the tone for subsequent critical opinion about "Mrs Gaskell," singling out what he saw as her quintessentially feminine characteristics: "She was all a woman was expected to be; gentle, domestic, tactful, unintellectual, prone to tears, easily shocked. So far from chafing at the limits imposed on her activities, she accepted them with serene satisfaction."[1] In accordance with this characterization of the author, *Cranford* was traditionally considered her finest work, appreciated for its simple charm, warm humanity, and nostalgia in representing provincial village life.

Gaskell criticism entered a new phase in the 1950s when Raymond Williams and other Marxist/sociological critics read with interest her novels of industrial life, *Mary Barton* (1848) and *North and South* (1855). But even here, though Gaskell garnered praise for focusing on the condition of the working classes, she drew criticism for offering personal rather than systemic solutions to class conflict. More recently, however, critics such as Patsy Stoneman have reread Gaskell's work in the light of feminist theory and revised the assessment of Gaskell as socially conservative, drawing attention rather to her critique of power relations and traditional family structures. Once patronized for her artlessness and the formal untidiness of her work – Elizabeth Barrett Browning thought *Mary Barton* a "slovenly" work – as well as her ideological confusion, she has emerged in the late twentieth century as an author of works richly ambivalent, transgressive, and formally sophisticated.

Gaskell responded energetically and perceptively to the many different realms of experience that came with her position as the mother of four daughters, the wife of a clergyman, and an active member of the Unitarian Manchester community. As a writer, she drew experimentally on a wide range of literary forms and antecedents. Central to this *Companion* is a recognition of Gaskell's diversity and complexity. The volume focuses throughout on her narrative versatility and aesthetics as a response to the social, cultural, and intellectual transformations of the period in which she wrote. The first chapter introduces the reader to Gaskell's life and her marvellously expressive letters. There follow chapters devoted to the individual texts, often paired in order to elicit comparative new readings. Subsequent essays on Gaskell and social transformation, on the family, domesticity and gender, and on the social and religious contexts of Unitarianism offer more general, wide-ranging explorations of key issues in her work. Other perennial and newer areas of interest in Gaskell scholarship (class relations, the psyche and the supernatural, print culture and the publishing market, consumer culture, empire and emigration), while not the subject of separate chapters, are taken up by many essays in the volume. A final chapter surveys past criticism of Gaskell and offers an assessment of Gaskell studies today.

The *Companion* begins with Nancy Weyant's concise chronology, packed with information about Gaskell's life, publications, and social context. A chapter on Gaskell's life and times follows, in which Deirdre d'Albertis teases out the often contradictory multiplicity of Gaskell's self-representation in her fiction and letters. Even in her own day, and even to herself, Gaskell was a combination of seemingly opposing attributes. Genial, spontaneous, sympathetic and charming, she nevertheless inspired strong, controversial response – readers burned copies of the scandalous *Ruth* (1853); libel suits threatened after the publication of *The Life of Charlotte Brontë*. Pointing to some of the darker, and perhaps less compromising, parts of her character, d'Albertis deepens the traditional emphasis on Gaskell's geniality and sweet womanliness. Her attention to Gaskell's "many mes" provides an apposite segue to the ensuing chapter on *Mary Barton* and *North and South* in which I explore Gaskell's interest in psychological interiority – the nature of emotions and the destabilizing effect on the self of overpowering emotional experience. As novels of industrial life, *Mary Barton* and *North and South* have often been paired in critical discussions of Gaskell's understanding of capitalist political economy. I extend critical treatments of their relationship as condition-of-England novels by exploring the internal correlatives of external social upheaval. The chapter focuses on the ambivalent representation in *Mary Barton* of powerful and passionate working-class feelings and the stunning jolts to consciousness in *North and South* occasioned by grief, shock, and psychic pain. Calling for a revaluation of the critical commonplace that Gaskell is melodramatic or sentimental in depicting emotion, I argue further that the way Gaskell represents consciousness and its alterations under turbulent social and personal conditions is not an inward turn away from social representation, but an insistence on the interrelationships between inner and outer worlds. Whereas in *Mary Barton* the representation of strong emotion is often revelatory of class stratification, in *North and South* overwhelming emotion is shown to undermine will and control, revealing at times an alarmingly unintegrated self. Rather than responding with denial or anxiety to disruptive emotional and psychic experience, Gaskell explores these moments as opportunities for self-reflection, confrontation, and renewed responsibility for action.

Unlike the two industrial novels, *Cranford* and *Ruth* have not traditionally been discussed in tandem, and at first sight appear to have little in common. The former is Gaskell's most popular novel, the latter her least. Gaskell was writing *Ruth* when *Cranford* was being serialized in *Household Words* (December 1851 to May 1853); it is therefore worth considering how two such different works issued from the same pen at roughly the same time. Resisting the critical tradition of regarding them as, on the one hand, a charming and nostalgic account of rural life, and, on the other, an uncomfortable social-problem novel, Audrey Jaffe argues that both texts are canonical oddities: *Cranford's* generic affiliations are more with the sketch or short story than with the novel and *Ruth* is less an example of mainstream Victorian realism than a moral tale, in which errant female sexuality is disciplined and inevitably punished. Jaffe examines their departures from conventional fictional forms in terms of their representation of female stereotypes – the spinster and the fallen woman, respectively – and their exploration of the idea of feminine community. In each case the text seeks to raise questions about the stereotypic figure on which it focuses and suggests how the male-dominated culture that produces it might be replaced by alternatives built around women or female sensibilities. Jaffe argues that in both novels an awareness of the constructed and indeed artificial nature of social identities sets them outside the realm of conventional realist fiction. Although neither text seems able to free its female characters from fantasy and self-delusion, each offers implicitly a radical critique of both realism and gender roles. Each suggests that an acknowledgment of what Jaffe calls "the artificiality of social structures, including literary ones" may be a way out of the prison-house of gender that constrains both these texts and the larger culture that produced them.

Gaskell's continued engagement with questions of gender, this time in relation to the woman writer and the need to reconcile the relations of literary and domestic life, informs her biography of Charlotte Brontë. Placing this work in the context of biographical writing at the mid-century, Linda Peterson emphasizes the extent of Gaskell's achievement by observing that at this time there were no biographies by women writers equal to the accomplishment of James Boswell's *Life of Samuel Johnson* (1791) or John Gibson Lockhart's *Memoirs of the Life of Sir Walter Scott, Bart.* (1837–8). There may have been fictional accounts of women artists and writers, such as those by Madame de Staël and Elizabeth Barrett Browning, as well as autobiographies, such as that of Harriet Martineau, but it was Gaskell herself, drawing together aspects of earlier forms of life-writing, who composed the most important nineteenth-century biography of a woman writer. Published in two volumes by Smith, Elder, this controversial foray into the genre of literary biography took Gaskell two years to write and drew on all her powers of research and narrative as she constructed her subject. While Gaskell insisted on speaking out on controversial issues and figures in her biography, she also suppressed information and evidence. In accordance with her representation of Brontë's modesty and propriety and in order to protect her subject from the charges of sensuality or grossness leveled at her novels, Gaskell omitted an account of Brontë's relationship with Monsieur Heger. There were other silences and evasions. The chapter shows how Gaskell shaped her account of Brontë in terms of the dichotomies she experienced in her own life and the patterns already established in her fiction. Brontë became the heroine of a life in which she was called on to play dual roles – the woman Charlotte Brontë and the artist Currer Bell. Peterson argues that Gaskell's engagement with the idea of "genius" suggests that she meant not only to claim this trait for women writers, but also to display her own genius in writing this biography. Patrick Brontë himself judged that it was just "what one Great Woman, should have written of Another, and . . . it ought to stand, and will stand, in the first rank of Biographies, till the end of time" (*CH*, 373–4).

As the opening of *The Life of Charlotte Brontë* shows, Gaskell set her subject in the context of Keighley as a town "in process of transformation" without which context it would not be possible to understand her friend correctly (*LCB*, I, 1:11). Attentive to the shaping power of the past and the nature of change, all Gaskell's work is informed by a strong sense of history. Sir Walter Scott's historical fiction, which flourished at the beginning of the century, gave impetus to the Victorian historical novel. William Makepeace Thackeray, Charles Dickens, Charles Reade and George Eliot were publishing important examples of the genre around the time that Gaskell wrote *Sylvia's Lovers* (1863). Marion Shaw further contextualizes Gaskell's historical fiction in relation to the new historiographies of the nineteenth century, which emphasized the details of ordinary life, and the Darwinian example of drawing from a mass of detail the laws that governed its organization. The chapter focuses on Gaskell's darkening vision of change and the struggle for existence in three historical fictions. Whereas historical process is celebrated in *My Lady Ludlow* (1858) set during the French Revolution, and society moves toward greater diversity, the ending of *Lois the Witch* (1859), which looks back to the time of the Salem witch trials of 1692, is equivocal. Gaskell imaginatively interpellates a fictional heroine into historical data, and critically explores the way a woman becomes the object of superstitious and hysterical persecution. Lois's death, as her lover insists, is unredeemable, despite the confession and plea for forgiveness of the persecutors. Set in 1793, during Britain's war with

France, *Sylvia's Lovers* is grounded in an actual case of a man hanged for incitement against the press gangs that captured and compelled young men into naval service. Around this incident Gaskell develops a story of how the lives of ordinary people are shaped by events beyond their control. As Shaw shows, she confronts the clash between private and public history. The novel's vision is arguably a dark one; its ultimate movement is toward resignation, and its consolations are beyond the reach of time-bound history.

Shirley Foster does not dispel the version of Gaskell as a writer pre-eminently known for her warm humanity and genial affections, but her analysis of the short narratives also reveals an author drawn to explore violent emotions and powerful psychological forces, the uncanny and otherworldly, the dark and more complex aspects of human relationship, and the jarring elements of human life. In addition to seven novels and four novellas, Gaskell published more than forty shorter works: stories, essays, autobiographical reminiscences and travelogues. Until recently, these have remained relatively obscure – some have not been reprinted since their original publication. This is perhaps because their generic variety and narrative versatility defy easy categorization. The chapter on Gaskell's short fiction and narrative considers her innovations in fictional form and the scope – ghost tale, Gothic, melodrama, mystery story, fantasy, nonfictional narrative – of her oeuvre of shorter works. To some extent the form of her short fiction was determined by the publishing venues it found. She began with pieces in *Howitt's Journal* and *Sartain's Union Magazine* (an American periodical) and by 1850 was contributing to the recently established *Household Words* edited by Dickens. Later she wrote for his *All the Year Round*, as well as for *Fraser's Magazine* and *The Ladies' Companion*, *Cornhill Magazine* and finally the *Pall Mall Gazette*. The short pieces suited her talents and temperament, allowing her to experiment with multiple narrators and multilayered narration. They also allowed her to blur the boundaries between fact and fiction. As Foster shows, they foreground the act of creativity itself by suggesting how the imagination can provoke the reinterpretation of history, as memory exhumes the past and recreates it in a new form.

Cousin Phillis (1864) and the all-but-completed novel *Wives and Daughters* (1866) are Gaskell's most mature work. Both engage closely with the question of change and social transformation. In the pastoral idyll of Hope Farm, the technology of the railroad and transatlantic travel interrupt a static, edenic life; that impossible and therefore disrupted stasis is mirrored in the way the daughter's denied sexuality disrupts the position of child in which Phillis's parents wish to keep her. Similarly, in *Wives and*

Daughters, which has also been praised as an excursion to a faraway world, a small community registers the impact of outside shifts in values and the relationship between parent and child is scrutinized in terms of the daughter's growing sexuality and socialization into femininity. Indeed, Linda K. Hughes argues that Gaskell's pastoralism in *Cousin Phillis* and *Wives and Daughters* is inseparable from her representation of modernity and its effects. What is further distinctive in her later fiction is that Gaskell no longer needs to rely on oppositions such as worker and owner, or north and south, but shows a growing sophistication in creating a social world whose complexity and subtle movements of change are more fully realized. Hughes sees *The Life of Charlotte Brontë* as a turning point in that Gaskell had to ground her subject's life and works in a world shaped and influenced by myriad factors. Her delineation of agricultural and historical change in *Cousin Phillis* and *Wives and Daughters* underscores her modernity and the importance of these late works as precedents for later fiction such as Eliot's *Middlemarch* and Thomas Hardy's Wessex novels.

Gaskell's representation of nineteenth-century gender roles, family dynamics, and domestic ideology is the subject of Patsy Stoneman's chapter. Stoneman sees in Gaskell's busy life a blurring of private and public roles: in addition to running a busy household, and caring for and teaching her daughters, there were countless duties that can be understood as social work (teaching in Sunday schools and helping out in times of economic privation) or cultural work (finding publishers for her work, and socializing with prominent cultural thinkers who visited Manchester). Gaskell's fiction shows the family as the place where people become social beings – all those who raise and care for children influence the foundations of the polity. Offering a correction to Marxist criticism that has seen her emphasis on relationship and sympathy as sentimental, Stoneman puts Gaskell in the context of the emerging liberal project of the nineteenth century and draws on the work of Susan Johnston to show that the much-vaunted distinction between public and private is illusory, since as Johnston has argued, "the household [is] the originary space in which the liberal self comes to be."[2] In the light of contemporary concerns about the formation of the liberal individual, Gaskell's novels appear not only canny and insightful but in the vanguard of Victorian concerns about social responsibility.

The coexistence of revolutionary and evolutionary change in Gaskell's writing has raised questions for readers about the nature and consistency of her political sympathies. Alongside an abiding fear of revolution so ingrained in nineteenth-century English society, we find a staunch commitment to liberal reform. Nancy Henry's chapter considers both the conservative and radical aspects of her fiction. Henry suggests that Gaskell was well aware of how fiction might play an important role in the transformations of a society. Not only could it memorialize the past, it could interpret the reasons for and effects of change and initiate further change by drawing attention to social problems and enlisting sympathy for those whose lives lay beyond the experience of most readers. The complexity of Gaskell's attitudes to change may be seen in the different ways in which in *Mary Barton* and "The Moorland Cottage" she views the question of emigration to the British colonies as a solution to poverty, disgrace, or discontent with society at home. Similarly, Gaskell aims to change society's attitudes toward "fallen women" at home in *Ruth*, and yet she encouraged emigration for an actual seduced woman as her only hope of salvation. Gaskell's ability to represent both sides of an argument, considered in conjunction with her complaint that she did not know where she stood on the political spectrum, has led readers and critics to suppose that she was inconsistent. But guided by Unitarian and humanitarian principles, Gaskell valued open-mindedness and the ability to explore a problem from different points of view. Her apparently inconsistent attitudes reveal, on closer inspection, a grasp of the complexities of any situation rather than confusion about the issues involved. So, for example, Gaskell is consistent in her distaste for violence, but she will at times, as Henry shows, praise military heroism when the cause seems just. The American Civil War and the Crimean War provoked Gaskell to think about violent change but she is perhaps even more attuned to slow, gradual social transformations evident in changing habits of mind and ways of living as England moved from an agrarian to a manufacturing economy. Gaskell engages repeatedly with the changes wrought by industrialization, with developments in trade relations and financial matters, scientific advancements and technology, all the while observing closely the shifting social and gender roles that such changes occasion.

John Chapple's chapter on Unitarianism places Gaskell solidly within a tradition of Unitarian belief, which took the search for truth as its greatest value, and was consistent with free-thinking Enlightenment principles. While Gaskell does not write about Unitarianism specifically in her fiction, Chapple argues that its values inform all her work. Her stories consistently explore social problems, promote compassion for suffering, and return to the importance of trust in divine providence. The chapter gives a nuanced account of the many ways in which Unitarianism shaped Gaskell's life: her father's background; her mother's Cheshire family and aunts at Knutsford; William Gaskell's varieties of Unitarianism; and the extensive range of Unitarian social connections in both England and America that had an influence on her. After the repeal of disqualifications in the late 1820s,

Unitarians could stand for parliament and began to occupy positions in government and thrive as doctors, lawyers, and businessmen as well as publishers and booksellers. Yet Gaskell was never, as Chapple points out, narrowly confined to Unitarian society and, especially after the publication of *Mary Barton*, developed many sustaining non-Unitarian connections. If Gaskell demonstrates a range of qualities attributable to Unitarian principles and beliefs, she departs, Chapple suggests, from "the enlightenment lucidity of her Unitarian inheritance" in her love of terror and the supernatural. But as Gaskell herself once declared, "I am not (*Unitarianly*) orthodox" (*L*, 784–5).

In the final chapter, "Gaskell then and now," Susan Hamilton explores the place of Gaskell within the academy and outside it, tracing the history of Gaskell's critical reputation and analyzing recent developments in criticism. The critical heritage is particularly relevant in assessing the effects of gender biases in criticism and the influence of recent theory on critical practice. Hamilton's analysis of the construction of many Gaskells in the history of Gaskell criticism helps to explain why at this juncture Gaskell seems to have been liberated from past constraining versions and to elicit more complex and comprehensive assessments of her achievements. Hamilton's explanation of Gaskell's importance in Lancashire tourism and her part in British heritage drama as a response to continuing class division and growing globalization prompts an awareness of how, in diverse ways, Gaskell is enlisted in contemporary negotiations of nationhood, as well as gender and class identities.

The critical emphasis throughout these essays on a more diverse and complex Gaskell than was previously acknowledged is in no small measure attributable to the valuable biographical and bibliographic work in Gaskell studies over the past few decades, which has provided the materials for further scholarship and interpretation. It is hoped that this *Companion*, the beneficiary of those studies, will in turn enhance readerly enjoyment and sharpen understanding of Gaskell's rich and varied range.

Notes

1 Lord David Cecil, *Early Victorian Novelists: Essays in Revaluation* (London: Constable, 1934), 198.
2 Susan Johnston, *Women and Domestic Experience in Victorian Political Fiction* (Westport, CT: Greenwood Press, 2001), 10.

2

DEIRDRE D'ALBERTIS

The life and letters of E. C. Gaskell

"I have always felt deeply annoyed at anyone, or any set of people who chose to consider that I had manifested the whole truth; I do not think it is possible to do this in any *one* work of fiction."
– Elizabeth Gaskell to Lady Kay-Shuttleworth (?1850)

Elizabeth Gaskell is a writer for whom generations of readers, critics, and scholars have felt an undisguised tenderness. "She will be herself remembered with affectionate regret by all who knew her," stated Richard Monckton Milnes shortly after her death, "as a most genial and delightful lady, who gave light and comfort to her home and pleasure to every society she entered" (*CH*, 506). An unfeigned capacity for spontaneity, for sympathy, and for pleasure endeared her to her contemporaries; these same qualities have also powerfully influenced the tenor of historical reception of her work. Yet, for such a well-loved figure, Gaskell has also managed to excite an inordinate amount of controversy. We know that "Mrs. Gaskell" offended, even outraged critics with not one but several politically engaged works of fiction. She was threatened with libel suits by individuals angered over her handling of sensitive material in her role as biographer. Parishioners of her husband's congregation at Manchester's Cross Street Chapel actually burnt their copies of *Ruth* (1853), protesting against the perceived immorality of Gaskell's sympathetic portrayal of a "fallen woman." And a small but determined band of reviewers took her to task at various points in her career for "the recklessness with which she has seized on a subject ... which she has so misrepresented," whether it be the condition of the working classes in Manchester or the causes of "the great social evil," prostitution (*CH*, 124).

"She could be stubborn, prejudiced, over-whelming, and erratic," admits Gaskell's biographer Jenny Uglow, "but people forgave her because she was so clearly *involved*."[1] This capacity for involvement could lead to strife. The careful reader of Gaskell's letters learns of private disagreements – fallings-out, indiscretions, hasty judgments – as well as unpredictable response to criticism. Mary Taylor, commenting on the fracas over *The Life of Charlotte Brontë* (1857), observed to Ellen Nussey that Mrs. Gaskell was a "hasty, impulsive sort of person, and the needful drawing back after her warmth gives her an inconsistent look."[2] Inscrutable at times even to herself, Gaskell lamented to her dear friend Tottie Fox: "I think I must be an improper woman without knowing it, I do so manage to shock people" (*L*, 223). An enduring puzzle for any reader of Elizabeth Gaskell is how to reconcile the notorious charm of the woman with some darker – and ultimately more uncompromising – part of her character. Who was "Mrs. Gaskell"? Could she be "an improper woman without knowing it"? Geraldine Jewsbury archly summed up this biographical problem: "I have a notion that if one could get at the 'Mary Barton' that is the kernel of Mrs. Gaskell one would like her, but I have never done so yet? Have you?"[3]

"[T]he kernel of Mrs. Gaskell"

That elusive "kernel" of Mrs. Gaskell – associated by Jewsbury with the industrial protest fiction of *Mary Barton* (1848), but by others with the pastoral masterpieces of *Cranford* (1853) and *Wives and Daughters* (1866) – is difficult to "get at" for several reasons. The first is temperamental: reading Gaskell, either in works intended for publication or in her private correspondence, is a tantalizing exercise in limited intimacy. The letters, composed in domestic *medias res*, are detailed, colloquial, apparently unreserved. Alongside the current of friendly disclosure, however, is frequent allusion to what cannot be given direct expression: "I ... want sorely to send off this letter to assure you my dearest Annie," she writes in 1859 to a close friend, "you have not been forgotten at this time which I know has been one of great trial to you. Don't suppose I *don't* know it because I don't speak of it my dearest" (*L*, 97). Gaskell's prose conveys great warmth and sympathy while at the same time preserving a note of reticence.

Would-be biographers are confronted with daunting gaps in the historical record: we know very little about what Gaskell thought of her childhood adoption into her mother's family, the disappearance of a beloved brother, John Stevenson, the death of her father, or her marriage in 1832 to the Reverend William Gaskell. As a chronicler of her own life, in other words, Gaskell practiced self-censorship to a surprising degree. Inevitably, her fictional representations of motherless daughters or of young men lost at sea – motifs that echo what we know of the outlines of her own experience – have been consulted, not without peril, in biographers' attempts to interpret such silences.

The second, entirely practical, reason we know so little about Gaskell's most private thoughts and relations is that she habitually requested that correspondents destroy her letters. Gaskell enjoined not only her children, but also her professional associates to discretion. She implored publisher George Smith in 1856, for instance, to protect her privacy, devising an elaborate system of coding that signaled which letters might be sent to the publisher's archive and which should be destroyed: "please when I write a letter beginning with a star like this on its front [drawing of a star], you may treasure up my letter; otherwise *please burn them, & don't* send them to the terrible warehouse where the 20000 letters a year are kept. It is like a nightmare to think of it" (*L*, 425).

In attempting to control access to her letters, Gaskell consciously resisted what she saw as "the impertinent custom" of biographical criticism, regarding it as "so objectionable & indelicate a practice" that she claimed to want nothing to do with it: "I do not see why the public have any more to do with me than to buy /or reject/ the wares I supply to them" (*L*, 761). "Her mother's wish that no biography should be written of her" certainly governed Meta Gaskell's decision late in life to burn most of the letters in her possession, perpetuating Elizabeth Gaskell's general refusal to cooperate with journalists eager for interviews during her lifetime.[4] "[E]*very* printed account of myself that I have seen have [*sic*] been laughably inaccurate," she objects to one supplicant; of another, she writes, "Mrs. Watts need not write to me – for I HATE photographs & moreover disapprove of biographies of *living* people. I always let people *invent* mine, & have often learnt some curious peculiars about myself from what they choose to say" (*L*, 762, 761).

The strong desire to "invent" a biographical subject's life was something Gaskell well understood. After her foray into literary biography with *The Life of Charlotte Brontë*, an exercise that impressed upon her the fragility of reputation, Gaskell became progressively more hostile to the prospect of anyone telling her life story. One of the greatest challenges she had faced as a novice biographer was how to present data objectively and to respect the testimony of interested sources, whether it be Brontë's fiercely possessive husband or her eccentric father, without ceding authorial privilege. Most famously, the issue of Brontë's suppressed passion for Constantin Heger, her former teacher and a married man, posed a formidable challenge to the biographer determined to represent her subject as eminently respectable. If she had been writing a novel, Gaskell would have been free to place whatever constructions she liked on Brontë's actions. But as a biographer – and an authorized biographer at that – she was held accountable by living participants in the history with which she was entrusted. Writing to Harriet Anderson in 1856, Gaskell chafed at both the responsibility and the restrictions of the form: "And I never *did* write a biography, and I don't exactly know how to set about it; you see you have to be accurate and keep to facts; a most difficult thing for a writer of fiction" (*FL*, 155). The blurring of fiction and fact is one of the remarkable, if inadvertent, achievements of *The Life of Charlotte Brontë*; getting at the truth of Brontë's life, as Gaskell saw it, required various choices either to emphasize or to downplay documents she found in her research. There was – and is – nothing straightforward about fashioning a narrative out of biographical "facts."

Given her troubles as a biographer and her anxieties over her own life being represented to the reading public, it may be surprising to learn that Gaskell eagerly collected biographical information about other novelists. Certainly she had no scruples when it came to speculating about the private lives of fellow writers. She reveled in literary gossip, for instance, longing to pierce the veil of anonymity assumed by George Eliot. In this she participated in her culture's shamefaced craving for *biographia literaria*. Literary circles were hardly immune to this desire (remember Geraldine Jewsbury's disappointment when Elizabeth Gaskell does not match her idea of "Mary Barton"). Charles Eliot Norton, upon meeting Gaskell, praised her as "full of generous and tender sympathies, of thoughtful kindness, of pleasant humor, or quick appreciation, of utmost simplicity and truthfulness," attributes he explicitly associated *first* with her fiction.[5]

This desire to "know" an author was evident in a fascination with the traces of the writing process itself. Gaskell actively participated in the popular pastime of collecting autographs, one obvious material relic of the writer's work, even trading in such literary ephemera:

> I cannot tell you how I feasted on the consciousness of the possession of these, even when I was quite too blinded by head-ache to read them. *Pray*, ask me to get you some; I shall so like doing something for you. I have copied S. T. Coleridge's letter; and only wait for your reply to send any or all the duplicates on the list.   (*L*, 502)

Remnants of the writer's text intrigued Gaskell, stimulating her appetite to circulate both the original object – in return for the loan of other originals – and precious copies of the autograph. Gaskell's fixation upon the biographical trace is hardly unique; arguably we still share in this desire today in our attempts to make available new source materials for Gaskell studies.

Was the Mrs. Gaskell who engaged Geraldine Jewsbury's curiosity the same Mrs. Gaskell we seek to recover today? Shifts over time in our picture of this author can be registered by something as seemingly fixed as a name.[6] From 1810 to 1865 she was known variously to her contemporaries as Elizabeth Cleghorn Stevenson, Mrs. Gaskell, E. C. Gaskell (as she generally signed herself), and – least frequently – Elizabeth Gaskell. Inaugurating her career with a soon-to-be-abandoned pseudonym "Cotton Mather Mills" (and later contemplating the moniker "Stephen Berwick"), she went on to publish *Mary Barton* in 1848 anonymously; the name E. C. Gaskell appeared first on the title page not of a novel, but of the biography of Brontë in 1857. For much of the nineteenth and early twentieth centuries, critics tended to refer to her as Mrs. Gaskell; only with the advent of feminist criticism in the late twentieth century did Mrs. Gaskell ultimately become canonized as "Elizabeth Gaskell." We have reason to believe, however, that she would have signed herself neither as Elizabeth Gaskell nor as Mrs. Gaskell had it not been for the marketing concerns of publishers. In a letter to her sister-in-law, Elizabeth Gaskell Holland, she teases, "It is a *silly piece* of *bride-like affectation* my dear, not to sign yourself by your proper name" (*L*, 40). Overcoming her doubts about such "bride-like affectation" was a gradual process; not until the 1860s was her work being published by Smith, Elder with the name "Mrs. Gaskell" firmly ensconced on the title page.

Scholars and critics who work with Gaskell's biography often seek to enforce a distinction between two incompatible selves, one public and the other private (something Gaskell herself helped to institutionalize with her polarized treatment of Brontë's life and work). "While I might be said to wish to 'deconstruct' the ideal Mrs. Gaskell," Felicia Bonaparte has argued influentially, "my real intention is to 'construct' the inner Gaskell I see revealed."[7] The notion that an authentic, "inner" Gaskell has been secreted – whether consciously or unconsciously – behind a screen of respectability lends credence to the theory that inconsistencies in her writing are explicable in terms either of a history of repression or of personal psychology.

Yet Gaskell's sense of her own life was more open-ended than this account suggests. In 1850, two years after the publication of the contentious *Mary Barton*, Gaskell presents the relation between her literary endeavors and a private sense of her own being as more complex than the model of "writer *contra* woman" allows:

> One of my mes is, I do believe, a true Christian – (only people call her socialist and communist), another of my mes is a wife and mother, and highly delighted at the delight of everyone else in the house … Now that's my "social" self I suppose. Then again I've another self with a full taste for beauty and convenience whh is pleased on its own account. How am I to reconcile all these warring members? I try to drown myself (my *first* self,) by saying it's Wm who is to decide on all these things, and his feeling it right ought to be my rule. And so it is – only that does not quite do. (*L*, 108)

Here Gaskell hypothesizes a sense of self that is shifting, subject to external pressures, and always responsive to circumstance. Contestation is implicit within each identity. Is she a Christian (as she sees it) or a socialist and communist, as critics of *Mary Barton* would maintain? So, too, conflict is staged among "these warring members." Can she go so far as to deploy one member against another? Is it possible to "drown" one part, "my *first* self," by abdicating altogether and hiding in the relational identity of the *femme couverte* dictated by convention ("it's Wm. who is to decide on all these things")? Clearly, subordination to patriarchal authority did not sit well with her Unitarian conviction that each soul, male or female, is equally accountable to God.

Stories about Gaskell's "essential" character often founder on the difficulty of reconciling what she openly recognized as irreconcilable imperatives. Thus we can see her as simultaneously managing and melancholy; pragmatic and impulsive; prone to physical or mental collapse and marked by resilience. To an extraordinary degree, Gaskell understood truth and meaning as stable concepts, but – and here is the rub – these concepts were knowable only by God. For human beings, true understanding was arrived at primarily through negotiation of conflict: "I take the opposite side to the person I am talking with always," she observed with jocular frankness to her friend Annie Shaen, "in order to hear some convincing arguments to clear up my opinions" (*L*, 57). Knowing her own mind, indeed knowing herself, was always connected to reciprocal recognition of another.

The making of E. C. Gaskell: "another of my mes"

In settling on E. C. Gaskell as her professional name, Gaskell gestured toward her readers rather than expressed any fixed notion of her own identity. The signature, in other words, is a form of address, a way of announcing herself to a world beyond any essential self. Charlotte Brontë once inquired of her point blank:

> Do you, who have so many friends, – so large a circle of acquaintance, – find it easy, when you sit down to write, to isolate yourself from all those ties, and their sweet associations, so as to be your *own woman*, uninfluenced or swayed by the consciousness of how your work may affect other minds; what blame or what sympathy it may call forth? (*LCB* II, 13:409)

A major difference between Gaskell and Brontë was that in order to be her "own woman," or to write, Gaskell never felt it necessary to "isolate" herself "from all those ties." To examine Gaskell's life and her literary achievement is to discover a series of selves, and corresponding names, that emerge out of the rich and ever-changing context of her encounter with "other minds." Tracing her development from E. C. Stevenson to E. C. Gaskell or, in her critical afterlife, from Mrs. Gaskell to Elizabeth Gaskell, challenges biographers and critics to grapple with a writer who evaded convention by assuming different identities without clearly privileging one over the others.

E. C. Stevenson: "craving after the lost mother"

Beginning life on September 29, 1810 as Elizabeth Cleghorn Stevenson, the future woman of letters was born to a mother whom she would never be able to recall. Elizabeth Holland Stevenson (1771–1811) died at the age of forty, having given birth eight times during her fourteen-year marriage to William Stevenson. Only two of their children survived to adulthood, a son, John, born in 1798, and Elizabeth, who was to spend thirteen months with her mother before the latter's untimely death. Although it was not particularly unusual for a child to be raised by relatives other than her mother in the early nineteenth century, young Elizabeth Stevenson felt the absence of maternal nurturance sharply and idealized the role of maternity throughout her life. Having no memories of her absent mother, Gaskell could only dream of a mother's elusive presence, much as her disconsolate heroines do in times of trouble: "when I tried to take hold of her," sobs the protagonist of *Ruth* (1853), "she went away and left me alone – I don't know where; so strange!" (*R*, 1:9). As an adult, Gaskell rarely alluded to her early life: childhood memories are recounted chiefly through the refracted lens of *Cranford* (1853) and *Wives and Daughters* (1866). John Chapple points out that a "composite history of the circles in which she was brought up" may be the closest we can come to understanding the character formation of E. C. Stevenson (as she began to sign herself once she reached the age of majority).[8]

Strangely, the child was given no keepsake of her mother. In a rare moment of vulnerability, at the age of thirty-eight Gaskell wrote to George Hope to thank him for forwarding a packet of her mother's letters:

> I have so often longed for some little thing that had once been hers or been touched by her. I think no one but one so unfortunate to be early motherless can enter into the craving after the lost mother ... I have been brought up away from all those who knew my parents, and therefore those who come to me with a remembrance of them as an introduction seem to have a holy claim on my regard.
> (*L*, 796–7)

Gaskell's statement that she was "brought up away from all those who knew my parents" is not entirely accurate: she occasionally saw her father

William Stevenson in Chelsea after his second marriage, and spent what was by all accounts a comfortable childhood with her mother's sister (who surely must have spoken often of Elizabeth Holland). Yet the sense that she was orphaned by circumstances, exiled from a bond that exists uniquely between mother and child, persisted throughout Gaskell's life.

Rather than remain in her father's unsettled London household, Elizabeth was adopted into her mother's clan, the Hollands, and cared for by a maternal aunt, Hannah Lumb, her "more than mother."[9] The prosperous middle-class Hollands were members of the well-established Unitarian community in Cheshire, with links to other leading families such as the Wedgwoods, Turners, and Darwins through shared faith, intermarriage, and commerce. The importance of this religious and social milieu, in terms of the young girl's education and assumptions, is hard to overstate. Elizabeth Stevenson was brought up within a theological tradition that emphasized free thought, tolerance, rationalism, and reform rather than religious "enthusiasm."

Surrounded from infancy by uncles, aunts, and cousins at Sandlebridge, the farm of her mother's parents, and in Knutsford, where she lived with her beloved Aunt Lumb, Elizabeth Stevenson was received without ceremony into a warmly supportive kinship network. Yet she also felt herself to be fundamentally alone in the world. "I have heard that Mrs. Gaskell was not always happy in those days," recollected Anne Thackeray Ritchie, "in her hours of childish sorrow and trouble she used to run away from her aunt's house across the Heath and hide herself in one of its many green hollows, finding comfort in silence, and in the company of birds and insects and natural things."[10] The sensitivity with which Gaskell portrayed the private – and often overlooked – emotional fragility of young girls – for instance, Sylvia Robson or Molly Gibson – derives force and authority from the remembrance of such apparently unwarranted, but nonetheless very real moments of "sorrow and trouble."

One may wonder how young Elizabeth's religious and intellectual training – and indeed her emotional development – might have differed if she had remained in her father's house. William Stevenson (1770–1829) gravitated initially to the Unitarian clergy, but left the ministry as a principled act of conscience (he objected to receiving payment for preaching of the gospel). In *North and South* (1855) we see an ambivalent version of Gaskell's father in Reverend Hale, a learned man whose religious scruples lead him to uproot his entire family. Although her father's crisis of conscience occurred before her birth, Gaskell's childhood was shaped by the consequences of her father's idiosyncratic nonconformity.

After he left the clergy, Stevenson tried his hand unsuccessfully at experimental farming at Saughton Mills, Midlothian. Having relocated his wife and one surviving child, John, first to Edinburgh and then to London, he parlayed whatever influence he could into a minor civil service post as Keeper of the Records at the Treasury. The restless temperament that bedevilled his early career expressed itself in later life through prolific contributions to periodical literature. During Elizabeth's sporadic visits to Chelsea, she would have seen an important precedent for writing professionally in the example of her father.

The adolescent Elizabeth Stevenson spent what were by all accounts some rather difficult hours with her father's family at 3 Beaufort Row. "Long ago I lived in Chelsea occasionally with my father and stepmother, and *very, very* unhappy I used to be," Gaskell recalled in a letter to Mary Howitt, "and if it had not been for the beautiful, grand river, which was an inexplicable comfort to me, and a family of the name of Kennett, I think my child's heart would have broken" (*L*, 797–8). The cause of her misery was undoubtedly the presence of her stepmother, Catherine Thomson Stevenson. William Stevenson remarried when Elizabeth was very young, but he did not invite her – as she may well have expected – to return from Knutsford to rejoin his household. In fact, Elizabeth was not summoned to meet the second Mrs. Stevenson, or her half-siblings, until she was twelve years old. The occasion for this first visit was the departure of John Stevenson, now a young man, for India with the Merchant Navy. Although Gaskell's daughters maintained that their mother scarcely knew her brother, their correspondence reveals that Elizabeth was genuinely attached to her older sibling, most likely because of the shared connection to their dead mother. Twelve years older than Elizabeth, John recognized her nascent literary talents, exchanging lively, affectionate letters with his impressionable sister. Thus it was a heavy blow when, at the age of eighteen, Elizabeth suddenly lost her brother as well. His disappearance overseas remained unexplained, and, as Gaskell's fiction attests, mysterious maritime figures continued to fascinate her until the end of her days. With the miraculous return home of lost men – Peter Jenkyns in *Cranford* or Charley Kinraid in *Sylvia's Lovers* (1863) – Gaskell sought to repair imaginatively a rupture in her own family that could never be healed, or – if the letters we possess are any indication – directly spoken of again.

Within the year William Stevenson, too, would be gone, dying from complications of a stroke in the spring of 1829. Her stepmother disingenuously assured Hannah Lumb that "I shall ever love Elizabeth as my own child, and trust that nothing will ever break that friendship which I trust is between us at this time, and also the love that she and her brother and sister have for each other," yet we know that Catherine Stevenson did not see her stepdaughter again for a good twenty-five years after her husband's death.[11] Gaskell's fiction bears witness to the difficulties of the relationship between stepmother and daughter, the worldly, self-interested Mrs. Gibson in *Wives and Daughters* offering a censorious portrait of the stepmother she knew and resented when she was a girl. By the age of nineteen, Elizabeth Stevenson understood the ephemeral nature of human ties. Biographers have generally contrasted the relatively sheltered early life she spent in the provinces with an expanded awareness that came to her in adulthood. Yet such a reading of the (admittedly) scant record of Elizabeth Stevenson's early childhood and adolescence does not give full weight to a history of dislocation, of foster care, and of broken (as well as painfully reformed) family bonds. Gaskell's beginnings as a writer were intertwined with a persistent conviction of loss. Transience, rather than permanence, would be the dominant rule of her experience.

"To knit our souls together": William and E. C. Gaskell

Scholars have sought in vain for one clear explanation of the emergence of Gaskell's public identity and the transformation of "E. C. Stevenson" from a girl described by her Aunt Lumb as "such a little giddy thoughtless thing" into the woman who was eventually to become the writer "E. C. Gaskell" (*L*, 1). We know that between 1832 (a year of sweeping electoral reform and cholera epidemics), when she married, and 1848 (a year of widespread political unrest in Britain and revolutions abroad), when she published her first novel, a sea change took place. Marriage at the age of twenty-one was pivotal in initiating Elizabeth Stevenson's development as a writer. Her suitor, William Gaskell (1805–84), was a gifted scholar, as well as a preacher of some eloquence: at the time of their engagement, he was capably manning his post as second minister of Manchester's Cross Street Chapel. In what has become known as the Gaskells' "joint engagement letter," we see a striking difference in the style and voice of each half of the betrothed couple. Elizabeth writes to her future sister-in-law with haste and typical irreverence, "I can't write a word more now, seeing I have 150 things to say to this disagreeable brother of yours" (*L*, 2). William, on the other hand, decorously alludes to the "still more lovely and endearing light" in which he regards his future bride after their first visit together to Knutsford. The experience, he writes, has served "to knit our souls together."[12] William's gravity had the general effect of strengthening the seriousness latent in his wife's character, even as her playfulness caused him, however slightly, to unbend.

The eldest son of a respected Lancashire Unitarian family based in the manufacturing centre of Warrington, William Gaskell was educated within the same tolerant, rational religious tradition as his bride-to-be. Ethically and intellectually, there is no question that William influenced his new partner. Very little is known of Elizabeth's religious views prior to 1832; yet by the time she was publishing fiction for the Howitts ("Clopton Hall" appearing in 1840 and "Libbie Marsh's Three Eras," among other stories, in 1847–8), her faith was clearly central to her conception of the work of artistic representation. The Gaskells shared a coherent worldview that nurtured the future novelist. "E. C. Gaskell" came into existence arguably through this first engagement with another mind, that of her spouse. Preparing her trousseau for the wedding ceremony, she jokingly writes to her friend Harriet Carr: "I fancy 'to learn obedience' is something new: to me at least it is ... I smell nothing but marking-ink and see nothing but E.C.S. everywhere" (FL, 19). Jenny Uglow remarks of this passage that as Miss Stevenson "tries on her bonnets and looks at her old initials, she is watching herself indelibly changing her identity."[13] Such change was to be repeated, with variations, more than once.

It is tempting to construe the provincial youth of E. C. Stevenson as incompatible with the urban, adult world that E. C. Gaskell inhabited in Manchester. "E.C.S.," presumably, would need to "learn obedience," in order to become "E.C.G." She would also subsume her identity in that of her husband. But that never happened: Gaskell retained her autonomy. Taking up residence first in Dover Street and then in Upper Rumford Street, the young minister's wife was transformed through her exposure to industrialization, as well as married life. Yet the Manchester self that came into being as a result never canceled an enduringly strong sense of herself as still belonging to the rural society of Cheshire. Gaskell moved between these poles throughout her life – North and South, public and private life, political engagement and pastoral retreat – without ultimately settling on one or the other.

This new identity, which we might call a "matrimonial" self, helped to produce E. C. Gaskell, the writer. Looking at the Gaskell marriage closely, we see that it was based not so much on compromise or subordination as on compatibility and an acceptance of parallel lives. In her fiction Gaskell's view of marriage was never particularly optimistic: from the overbearing patriarchal oppression of "Lizzie Leigh" (a story begun in the late 1830s) to the tragic misunderstandings of "The Manchester Marriage" (1858) and Sylvia's Lovers, to the diminished expectations of the Gibson misalliance in Wives and Daughters, the union of man and wife is more often portrayed as unhappy than otherwise. Her Aunt Lumb's troubled wedlock as a young woman to a husband suffering from mental illness, her father's painful remarriage, and later her own daughters' love troubles – Meta's canceled engagement to Captain Charles Hill, and Marianne's protracted romance with a second cousin, Thurstan Holland – alerted Gaskell to the risks associated with the legal contract, as well as the religious sacrament, of marriage. Sceptical of attempts to reform marriage law in order to make it a more equitable institution, she observed in a letter to Tottie Fox that "a husband can coax, wheedle, beat or tyrannize his wife out of something and no law whatever will help this that I see," adding mischievously, "(Mr Gaskell begs Mr Fox to draw up a bill for the protection of *husbands* against wives who will spend all their earnings)" (*L*, 379). Equilibrium, for this couple, was guaranteed by separation with connection. Given their temperamental differences, William and Elizabeth eventually maintained divergent work lives, social schedules, friendships, and travel itineraries. The unusual measure of E. C. Gaskell's independence may best be indicated by the fact that when she died unexpectedly of a heart attack, she was taking tea in a second home acquired without her husband's knowledge or consent. The Lawn was ostensibly purchased as a surprise for her husband on his retirement. Yet the Reverend Gaskell had no intention of retiring. After his wife's funeral, he resolutely continued working on at Plymouth Grove for another two decades until his own death in 1884; contrary to her fond wishes, the "secret" house at Alton was never inhabited by any of the Gaskells.

E. C. G: "Your ever affect. Mother"

Soon after her move to Manchester, E. C. Gaskell expanded her repertoire of roles by becoming a mother. Her first sustained effort as a writer – the diary she began keeping in 1835 for her infant daughter, Marianne – grew out of her anxiety over parenting. The motive for composition was personal: "as a token of her mother's love" (*PV*, 50). But Gaskell also used the text to explore the genesis of character, a sense of self formed explicitly through identity with another: "if that little daughter should in time become a mother herself, she may take an interest in the experience of another" (*PV*, 50). The diary presents a compelling portrait of the mother Gaskell hoped to become – wise, tolerant, nurturing – and whose devotion she prized beyond all other forms of love. Even more importantly, in this work we see writing as a discipline that produces, rather than detracts from, domestic sympathy.

Motherhood dramatically shaped the contours of E. C. Gaskell's life. She carried to term seven pregnancies: her first child was stillborn in 1833 and two sons died in infancy (her second boy, Willie, at the age of nine months from an attack of scarlet fever). Gaskell's remaining four daughters grew to maturity, but she was never free from worry over their health or welfare. The care she lavished on her girls was mirrored in her preoccupation with the theme of mothering in her fiction. Yet the image of the mother as pure, self-sacrificing, even beatific coincides with an answering sense of lack or loss in the stories and novels. More often than not, the beloved mother is powerless, dead, or dying; motherless daughters are left to fend for themselves or to seek out surrogates in kindly spinsters and rough, homespun domestics. Gaskell's own dependence on Ann Hearn, fifty years in service with the Gaskell family, and on "her dear household friend," the nursery governess Barbara Fergusson who attended Willie in his final illness, gave rise to some of the most sympathetic portraits of servants in Victorian literature (*FL*, 34). She was well aware that the work of mothering had a solid basis in material practices, many of which she – like most women of her time and class – was unable or unwilling to perform.

Describing the two forms of work as mutually exclusive, Gaskell proposed a successive staging of childrearing and artistic production:

> When I had *little* children I do not think I could have written stories, because I should have become too much absorbed in my *fictitious* people to attend to my *real* ones ... When you are forty, and if you have a gift for being an authoress you will write ten times as good a novel as you could do now, just because you will have gone through so much more of the interests of a wife and a mother.
>
> (*L*, 694–5)

Written in 1862, in what appears to be a dictated letter, Gaskell's counsel to this unknown female literary aspirant cannot be taken simply at face value. First of all, we know that Gaskell *did* write when her children were very small, not only the diary but "Clopton Hall," and several short stories that were published years later. Indeed, her youngest child, Julia, was only two years old when she published *Mary Barton*. In spite of her domestic obligations, Gaskell *always* wrote.

Second, we know that her absorption in fictitious people was importantly connected – rather than opposed – to Gaskell's loving ties with real ones. Most likely, for instance, this very letter was dictated to a member of her household. Rarely recognized is the way in which her work as an author was sustained by close relations with her daughters. Marianne and Meta were frequently drafted to help in managing both William's and Elizabeth's correspondence; as secretaries, the girls participated in the labour-intensive work of copying documents and preparing manuscripts. The role in Gaskell's aesthetics of what feminist philosopher Sara Ruddick calls "maternal thinking," as Patsy Stoneman has argued, can be seen in her fiction as an "ideal receptivity" that "has nurturance rather than control as its object."[14] Yet maternalism for Gaskell was also a mode of literary production. Not only did she employ her daughters when work was pressing, she also enlisted the aid of other young women attached to the family circle (such as the Winkworth sisters) with her literary projects. Gaskell's role as a mother, contrary to some of her statements, was never one that fundamentally detracted from her focus on writing. Moreover, passages on the craft of fiction in her letters – for instance, her advice to Herbert Grey to "observe what is *out* of you" – are framed by pungent shop-talk in the voice of "E.C.G" with her daughters: "I pity the man don't you? But it is good advice after all ... Show it to Mr H A B – as a 'specimen of *reviewing*'" (L, 541, 542).

One of the enduring myths about the maternal origins of Gaskell's creativity is that after the death of her son she turned (at her husband's insistence) to the cathartic release of writing *Mary Barton*. In this narrative the novelist is naive, untutored, not motivated by her own ambition. As we have already seen, however, this account suppresses evidence of E. C. Gaskell's apprentice literary efforts in the 1830s. The myth also assigns authorial agency to William, rather than to Elizabeth: she merely accedes to his promptings that she should write. Although misleading, this story unexpectedly emphasizes a radical continuity of subjectivity between the life and work of E. C. Gaskell. In seeking public redress for her private pain, Gaskell saw the one realm as necessarily contiguous with the other. Her own suffering made her all "the more anxious to give some utterance to the agony which, from time to time, convulses this dumb people; the agony of suffering without the sympathy of the happy" (*MB*, xxxvi). Gaskell's claim that fictitious people absorb the writer's attention at the expense of real ones falls apart when tested against the preface of *Mary Barton*, because real people in her work are – in this sense – no different from fictitious people. The laborers she represents in the industrial fiction exist because of Gaskell's realist intentions: the suffering of those fictitious people is conflated with the suffering of real people the author has known. To separate the two, in short, is seriously to misrepresent the ethical and imaginative wellspring of Gaskell's art.

Mrs. Gaskell: "If I were Mr. G. O Heaven how I would beat her!"

In becoming "Mrs. Gaskell," when she was well into middle age, the transformation of the private woman into a celebrated novelist was complete. Being Mrs. Gaskell could be taxing: critics have often described this self as Gaskell's concession to convention. Jane Carlyle dismissed her in this guise as "a very kind cheery woman in her own house; but there is an atmosphere of moral dulness about her, as about all Socinian women."[15] And Mrs. Gaskell could be provoking: Charles Dickens, her oft-frustrated editor, famously ranted, "Oh, Mrs. Gaskell, fearful – fearful! If I were Mr. G. O Heaven how I would beat her!"[16] Just as being married played a decisive part in the early reception of E. C. Gaskell's writing, so, too, it shaped her contemporaries' sense of who she was as a public figure. "*What* women ought to write novels, that novels may be such as really ought to be written?" mused John Malcolm Ludlow in his critique of *Ruth*. "When we look at female writers, we cannot help being struck by the vast superiority of the married as a class, over the single" (*CH*, 285). A designation of "Mrs." was integral, I want to suggest, not only to Gaskell's imagination of herself and of others, but also to negotiation of the marketplace in which her writing circulated.

Having weathered the firestorm of criticism over *Mary Barton* and then *Ruth*, Gaskell had "arrived" as a novelist. She consolidated her standing by accepting the commission in 1855 to write *The Life of Charlotte Brontë*. Although she prided herself on her ability to integrate household responsibilities with literary ones, Gaskell came increasingly to absent herself from home cares and to set aside large blocks of time to meet publishers' deadlines: first in conformity to Dickens's schedule for the stressful serialization in *Household Words* of *North and South* (September 1854–January 1855), and then for the biography, under pressure to rush into print as soon as possible after Brontë's death.

Fame brought Gaskell greater mobility and self-confidence than she had ever known before: in the 1850s she formed important friendships in Paris with *salonnière* Mary Clarke Mohl, wife of the German Orientalist Julius von Mohl, and in Rome with the American art historian Charles Eliot Norton. These mature relationships encouraged Gaskell to take herself seriously as an artist, as well as to broaden her perspective beyond earlier regional and national identifications. By the time she was researching the ambitious historical novel *Sylvia's Lovers*, Gaskell was traveling specifically for the purpose of her work and sought out retirement for sustained periods of productivity, coming late in life to appreciate "the wisdom of French ladies going into retraite."[17] So, too, Gaskell's relations with her publishers over fifteen years represented an education in professionalism, from the early patronage of the Howitts and her first tentatively brokered arrangements with Chapman and Hall, through her instructive dealings with John Forster, to the collegiality and friendship she enjoyed with George Smith. As her reputation grew, Gaskell proved to be an increasingly canny negotiator, openly bargaining over the sale of copyright for *Sylvia's Lovers*, taking an active interest in American editions of various works, and arranging for translations into French (with Hachette) and German (with Tauchnitz) of her novels.

E. C. Gaskell has not survived the term of her natural life. Readers today know this enigmatic figure either as "Mrs. Gaskell" or as "Elizabeth Gaskell." In losing "E. C. Gaskell," literary history has also lost some of the unsettling motility of her multiple self-declarations. Gaskell's power to anger, move, and disturb as well as to seduce and charm her readers has often been explained away in an attempt to name her finally and for all purposes. Yet she bristled at the notion that she or anyone had "manifested the whole truth" with a single name or work of fiction (*L*, 119). "I think that is one evil of this bustling life that one has never time calmly and bravely to face a great grief," she wrote after the death of her cherished son, "and to view it on every side as to bring the harmony out of it" (*L*, 111). Incapable fully of bringing "the harmony" out of her own or another's "great grief," for E. C. Gaskell, her life and work were predicated upon the impossibility of – and yet the longing after – achieving such "a view on every side." It was in the trying that her achievement rests.

Notes

1 Jenny Uglow, *Elizabeth Gaskell: A Habit of Stories* (London: Faber and Faber, 1993), 604.
2 Mary Taylor to Ellen Nussey, January 28, 1858, in T. J. Wise and J. A. Symington, eds., *The Brontës: Their Lives, Friendships and Correspondence*, 4 vols. (Oxford: Basil Blackwell, 1933), IV, 229.
3 Geraldine Jewsbury to Jane Carlyle, December 1850, in Mrs. Alexander Ireland, ed., *Selections from the Letters of Geraldine Endor Jewsbury to Jane Welsh Carlyle* (London: Longmans, Green, 1892), 383.
4 Meta Gaskell, letter to the *Guardian*, September 30, 1910, quoted in John Chapple, *Elizabeth Gaskell: The Early Years* (Manchester: Manchester University Press, 1997), 4. It should be noted that the Gaskell daughters did not uniformly repel such requests: Meta and Julia aided A. W. Ward with his biographical research on their mother and Marianne preserved a cache of letters in spite of Gaskell's injunctions to destroy such personal correspondence.
5 Charles Eliot Norton to James Lowell, June 20, 1857, in *The Letters of Charles Eliot Norton*, ed. Sara Norton and M. A. de Wolfe (Boston: Houghton Mifflin, 1913), 171.
6 I am very grateful to Josie Billington for her discussion with me of what is at stake in our uses of Gaskell's many names. As she has noticed, Christopher Ricks made the first case for preferring E. C. Gaskell, a practice I follow here.
7 Felicia Bonaparte, *The Gypsy-Bachelor of Manchester: The Life of Mrs. Gaskell's Demon* (Charlottesville: University of Virginia Press, 1992), 11.

8 Chapple, *Elizabeth Gaskell*, 5. For the few early letters we know of, see *FL*.

9 Quoted in Uglow, *Elizabeth Gaskell*, 12.

10 Anne Thackeray Ritchie, preface to Elizabeth Gaskell, *Cranford* (London: Macmillan, 1891), xii.

11 Catherine Stevenson to Hannah Lumb, June 18, 1829, quoted in Uglow, *Elizabeth Gaskell*, 55.

12 William Gaskell, quoted in Chapple, *Elizabeth Gaskell*, 419.

13 Uglow, *Elizabeth Gaskell*, 76.

14 Patsy Stoneman, *Elizabeth Gaskell* (Bloomington: Indiana University Press, 1987), 37.

15 Jane Carlyle to Thomas Carlyle, September 12, 1851, in *New Letters and Memorials of Jane Welsh Carlyle, annotated by Thomas Carlyle and edited by Alexander Carlyle*, 2 vols. (London: John Lane, 1903), II:29.

16 Charles Dickens to W. H. Wills, September 11, 1855, in *The Letters of Charles Dickens*, 12 vols., VII, ed. Graham Storey, Kathleen Tillotson, and Angus Easson (Oxford: Clarendon, 1993), 700.

17 Elizabeth Gaskell to Charles Eliot Norton, quoted in Uglow, *Elizabeth Gaskell*, 490.

3

Mary Barton and *North and South*

Elizabeth Gaskell's two "Manchester" novels have often been paired in critical discussion in order to compare their representation of industrial life and their purchase on the relations of workers and masters, labor and capital. The process of industrialization in Britain had precipitated rapid shifts of population into the cities to seek work in the factories. Crowding, lack of sanitation, and other ills of urban expansion gave rise to concerns about "the condition of England," as Thomas Carlyle famously put it. Fluctuations in the economy had in the 1830s and 1840s resulted in poverty and starvation among the laboring classes, leading to protests and demands for reform on the part of workers and fears of social unrest or, worse, revolution on the part of the middle and upper classes.

Until lately Gaskell's engagement with political economy, class conflict, and industrial conditions was rather narrowly construed, but recent feminist criticism has argued for wider definitions of the political and examined the novels as much for the political implications of gender and domestic life as for their factory, riot, and strike scenes.[1] Taking my cue from a broadening sense of the way social conditions shape how subjects experience gender and class as aspects of identity, I propose in this chapter to look at what has been rather less discussed – Gaskell's representation of emotional and psychic states in the context of social change and the upheavals of modernity. Written with an eye on revolution abroad and Chartism at home, *Mary Barton* (1848) pleads with its middle-class readers for a sympathetic response to turbulent working-class feelings, even as it also represents the working classes as lacking in control over their emotions. Powerful and excessive emotion, it seems to warn through John Barton's "monomania" and Mary's brain fever after her crisis in court, can precipitate pathological effects. In *North and South* (1855), perhaps because a middle-class lapse of self-control does not seem to Gaskell an obvious social danger, she allows herself to explore the power of overwhelming emotion and its aftermath as less threatening to sanity. But in scrutinizing emotional experience that unsettles so deeply that it stuns memory and volition, and results in trance or troubled dreams, Gaskell also implies a (middle-class) self that is less unified and governable than much mid-century psychological discourse would allow. The way she represents consciousness and its alterations under turbulent social and personal conditions is not an inward turn away from social representation, but an insistence on the connectedness, if not inseparability, of inner and outer worlds. Yet even as vicissitudes in both psychological and social zones buffet and shock the subject, they open up possibilities for growth.

Mary Barton: "the deep suffering of the heart"

A common account of the genesis of *Mary Barton* is that Gaskell wrote it to soothe her sorrow. Urged by her husband, Reverend William Gaskell, to turn to writing as a distraction from grief after her young son Willie had died of scarlet fever in 1845, Gaskell began her story of working-class suffering to keep at bay "the memory of painful scenes which would force themselves upon my remembrance" (*L*, 74). The preface to *Mary Barton* gestures to these circumstances as if to dispel any further reference to them: "three years ago I became anxious (from circumstances that need not be more fully alluded to) to employ myself in writing a work of fiction" (*MB*, xxxv). In the course of the novel, however, painful remembrances occasionally obtrude themselves, triggered by the narrative and apparently disrupting it as the narrator shifts momentarily into a first-person mode to articulate her own feelings of loss. So the narrator turns from describing Mrs. Wilson's disturbing dreams to an account of her own precious but bittersweet dreams:

> What if in dreams (that land into which no sympathy nor love can penetrate with another, either to share its bliss or its agony, – that land whose scenes are unspeakable terrors, are hidden mysteries, are priceless treasures to one alone, – that land where alone I may see, while yet I tarry here, the sweet looks of my dear child), what if, in the horrors of her dreams, her brain should go still more astray, and she should waken crazy with her visions, and the terrible reality that begot them? (*MB*, 24:316)

The reference to "my dear child" occurs embedded – one might say "buried" – in parentheses after the third repetition of "that land" as if in each description of the dream world we spiral out of the fictional universe and into the world of the writing "I." Another example occurs when Mary has made the shocking realization that her father is the murderer of Harry Carson. Gaskell imagines her heroine's surroundings as unsympathetic to her state of mind, a contrast to the lovely night that surrounds the author as she writes:

> There was little sympathy in the outward scene, with the internal trouble. All was so still, so motionless, so hard! Very different to this lovely night in the country in which I am now writing, where the distant horizon is soft and undulating in the moonlight, and the nearer trees sway gently to and fro in the night-wind with something of almost human motion; and the rustling air makes music among their branches, as if speaking soothingly to the weary ones who lie awake in heaviness of heart. The sights and sounds of such a night lull pain and grief to rest. (*MB*, 22:200)

The metafictional reference to the circumstances of writing reinforces the sense of the narrator as one of the weary ones who knows what it is to "lie awake in heaviness of heart" and need the night (and writing) to "lull pain and grief to rest."

Read alongside Gaskell's advice to a fellow novelist more than a decade later, these confessional moments would seem to be lapses, contraventions of her artistic principles. "I think you must observe what is *out* of you, instead of examining what is *in* you," she writes, advocating a novelistic reference for setting "*objects* not *feelings*" before the reader (*L*, 451). The advice later in the letter not to "intrude yourself in your descriptions" may have been better followed in her more mature works. But I would argue that in *Mary Barton* the moments when the novelist's feelings bubble up into the narrative are important in demonstrating the process by which Gaskell found her subject and focus in this first novel. To go further, one might say that the autobiographical hint or turn at these moments is perhaps less artless and more aesthetically considered than we may initially think, for it is through these disclosures of her own experience of grief that Gaskell establishes her credentials as a sympathetic witness. The confessional intrusions invite readers, too, to move from the narrative to their own experience of grief or pain and hence to a sense of connectedness with the working-class subjects of the novel. On many occasions Gaskell writes inclusively about "our" suffering, including the reader in a more generalized commentary on the nature of grief: "Our very excess of grief rocks itself to sleep, before we have had time to realise its cause; and we waken, with a start of agony like a fresh stab, to the consciousness of the one awful vacancy, which shall never, while the world endures, be filled again" (*MB*, 36:440). Without dispelling the specificity of industrial problems and the plight of the working classes, Gaskell works to establish a sense of the commonality of suffering. And, consonantly, what she offers in the moment of understanding and forgiveness between Carson and Barton at the novel's end is not an economic plan for systemic reform but a connection based on the mutual knowledge of suffering: "Rich and poor, masters and men, were then brothers in the deep suffering of the heart" (*MB*, 35:431). They are united in their common grief, for each knows what it is to lose a son. Behind their dead sons stands the shadow of Willie Gaskell, a symbol of the humanizing power of suffering.[2]

Gaskell's own search for an outlet from personal pain did not just coincide with the wish to give utterance to the suffering of working classes: the two experiences were indissolubly linked.[3] In acknowledging that there was a "morbid" element in *Mary Barton*, Gaskell also perceptively recognized the inextricability of her own suffering from that which she represents in the novel: there is "too heavy a shadow over the book," she conceded, "but I doubt if the story could have been deeply realized without these shadows" (*L*, 75). Gaskell was by no means the first woman novelist to concern herself with the plight of the poor. Industrial fiction by Charlotte Elizabeth Tonna, Frances Trollope, and Harriet Martineau had already established a genre of writing sympathetically about the social ills of industrialism. Gaskell entered this developing tradition primed by what she had witnessed in Manchester and by her own experience of suffering. While the preface makes only the briefest of allusions to those personal circumstances of grief which prompted her writing, it does go on to dwell on the question of sympathy. Gaskell writes of the "deep sympathy" she had always felt with "the care-worn men" and how "[a] little manifestation of this sympathy and a little attention to the expression of feelings" opened their hearts to her (*MB*, xxxv). She writes also of the "agony of suffering without the sympathy of the happy" (*MB*, xxxvi). In the world of the novel, sympathy is of the highest order of feeling: despite her irritability and occasional waspishness, Mrs. Wilson is redeemed by her ultimate compassion toward Mary and "a deep and noble sympathy with great sorrows" (*MB*, 36:446).

Closely bound up with Gaskell's investment in sympathy is a commitment to listening to feelings, evident in the preface where Gaskell hints darkly that the failure to do so may result in revolution – "the events which have so recently occurred among a similar class on the continent" (*MB*, xxxvi). But while she establishes her narrative ground in attending to feelings, it is also significant that in the course of the novel she registers considerable ambivalence about their collective working-class expression. The strike, for example, is attributed to overheated emotions: "when men get excited, they know not what they do" (*MB*, 15:202). Chartism, resulting in the petition of 1839, is framed as a movement built on "excited feelings" (*MB*, 6:97). There are also unscrupulous troublemakers who "cherish such feelings" of vengeance and antagonism in the working classes and who know how to use rhetoric to rouse "the dangerous power at their command" (*MB*, 3:25).

The great caveat about feelings and passions is that they need to be educated, reflected upon, and wrought into thoughtful conclusions. Hence Gaskell's fear of the trade union, likened to the "mighty agency of steam, capable of unlimited good or evil. But to obtain a blessing on its labours, it must work under the direction of a high and intelligent will; incapable of being misled by passion or excitement. The will of the operatives had not been guided to the calmness of wisdom" (*MB*, 15:203). Many Victorian psychologists regarded the will or volition as the seat of reasoned self-governance. Without the exercise of will, one authoritative mental physiologist explained, "the individual becomes a thinking automaton, destitute of the power to withdraw his attention from any idea or feeling by which his mind may be possessed, and is as irresistibly impelled, therefore to act in accordance with this, as the lower animals are to act in obedience to their instincts."[4] Accordingly, Gaskell's remarks about the absence of a "high and intelligent will" are revelatory of middle-class fears that working-class resistance and solidarity is likely to be unreasoned or misguided. Just as will is necessary to govern passions and excitement, sympathy must be educated in order to be effective. John Barton feels keenly for his fellow laborers, but, the narrator asks, "What availed his sympathy? No education had given him wisdom; and without wisdom, even love, with all its effects, too often works but harm" (*MB*, 15:199). And in a letter describing the genesis of the novel, Gaskell writes that she tried to imagine what the inequalities of fortune would seem like to a man "full of rude illogical thought, and full also of sympathy for suffering, which appealed to him through his senses" (*L*, 74). The hierarchical relationship between "senses" and "intelligent will" not only governed mid-century ideas about the functioning of the mind, but also informed conceptions of class stratification. A sense of class distinction, in turn, infiltrated the understanding of "sympathy" in psychological discourse of the mid-century. In a chapter on "Sympathy and Imitation" in *The Emotions and the Will* (1859), Alexander Bain warned that actors could transfer emotions to others – even false emotions. Those weak in character or of a susceptible nature were prey therefore to the influence of any popular demagogue.

The underlying association of the working classes with a lack of disciplined will and an inability to govern powerful feelings makes itself felt in the novel in the representation of pathological states of mind. After the deaths of his wife and son, John Barton becomes bitter and morose, takes to opium, and even beats his daughter once. His fixation on the disparity between rich and poor becomes a pathological condition: "The same state of feeling which John Barton entertained, if belonging to one who had had leisure to think of such things, and physicians to give names to them, would have been called monomania" (MB, 15:198). Similarly, Mary's enormous exertions to save Jem Wilson from a murder charge without inculpating her father lead to her collapse in court. An ensuing brain fever puts her life and sanity in jeopardy so that Jem worries lest she may remain "a poor gibbering maniac all her life long" (MB, 33:398). Mary's Aunt Esther, it is suggested, is deranged as a result of the loss of her daughter, and the life of prostitution and addiction she adopted to try to save the child. She has a "violent and unregulated" nature and speaks with "a wild vehemence, almost amounting to insanity" (MB, 21:276; 14:189). It is feared that Jane Wilson's shock at Jem's arraignment will cause delirium and send her brain astray. While such representation of emotional states may appear simply to be part of the novelist's repertoire of melodramatic devices, the linkage of disorderly working-class subjects with pathological psychic states is indicative of a larger pattern in which excessive feeling and lack of control are coded as a working-class problem.

Although psychic distress in *Mary Barton* may be a prelude to madness or monomania, Gaskell dwells far more on the bodily signs of suffering in her working-class subjects than its effects on their interiority and consciousness. The suffering of the poor is for the most part to be read on starving or diseased bodies or metonymically represented through the state of the home. Even John Barton's condition of monomania is explained in an architectural metaphor through a story about a narrowing room in which a criminal is shut up. "Day by day he became aware that the space between the walls of his apartment was narrowing, and then he understood the end. Those painted walls would come into hideous nearness and at last crush the life out of him. And so day by day, nearer and nearer, came the diseased thoughts of John Barton" (MB, 15:198).[5] The several descriptions of homes and dwellings in *Mary Barton* offer spatial representations of their inhabitants. Alice Wilson's humble scrubbed and spotless cellar with its drying herbs shows her straitened circumstances but assures us of her simple purity, orderliness, and old country ways. Tea at the working-class but respectable home of the Bartons in the opening scenes emphasizes domestic comfort and adequacy, which later contrasts with what the home becomes after John Barton's wife and son die and his fortunes decline. The physical squalor of the Davenports' fetid and rank cellar bespeaks their helpless indigence and suffering.

In accordance with the greater focus on bodies rather than minds, Gaskell's working-class subjects are also associated with orality and speech rather than textuality and writing. Her stated aim in *Mary Barton* is to "give some utterance to the agony which, from time to time, convulses this dumb people," whom she later says wanted a "Dante to record their sufferings" (*MB*, xxxvi; 8:96). But one may pause over the label "dumb," for Gaskell represents a vocal and articulate working-class society. The rich Lancashire dialect of some of her characters (notably not Mary herself) is faithfully represented (with notes by William Gaskell accompanying the fourth edition), and working-class poems by Samuel Bamford are included in the text, as are a plethora of stories, like the touching and comic account of how Job Legh brought his baby granddaughter home, or the one by Margaret of how she discovered a scorpion (thought to be dead) running about on the hearth. Lively conversation abounds with evidence of supple means of self-expression, as is seen in the discussion between Mrs. Wilson and Alice on the subject of Queen Victoria, or between Will Wilson and Job on the scientific credibility of mermaids. Although we encounter John Barton for the most part as a taciturn and morose man, he has a reputation of being very articulate, and is chosen as a Chartist delegate to London because he has the eloquence enabling him to "put the feelings of his fellows into words" (*MB*, 15:199).

Gaskell's aim of giving "utterance to the agony ... [of] this dumb people" addresses not so much the opposition of speech and silence but that of orality and textuality. Her novelistic aim is to provide a written articulation of the working-class plight for middle-class readers; in referring to "utterance," therefore, she draws on the elision of written and spoken word that occurs when we represent a text as "speaking" to us. Beyond serving Gaskell in addressing her readers as if she were talking to them, this elision marks an important class-inflected opposition in the novel between talking and writing. Not only does Job Legh feel the "want of power in words while the feeling within him was so strong and clear," he has little use for writing: "Writing was to him little more than an auxiliary to natural history; a way of ticketing specimens, not of expressing thoughts" (*MB*, 37:455; 33:400). If this autodidact is sceptical about the value of writing when trying to communicate feeling, the issue is not illiteracy, but a greater trust in presence and orality. Similarly uneasy about the value of writing as a means of conveying one's feelings, Margaret urges Mary not to write to Jem, warning that it will not express her feelings properly and "[t]'would be hard to say neither too much nor too little" (*MB*, 12:167).

A working-class mistrust of writing is evident in several ways. Written words are responsible for a great deal of confusion and danger in the novel. The beautifully inscribed valentine that Jem gives Mary is then used by her to copy out Samuel Bamford's verses, and ends up as the wadding in a murder weapon. When Esther recognizes Jem's fine handwriting, she concludes that he is the murderer. Writing can be severed from its author and yet incriminate him. Subpoenas cause much dread in the novel, seeming to be only bits of paper but signifying the compelling authority of the law. Although the narrator confesses to having a "dread of parchment" and generalizes about the fear it inspires – "Many people have it, I am one, Mary was another" – working-class subjects have far more reason to mistrust official paper since the command and authority it conveys is never at their disposal and rarely works to their advantage (*MB*, 23:301). Thus Tom Wilson has to see Mr. Carson in order to obtain an infirmary order – Davenport's admission to the hospital is contingent on it – and because Carson has "no in-patient's order to spare at present," he gives him an out-patient's form for the following Monday, by which time, of course, the perilously ill Davenport is dead (*MB*, 6:79). And later, before Jem's trial, Carson calls his lawyer up at night to suggest that "some letter should be written or something done to secure the verdict" (*MB*, 26:333).

Writing and literacy are a means of access to information and hence power, as John Barton's story about the surgeon's notes makes clear. Barton explains how he was once ill and allowed to stay an extra week in the infirmary because he could write. Set to do sorting work for the surgeon, he read that all the accidents the doctor had seen happened in the last two hours of the day's work. Such evidence, the novel suggests, helped to introduce the Ten Hours Bill. On the one hand, Gaskell is establishing John Barton as privy to history in the making, but on the other, she suggests indirectly that reading and writing are tools of knowledge and power. As we see, however, writing is associated largely with the middle classes: Harry Carson writes letters to Mary; the lawyer Mr. Bridgenorth is mostly represented while writing, and although, in the final pages of the novel, Jem and Mary receive a letter from Job Legh, its main purpose is to announce presence – a visit from Margaret and Will and possibly Job himself. Despite the fact that Gaskell allows her working-class subjects a richness of oral culture and learning, she does not permit writing to be an important or defining part of that culture. Feeling rather than thought, presence and orality rather than writing, define the representation of working-class subjects. In line with these ascriptions, the articulation of their distress in literary form is the task of the middle-class novelist addressing her largely middle-class readers. The noble aim of mobilizing the feelings of middle-class readers on behalf of the suffering lower classes thus produces a novel in which the representation of feeling itself is tinged with prevailing class conceptions. Feeling may be the means of connection among classes, a common language and a leveler of class difference, but the way emotions are understood and represented often reinforces class stratification.

Psychic pain and its aftermath in *North and South*

As a social-problem novel, or a novel of industrial life, *North and South* has traditionally received much critical attention for its concern with the relations of labor and capital. It is also, I will argue, a novel profoundly interested in the effect of very powerful feelings on psychic functioning and in the haunting aftermath of intense emotional experience.[6] In its attention to dream and the power of unconscious processes, the novel seems as interested in the nature of the psyche as it is in social problems. Indeed, the two concerns are closely related. Gaskell shows the turbulence, upheaval, and disruption in changing social conditions, all of which affect the mind in destabilizing ways. Attentive to the social as well as the physiological bases of mind, the amateur psychologist George Henry Lewes remarked that "to understand the Human Mind we must study it under normal conditions, and these are social conditions."[7] Studying the human mind under social conditions in mid-century England, *North and South* suggests, we may learn more about both.

Again and again, *North and South* explores how people cope with emotional shock and pain – what Shakespeare's Hamlet calls the "heart ache and the thousand natural shocks" that the mind (and through it the flesh) is heir to. But psychic suffering here is no prelude to madness or unhinging as it is in *Mary Barton*, where Mary's extreme emotional stress after her public appearance in court sends her into a brain fever. Gaskell deliberately avoids pathologizing strong feelings and their effects, rather seeing the negotiation of painful feelings occasioned by love, death, and moral crisis as ordinary, even daily, business.[8] Gaskell's avowed subject in *Mary Barton* is working-class woes "which come with ever-returning tide-like flood to overwhelm the workmen" (*MB*, xxxvi). This focus gives way in *North and South* to a less overtly historical treatment of suffering and a more generalized interest in the psychic effects of different kinds of pain – a scrutiny that crosses gender and, to a much lesser extent, class lines.

Mary Barton seems almost relentless in detailing a succession of deaths, the preeminent causes of which are starvation and disease among the indigent working classes. Although *North and South* is not focused to the same extent on working-class poverty, its death toll is similarly high – Mrs. Hale, Bessy Higgins, Mr. Hale, Boucher, his wife, Mr. Bell. In December 1854 Gaskell wrote to Charles Dickens, who, as editor of *Household Words*, where the novel was being published, had given it the title *North and South*, "I think a better title than N & S would have been 'Death & Variations.' There are 5 deaths, each beautifully suited to the character of the individual" (*L*, 324). While many would disagree with Gaskell on the "better title," her comment does serve to highlight her own, possibly self-ironic, awareness of the centrality of death in this novel – a novel written, we might remember, during the Crimean War when reports of casualties and disease increasingly dominated the press. "Beautifully suited to the character of the individual," the deaths also frequently implicate the social conditions in the industrial north, from Bessy, who dies of the cotton fluff in her lungs, to Mrs. Hale, who is rendered frail and sickly by the move to Milton. The deaths are often occasions of sentimentality and pathos, but also, in so far as they affect Margaret, opportunities for education and instruction, and spurs to independence. And further, in provoking strong reactions among affected characters, they offer the third-person narrator a reason to move in and out of her characters' minds, probing the nature of consciousness in the aftermath of distress.

In the turbulent world of *North and South*, death is, however, only one among several events that produce emotional upheaval and provoke a response of shock and pain. There is also Mr. Hale's decision to leave the Church; Frederick's discredited and fugitive status; Margaret's encounter with the mob; her lie to protect Frederick; her painful response to cruel local superstitions on her return to the South. More private and less obviously eventful are Margaret's responses to the proposals by Mr. Lennox and Mr. Thornton and Thornton's experience of rejection in love. Furthermore, the experience of and response to powerful emotion are not conventionally gendered in this novel. In *Mary Barton* Gaskell shows working-class men as emotional and feeling, indicating the maternal, feminized, and nurturing aspects of working-class culture.[9] In *North and South* the experience and exhibition of powerful emotion is less about an ethic of feeling and caring and more about the destabilizing effects of emotion on consciousness. After Mrs. Hale dies, Dixon the maid is concerned for the health of Margaret's father: "I was really afraid for master, that he'd have a stroke with grief . . . [H]e ought to be roused; and if it gives him a shock at first, it will, maybe be better afterwards" (*NS*, II, 6:253); when Frederick arrives to see his dying mother, Mr. Hale begins to "cry and wail like a child" (*NS*, II, 5:245); Frederick sobs in the night after his mother's death; and the painful effects of passionate love on John Thornton leave him stunned and dizzy, with a violent headache and a throbbing intermittent pulse. Although some critics have pointed to Mr. Hale's effeminacy in contrast to Thornton's masculine power and control, a close look at the text's rendering of emotion suggests that it is not necessarily unmanly for men to experience powerful, even uncontrollable, feelings.[10] "I am a man. I claim the right of expressing my feelings," Thornton declares (*NS*, I, 25:195). And although working-class men are more frequently represented as susceptible to strong emotion, it is in fact Nicholas Higgins who is "ashamed of his suffering" and shakes off "the emotion after Bessy's death" (*NS*, I, 15:122).

As if to bring home the double standard of her culture's way of coding the exhibition of overwhelming emotion as feminine and working-class, Gaskell describes Mr. Hale's fear of breaking down entirely at his wife's funeral and therefore wanting Thornton to accompany him. When Margaret asks to go with him, he says, "You! My dear, women do not generally go" (*NS*, II, 8:266). Margaret explains that she knows that is the case and it is so because "women of our class have no power over their emotions and are ashamed of showing them. Poor women go, and don't care if they are seen overwhelmed with grief" (*NS*, II, 8:267). Two things emerge here: first, men of her class may also have difficulty retaining power over their emotions, and second, from Margaret's point of view poor women are right in not caring if they are seen overwhelmed with grief. The implicit critique here of emotional control suggests that the social injunction to keep strong feelings in check is a class convention, which may be as bad in its way as the tendency to surrender to excessive emotion.

Gaskell's focus on interiority in this novel continues her emphasis on the importance of feeling and emotion that I have discussed in relation to *Mary Barton*, but one marked difference between the two novels is Gaskell's interest in *North and South* in unconscious processes. The narrator draws consistently on the language of dream and trance, and the idea of being "beside oneself" or "not oneself." This focus puts Gaskell in the company of mid-century mental physiologists such as William Carpenter, a Unitarian and one of the Gaskells' acquaintances. In 1855 he published the fifth edition of *Principles of Human Physiology*, in which he paid close attention to various states of consciousness and coined the term "unconscious cerebration" to express the idea of unconscious processes akin to thinking.[11] Writing about the mind and its operations, Carpenter explains how consciousness ordinarily works and under what conditions it gives way to altered states, such as sleep, somnambulism and mesmeric trance, until it can be seen as pathologically disturbed in states such as mania or delirium. If, in *Mary Barton*, Gaskell drew on mania and delirium to represent the psychic states of John and Mary Barton, in *North and South*, she is more concerned with slightly altered states of mind than with pathological disturbances. Gaskell is unusual among mid-century novelists in exploring the stunning or numbing effects of shock and emotional upheaval. She seems also in advance of medico-psychological discourse, which, although very interested in mesmerism and altered states of mind, paid little attention at this time to the altering effects of shock on psychic states.

In order to represent the psychic consequences of overwhelming experience, Gaskell draws, often analogically, on the language of dream and trance. Through this she implies that the experience of emotional upheaval can be tantamount to entering an altered state of consciousness. So, for example, "Mr Hale came as if in a dream, or rather with the unconscious motion of a sleepwalker, whose eyes and mind perceive other things than what are present" (NS, II, 6:252). And Margaret, lying insensible, a stone from one in the mob having grazed her temple, is described as one "in death-like trance," unable to move or speak, yet fully aware of what is going on around her (NS, I, 22:183). Margaret likens the news of Mr. Hale's decision to leave the Church as "a night-mare – a horrid dream – not the real waking truth!"(NS, I, 4:40). Gaskell implies that so powerful is the experience of strong emotion, it can distort one's sense of reality and identity. When Mrs. Hale is ill, Margaret spends the night watching over her, thinking of the recent past as if it were "unreal" and "a dreaming memory of some former life," then when the morning comes, "it seemed as if the terrible night were unreal as a dream; it too, was a shadow. It, too, was past" (NS, I, 21:170). Gaskell's recourse to the language of dreams allows her to suggest the jolt that Margaret's perception of reality has suffered as a result of her mother's illness.

Gaskell repeatedly evokes the sense of living a nightmare or bad dream in troubled times. Conversely, she also uses the contrast and continuity between dreaming and waking worlds to suggest that reality may be worse even than bad dreams. Several dreams in the novel are recounted in detail in such a way as to show Gaskell alive to a sense of psychic life beyond the conscious. Margaret dreams of Lennox falling from a tree after his proposal to her; Thornton dreams of Margaret as a lascivious temptress after he sees her with Frederick. A trance-like state of horror and thraldom, which is likened to a bad dream, is the aftermath of Thornton's proposal to Margaret. Gaskell deploys the most highly Gothicized imagery in the novel to express the spectre of sexuality and Margaret's repudiation of the taboo knowledge of her attraction to Thornton:

> The deep impression made by the interview, was like that of a horror in a dream; that will not leave the room although we waken up, and rub our eyes, and force a stiff rigid smile upon our lips. It is there – there, cowering and gibbering, with fixed ghastly eyes, in some corner of the chamber, listening to hear whether we dare to breathe of its presence to any one. And we dare not;

poor cowards that we are! ... Hitherto she had not stirred from where he had left her; no outward circumstances had roused her out of the trance of thought in which she had been plunged by his last words ...   (*NS*, I, 25:198)

Gaskell finds in the Gothic a vocabulary that allows her to convey the nightmarish cast of interiority in moments of emotional shock. She was, of course, no stranger to the ghost story or the supernatural tale, and she does in this novel occasionally deploy the accoutrements of Gothic horror to describe extreme states of mind. Her descriptions of powerful emotional response, especially taken out of context, do have an air of melodrama or exaggeration about them. When Thornton sees Margaret with a man he does not know to be her brother, Gaskell draws on a varied artillery of metaphor and simile relating to haunting, fantasy, dream, pain, and death to capture his agonized interior space:

[h]e was *haunted* by the remembrance of the handsome young man, with whom she stood in an attitude of such familiar confidence; and the remembrance *shot through him like an agony,* till it made him clench his hands tight in order to subdue the pain ... his trust dropped down *dead and powerless*: and all sorts of *wild fancies chased each other like dreams* through his mind.
(*NS*, II, 8:270, my emphasis)

But for the most part in *North and South*, the language of shock and horror is absorbed into the realist texture of the novel's narration so that it rarely produces a Gothic or melodramatic effect; the inner world's nightmare and fantasy are not aberrations but come to seem coextensive with the ordinary workaday world, and are often largely undetected by others.

Intense emotional experience such as Thornton experiences after Margaret's rejection has the effect of undoing the equanimity and balance of the self, disturbing bodily as well as psychic composure. In line with the emergent physiological psychology of the 1850s, Gaskell seems to emphasize the correlation between physiological and mental states, and the importance of the former in elucidating the latter:[12]

When Mr Thornton had left the house that morning he was almost blinded by his baffled passion. He was as dizzy as if Margaret, instead of looking, and speaking, and moving like a tender graceful woman, had been a sturdy fish-wife, and given him a sound blow with her fists. He had positive bodily pain, – a violent headache, and a throbbing intermittent pulse ... He called himself a fool for suffering so, and yet he could not, at the moment, recollect the cause of his suffering, and whether it was adequate to the consequences it had produced.
(*NS*, II, 1:207)

For a time the overpowering experience dominates consciousness, but then it seems to subside: "it seemed as if his deep mortification of yesterday, and the stunned purposeless course of the hours afterwards, had cleared away all the mists from his intellect" (*NS*, II, 2:212). Yet as Gaskell shows, Thornton's self-congratulation at dispelling the effects of the emotion is premature. Powerful feelings return, unbidden, to arrest the mind's focus once more:

> It seemed as though he gave way all at once; he was so languid that he could not control his thoughts; they would wander to her; they would bring back the scene, – not of his repulse and rejection the day before, but the looks, the actions of the day before that. He went along the crowded streets mechanically, winding in and out among the people, but never seeing them, – almost sick with longing for that one half hour. (*NS*, II, 2:213)

Gaskell's focus here on Thornton's wandering attention, and his lack of control over his mind, raises a well-aired question in mid-nineteenth-century physiology: the role of volition or will in controlling psychical states. Throughout Carpenter's discussion of abstracted states of mind, he draws reverential attention to "the Will" as the commander of the ship, in the absence of which it runs without steering or direction. States in which the will is suspended include wandering attention, reverie, abstraction, absence of mind, signs of functioning by rote or habit while the mind is otherwise occupied.

While Carpenter's focus on order and control and his advocacy of vigorous mental training has been linked to the Unitarian preoccupation with education and self-regulation, Gaskell, also a Unitarian, seems more ready to explore (at least in her middle-class characters) what may emerge in states where self-control is shaken. Her open-mindedness is here literally that – an attention to the mind opened to its unconscious processes. Significantly, only after the torment of love has opened Thornton up to his capacity to feel strongly is he capable of responding to Higgins. It is not so much Margaret's beneficent influence that is the cause of this transformation but the almost magical effect of his own powerful emotions that renders Thornton receptive. And although Gaskell uses the language of enchantment in describing the process, she is not being evasive or mystifying the nature of his changed attitude when she writes "then the conviction went in, *as if by some spell*, and touched the latent tenderness of his heart" (*NS*, II, 14:325, my emphasis).

The difference between Gaskell and Carpenter is her implicit sense that there may be times when the undermining of self-control and will can be useful and informative – a condition, even, for new growth and change. Gaskell would of course not dispute the importance of will and rational control. There are several examples in the novel of the dangers of intemperate response: Frederick, who commits mutiny in response to oppression and cruelty; the ancestor, "old Sir John" Beresford, who shot his steward for insulting him; and, in an especially stereotypic representation of primitive, working-class mob mentality, the strikers who "watch open-eyed and open-mouthed the thread of dark-red blood which wakened them up from their trance of passion" (*NS*, I, 22:179). While this collective "trance of passion" is a very dangerous thing, the many states of trance or abstraction that Gaskell evokes in the novel are not generally feared as dangerous paths to unreason and not seen as undermining the will in a threatening way. As we have seen in *Mary Barton*, passion and reason are opposed in working-class subjects; in *North and South* they are not so much oppositional as mutually informative. As if to acknowledge the precariousness of the coherent and stable subject, Gaskell inflects Carpenter's model of selfhood so that it can less threateningly accommodate the displacement of a vigilant, governing consciousness. Several recent critics have written about Gaskell's refusal of absolutes and embracing of complexity and even contradiction in this novel.[13] As Terence Wright notes, "We constantly witness the crumbling of absolutes, the clear becoming irresolute, the iron will a vulnerable flesh."[14] Deeply sceptical about solutions and abidingly interrogative, Gaskell implicitly questions the unitary and integrated nature of the self. The model of selfhood she implies has a place for the work of unconscious experience however problematically that may inflect questions of responsibility and accountability.

These questions obtain in relation to Margaret's two impulsive public actions – saving Thornton from the mob and lying to a policeman to save her brother – which seem both to arise, as a result of strong emotion, from a part of the self that is not under conscious control.[15] "You forgot yourself in thought for another," explains Mr. Bell, who helps Margaret to ratio-nalize the lie by referring to the "temptation" as "strong, instinctive motive" (*NS*, II, 21:396, 397). The self forgotten or possessed is invoked to explain both these impulsive actions: Margaret wonders "what possessed" her to defend Thornton. And after lying to save Frederick, "she tried to recall the force of her temptation by endeavouring to remember the details which had thrown her into such deadly fright; but she could not. She only understood two facts – that Frederick had been in danger of being pur-sued ... and that she had lied to save him" (*NS*, II, 10:277). Each of these occasions on which Margaret feels possessed or cannot recall what prompted her action is also accompanied by a scene of swooning or loss of consciousness, as if to signal the abdication of the ordinary volition or consciousness that produced the untoward action. Just as Thornton's experience of powerful emotion results in intense bodily symptoms as well as psychic pain, so Margaret's disruption of ordinary consciousness results in a condition of bodily collapse.

In the first instance, her action arises in part from unacknowledged feelings for Thornton. It is fitting that she lies apparently unconscious when she hears how her protection of Thornton has been construed as love. On the way home, struggling not to lose consciousness again, she tries not to think of "that ugly dream of insolent words ... and her mind sought for some present fact to steady itself upon, and keep it from utterly losing consciousness in another hideous, sickly swoon" (NS, I, 22:185). The "ugly dream," far more than the confrontation with a violent mob, threatens consciousness because it confronts her with forbidden knowledge. Often indicated by blushing and feelings of shame, Margaret's knowledge and awareness of herself as sexually attractive is repeatedly denied even as it is simultaneously recognized and commented on by others.[16] Lennox's proposal arouses her shame at being seen as a marriageable woman and the factory men who comment impertinently on her looks call up "a flash of indignation which made her face scarlet" (NS, I, 7:72). In Margaret's impulsive protectiveness and subsequent question – "what possessed me?" – Gaskell attempts to unpack the nature of dissociated or inadmissible knowledge. Without using the term "subconscious" or "unconscious," Gaskell is nevertheless drawing close to the idea they convey of a part of the mind that is not conscious, but is able to influence actions and behavior.

The second of the two scenes that show Margaret abstracted from herself deploys much the same language of altered states, and takes place after she is forced to lie about Frederick's presence. While Margaret's lie is impulsive, springing up from a need to protect Frederick, its execution makes of her an automaton, a somnambulist, whose actions come from another place than ordinary consciousness: "'I was not there,' said Margaret, still keeping her expressionless eyes fixed on his face, with the unconscious look of a sleep-walker" (NS, II, 9:273). She later repeats the lie, again with a "glassy, dream-like stare," so that the policeman's "quick suspicions were aroused by this dull echo of her former denial. It was as if she had forced herself to one untruth and had been stunned out of all power of varying it" (NS, II, 9:274). When the policeman leaves, "[s]he kept her eyes upon him in the same dull, fixed manner, until he was fairly out of the house. She shut the door, and went into the study, paused – tottered forward – paused again – swayed for an instant where she stood and fell prone on the floor in a dead swoon" (NS, II, 9:275). Margaret's loss of consciousness and stunned faculties make her seem a conventional, fainting Victorian heroine. But in several other situations of crisis, Margaret behaves with strength and fortitude where ordinary women might have succumbed. Confronted with

Boucher's bloated and disfigured body, she covers his face, and sets about breaking the news to his family. On a prior occasion, the doctor who tells her about her mother's poor health says to himself, "[I]t's astonishing how much those thorough-bred creatures can do and suffer. That girl's game to the back-bone. Another, who had gone that deadly colour, could never have come round without either fainting or hysterics. But she wouldn't do either ... And the very force of her will brought her round" (*NS*, I, 16:127). Such instances prompt us to look beyond the fainting fit as an occurrence of feminine wilting. While the narrator suggests that lying is so alien to Margaret that she is incapable of being inventive or varied, the text also shows that in lying Margaret is "not herself." The sense of dissociated consciousness that is conveyed serves to exculpate Margaret (though she roundly condemns herself) from full responsibility for her actions. But even so, her action muddies the ideal of clear moral behavior, straightforward and beyond reproach. The incident recalls Mary Barton's crisis in court when she attempts to defend Jem without divulging her father's guilt. Gaskell is less probing of Mary's decision to shield her father and more dramatic in imagining the threat to sanity that Mary's self-division entails. *North and South* explores Margaret's mind in the aftermath of the lie. Although Gaskell does not resolve the question of moral responsibility for actions that seem to contradict one's avowed and consciously held principles, she does use the experience to unsettle Margaret by opening her up to her own fallibility.

Gaskell's focus on the capacity of shock to stun the emotions looks forward to the development in the late nineteenth and early twentieth centuries of the concept of trauma. The discourse of trauma cohered around studies of the effects of stress or shock on memory and the incapacity of the subject to recollect, narrativize, or assimilate overwhelming experience. The traumatized individual typically experiences disruptions of memory in relation to the disastrous experience. Hallucinations, flashbacks, and emotional triggers of panic and powerlessness signal the presence yet inaccessibility of the dissociated knowledge. In Gaskell's novel experiences of shock, pain, and violence of feeling, though they may stun and numb the faculties, are not so extreme or cataclysmic. Emotional shocks or jolts are most closely explored and respected, painful as they are, as sources of information about a self that is less unified and governable than one would like, but must yet answer for its actions. If her representations of stunned consciousness do anticipate formulations of trauma, they are never simply or narrowly personal but always viewed in terms of their larger social implications. Reading *North and South* with attention to the movement of the narrator into the recesses of consciousness, reading with an ear for the language of dreams and abstracted states through which the narrator adumbrates the mysterious but influential realm beyond ordinary consciousness, we recover what a focus on external action and event cannot provide. Far from being mere melodramatic effects, the novel's crises of inner life and consciousness are an integral part of Gaskell's attempt to chart the social transformations of mid-century England and understand the forces of feeling and unconscious life that jolt the individual into self-scrutiny and renewed engagement with the outside world.

Notes

1 See, for example, Patsy Stoneman, *Elizabeth Gaskell* (Brighton: Harvester, 1987); Jill L. Matus, *Unstable Bodies: Victorian Representations of Sexuality and Maternity* (Manchester: Manchester University Press, 1995); and Susan Johnston, *Women and Domestic Experience in Victorian Political Fiction* (Westport, CT: Greenwood Press, 2001).

2 See Jane Spencer, *Elizabeth Gaskell* (Basingstoke: Macmillan, 1993), 33–6, who discusses the importance of children, and grief at their loss.

3 See Kate Flint, *Elizabeth Gaskell* (Plymouth: Northcote House, 1995), 11.

4 William Benjamin Carpenter, *Principles of Human Physiology*, 5th edn. (London: Churchill, 1855), 627.

5 Gaskell mentions an Italian origin for this tale of punishment; it is also the subject of a horror story, William Mudford's "The Iron Shroud," published in *Blackwood's Magazine* in 1830.

6 Other critics who have focused to some extent on the emotional economy of the novel include Rosemarie Bodenheimer, "*North and South*: A Permanent State of Change," *Nineteenth-Century Fiction* 34:3 (1979), 281–301, and Terence Wright, *Elizabeth Gaskell: We Are Not Angels: Realism, Gender, Values* (Houndmills: Palgrave Macmillan, 1995), 105, who observes that the novel is "a book full of pain ... of stress and disturbance, of pangs of conscience and sexual torment."

7 George Henry Lewes, *Problems of Life and Mind*, 5 vols. (London: Trubner and Co., 1874–9); first series, 2 vols., *The Foundations of a Creed* (1874), I, 127–8.

8 See Wright, *Elizabeth Gaskell*, 107, who focuses on the passage of days and nights and the novel's "painful sense of the monotony of ordinary existence."

9 See Stoneman, *Elizabeth Gaskell*, 68–86.

10 See, for example, Sally Shuttleworth (*NS*, xvi). Gaskell herself referred to Hale in a letter of 1855 as "weak and vacillating" (*L*, 353).

11 Gaskell reported in letters to Marianne that he stayed with them during a lecture tour in 1851 (*L*, 146–7, 831, 833).

12 See Alexander Bain, *The Senses and the Intellect* (1855), 3rd edn. (1855; London: Longmans, Green, and Co., 1868), and *The Emotions and the Will*, 3rd edn. (London: Longmans, Green, and Co., 1880).

13 See especially Hilary Schor, *Scheherezade in the Marketplace: Elizabeth Gaskell and the Victorian Novel* (New York: Oxford University Press, 1992).

14 Wright, *Elizabeth Gaskell*, 110.

15 See Bodenheimer, "*North and South*: A Permanent State of Change," 295–6, for an excellent discussion of these instances, which focuses on Margaret's foray into the public realm; while I am indebted to her discussion, my own focus is more on the altered states of consciousness produced in the aftermath of powerful emotion.

16 For further discussions of shame, see Stoneman, *Elizabeth Gaskell*, 128–38, and Shuttleworth, introduction to *NS*, xxix.

4

AUDREY JAFFE

Cranford and *Ruth*

"The use made of fragments and small opportunities; ... [t]hings that many would despise, and actions which it seemed scarcely worthwhile to perform, were all attended to in Cranford."
– Elizabeth Gaskell, *Cranford* (1853)

"[A] vision of a man seemed to haunt the kitchen."
– Elizabeth Gaskell, *Cranford* (1853)

Cranford and *Ruth* were written in tandem. For three years Gaskell "vibrated" back and forth between the two projects (to borrow the term she uses to describe the movement of *Cranford*'s narrator), and then *Cranford*, which began as a series of stories Gaskell wrote for Charles Dickens's weekly journal *Household Words*, was published in one volume in June of 1853, *Ruth* in January of that same year. Both texts are centrally concerned with the status of women and the nature of female community; both are said to draw on Gaskell's memories of having been raised in the all-female company of her aunts Hannah Lumb and Abigail Holland in the small town of Knutsford south of Manchester. But the two works differ radically from one another, offering alternative visions, genres, and sensibilities. One is satiric, the other fairly sentimental; one is generally comic, the other chiefly tragic. One explores the nature of village life while the other focuses on a few central characters and families; one is ostensibly though not exclusively interested in what are conventionally viewed as trivial feminine concerns (tea and headgear) while the other seeks to intervene in social debates crucial to the status of Victorian women (prostitution and philanthropy). And one has long been a popular and beloved example of the author's work, while the other was so reviled by contemporary readers that some burned their copies. Certainly, for many of her readers, the Gaskell who authored *Ruth* seemed difficult to reconcile with the one who penned *Cranford*. But it is precisely because these texts are apparently so opposed and issued from very different Gaskells that critical insight might be gained by juxtaposing them.

What *Cranford* and *Ruth* do share is their status as oddities within the Victorian literature canon: neither fits neatly within the usual categories of Victorian-novel criticism. *Cranford* is loose and episodic, its generic affiliations more with the sketch or short story than with the novel; *Ruth* is less an example of mainstream Victorian realism than a moral tale, the elaboration of a familiar Victorian disciplinary narrative in which female sexuality is exorcized via the familiar route of female punishment. It may be the case, then, that rather than any intrinsic qualities, a mere quirk of literary history – the status of these texts with respect to the canons of Victorian fiction and criticism – suggests a new approach to their combined assessment. For a departure from conventional narrative form in each work is accompanied by a concern with the detachment of characters, especially female characters, from dominant cultural narratives, especially those in which women play out their conventional roles as economically and socially subservient to men. Each text takes up a Victorian female stereo-type (*Cranford*, the spinster; *Ruth*, the fallen woman); each seeks to raise questions about that figure by proposing (more or less explicitly) the replacement of the male-dominated culture that produced it with a culture dominated by women and/or an alternative, feminine sensibility. Empha-sizing the harshness and destructiveness – in *Cranford*'s terms, the vulgarity – of male-dominated society, these texts thus propose the exchange of one set of societal rules for another. But the challenge posed by the idea of finding a realistic alternative to masculine rules (or masculine rule) within what remains is such that, even in the context of imaginative escape, a male-dominated structure is reflected in the derivative and fantastical quality of the oppositional worlds they proceed to construct. Indeed, within what seems to be an inescapable binary model, these works suggest that the granting of a dominant role to women is imaginable – even in fiction – only in fictional terms.

***

In anticipation of the visit of the renowned magician Signor Brunoni to the town of Cranford, one of that town's inhabitants seeks to "prime herself with scientific explanations for the tricks of the following evening" (*C*, 9:84). Wishing to decipher the rules that govern Brunoni's magic, Miss Pole hopes to avoid what she anticipates will be an unpleasant sensation of surprise: unpleasant not least, one might speculate – given the feminine emphasis of Cranford society – because it is to be offered by a man. That same Miss Pole, presented not only as an outwitter of magicians but also as a devotee of rules of all kinds, prevents the narrator from turning her head to survey the "merry chattering people" during the magician's perfor-mance, asserting that such behavior is "not the thing." "What 'the thing' was, I could never find out," observes Mary Smith drily, "but it must have been something eminently dull and tiresome" (C, 9:86).

If Miss Pole's caution seems strange in the context of a society whose most distinctive feature is its attempt to overturn that most prominent Victorian "thing" of all – the dominance of men – it also suggests the extent to which this redefinition leaves many aspects of social life unchanged. Indeed, Cranford may if anything be more rule-bound than the society it seeks to replace – perhaps necessarily so, given the uncharted territory that its denizens occupy. For if the magician's rules are somehow threatening in their mystery, the rules of Cranford – such as the diktat that one must not turn one's head in a crowded theater – are no less arbitrary and perhaps no more interesting than those made by men (and indeed, given her name and *Cranford*'s frequent evocation of gender disguise, it would not be so strange to discover that Miss Pole is a man). But the rules nevertheless perform their function, which is to offer a hedge against the terror invited by Cranford's societal experiment. For *Cranford* and *Ruth* seek to expel both men and what they identify as masculine sensibilities from worlds that have traditionally been governed by them. Separately and together, these texts ask whether the rules might be rewritten, and what in such an event "the thing" might turn out to be.

Much of *Cranford* consists of ethnographic excursions into Cranford life: descriptions of the manners and habits of the village's inhabitants. The narrator Mary Smith, who shuttles back and forth between Cranford and the world outside it, tells of "the use that was made of fragments and small opportunities in Cranford; the rose-leaves that were gathered ere they fell, to make into a pot-pourri ... ; the little bundles of lavender-flowers sent to strew the drawers of some town-dweller" (C, 2:15). We learn that the ladies of Cranford have a fashion sense all their own, focused chiefly on hats:

> If the heads were buried in smart new caps, the ladies were like ostriches, and cared not what became of their bodies. Old gowns, white and venerable collars, any number of brooches, up and down and everywhere ... – old brooches for a permanent ornament, and new caps to suit the fashion of the day; the ladies of Cranford always dressed with chaste elegance and propriety, as Miss Barker once prettily expressed it. (C, 8:73–4)

As she mediates between life outside Cranford and the village, with its special rules and customs, however, Mary also hints that Cranford's attention to detail, charming as it may be, points toward a deeply fictionalized view of the world.

> We had tacitly agreed to ignore that any with whom we associated on terms of visiting equality could ever be prevented by poverty from doing anything

that they wished. If we walked to or from a party, it was because the night was *so* fine, or the air *so* refreshing; not because sedan-chairs were expensive. If we wore prints, instead of summer silks, it was because we preferred a washing material; and so on, till we blinded ourselves to the vulgar fact that we were, all of us, people of very moderate means. (C, 1:4)

Even as she aligns herself with Cranford's women, Mary underscores their capacity for self-delusion. For despite the lightness and flexibility of her tone, her narrative is especially concerned with the townswomen's rigidity: their sensitivity to any behavior that seems to violate some Cranford-ordained rule, whether it be the wearing of hats, the telling of jokes, or the donning of clothing more commonly associated with the other sex. The townswomen are expected, for instance, to adhere to Cranford's "rules and regulations" in the matter of dress, avoiding above all anything " 'vulgar' (a tremendous word in Cranford)" (C, 1:2; 1:3). The term "vulgar" refers to that which would upset Cranford gentility, and especially to any direct mention of the subject of money. Gentility, Cranford's highest value, constitutes the blindness here described and the community's dominant fiction, embodying its beliefs about class, money, and the unshakable status of Cranford society.

Because they are not wedded to the rules that govern Cranford society, it is men who most threaten the town's hermetic social code, men who are most likely to be, in Cranford terms, vulgar: "We had congratulated ourselves upon the snugness of the evenings; and, in our love for gentility, and distaste of mankind, we had almost persuaded ourselves that to be a man was to be 'vulgar' " (C, 1:7). Indeed, what Mary conveys most vividly to her readers' consciousnesses as the *raison d'être* of both village and her reportage is the stipulation that in Cranford men remain subordinate to women: to those "Amazons" who are, as the insistently genteel first sentence puts it, in "possession." Not surprisingly, the first modern wave of *Cranford* criticism, prompted by feminist rereadings of the 1970s, lauded the story's focus on female community and ostensibly feminine values.[1] More recently, however, *Cranford* has been described as a critique of the constraints of Victorian ideology, particularly the destructive effects of the ideology of separate spheres (the widely accepted view that women ruled the domestic realm, men the world outside). The lives of Cranford's women have been seen as comic, energetic, and caring, but also as pathetic and devoid of energy, evidence of a moribund society and social code.[2] In particular, since Cranford's restrictions against men necessarily include, as belonging similarly in the category of the vulgar, knowledge of the workings of the larger world in which the townswomen are inevitably enmeshed, the women of Cranford remain unable to manipulate its terms and to save themselves from its machinations: to discover the whereabouts of Matty's brother after he disappears, for instance, or to comprehend the failure of the bank that holds her money. Such ignorance can be understood as either comic or tragic, or perhaps comic to the point of being tragic; for one critic, it emphasizes "the nineteenth-century's systematic infantilisation of women."[3] The use of the term "possession," as in Cranford is in possession of the Amazons, similarly elides the derivative, dependent quality of Cranford property: the reality that those who hold it are widows and spinsters, indebted to their husbands and fathers.

The construction of a microcosmic topsy-turvy Victorian England in which men are second-class citizens is, of course, a response to an actual Victorian England of which women can hardly be said to be "in possession"; it is the manifestation of anxiety about the power wielded by men in Victorian culture in general, the difficulty of keeping them in – or out of – any place they have not designated for themselves. The idea of a separate feminine society allows for an almost parodic critique of Victorian separate-spheres ideology, as if, to borrow a memorable twentieth-century formulation, men really are from Mars and women from Venus.[4] But *Cranford* is hardly devoid of men, and indeed both village and narrative are routinely enlivened by deviations from the Cranford "thing": masculine disruptions of the town's placid surface. Although "all the holders of houses, above a certain rent, are women," Cranford grants the few men who do appear an unusual degree of importance, and the story draws much of its narrative energy from the very intrusions of which "the ladies of Cranford" despair (C, 1:1).

The narrator's comment about the dullness of adhering to "the thing," especially when it inhibits her desire to look about her, speaks to her role as amateur ethnographer, observer and recorder of Cranford habits and codes; it also raises the stereotypical narrative problem of the all-female society: the question of whether the "fragments and small opportunities" that such a town offers have any hope of holding a reader's interest. Indeed, in Cranford violations of the rules frequently take the form – as the town's female-centeredness suggests they must – of men (or the idea or fantasy of men, since, as in the case of Signor Brunoni, their mystifying reputation tends to precede and surround them) out of place: the recurrent possibility of men "'where nae men should be'" (C, 10:93). Although it is staunchly on record as wishing to exclude men, that is, Cranford is both fascinated by them and unable to function without them: it is haunted by the possibilities, threats, and promises – the intimations of social and economic realities, of life on the outside – they represent. The story might be said, in fact, to illustrate the insufficiency of exclusion (or ownership of real estate) as a means of dealing with masculine power, suggesting that despite their prominence in Cranford, women exist less in some alternative position to that power than in continued subordination to it.

Thus it is perhaps not surprising that men frequently appear in the role of thieves, threatening the removal from Cranford of Cranford property – including its women. After the visit of Signor Brunoni, for instance (a figure representing two forms of alienness, sex and nationality), the inhabitants of Cranford imagine their town besieged by male robbers; they detect men's footsteps on flowerbeds and position fire-irons to fall on male intruders. The narrative tells of Miss Matty's recurrent fear of being "caught by her last leg, just as she was getting into bed, by some one concealed under it," and of her device for dealing with this problem:

> she had told Martha to buy her a penny ball, such as children play with – and now she rolled this ball under the bed every night; if it came out on the other side, well and good; if not, she always took care to have her hand on the bell-rope, and meant to call out John and Harry, just as if she expected men-servants to answer her ring. (C, 10:98)

The reliance on invisible men displayed on both sides of this scenario, and the replacement of men by bogeymen – men in the garden, men under the bed; men as sexual predators but also as rescuers – bespeaks the Cranford community's unavoidable ambivalence toward men in general. For even as it keeps men out, Cranford owes its existence to them: men control the joint-stock company responsible for the loss of Matty's money; men marry one's companions or perhaps even oneself, thereby not only depleting the town's supply of ostensibly self-sufficient women but also giving the lie to – and revealing the phantasmatic status of – the village's claims for self-sufficiency. In Cranford men steal what (and because) they already possess.

As if to banish this unsavory reality, *Cranford* is dominated not only by stories about men but also by fantasies of their violent eradication. Hardly has the narrative begun, for instance, than one Captain Brown is introduced as a respected authority on numerous matters – a "true man," in an unarguably complimentary epithet – despite what is described as resistance to his initial presence in the village (C, 1:7). But Captain Brown is soon felled by a passing train, as if in acknowledgment that, were he to remain, there would be no way to escape his narrative dominance. In a detail that suggests both the desire to eliminate men via sudden, fatal accidents, and the status of men as the cause of such accidents, Captain Brown's failure to anticipate his encounter with an oncoming train (doubtless driven by a man) is said to be a result of his absorption in the newest number of *Pickwick*. (Many critics note that the contrast between Dickens and Dr. Johnson, established as a point of enmity between Brown and Miss Jenkyns, emphasizes the conflict between new ways and old that becomes the narrative's ostensible central issue, with Mr. Brown's untimely end on the railway tracks effectively, if only temporarily, sealing the discussion by suggesting the violent destructiveness of modern ideas.) The demise of Captain Brown, however, is soon followed by the arrival of his erstwhile friend Major Gordon, who concludes this portion of the narrative by marrying the Captain's daughter Jessie and removing her from Cranford. Men, as representatives of the village's interactions with and dependence on the larger world it cannot control, are everywhere in evidence but also everywhere mystified and misunderstood; like Signor Brunoni, they embody rules that cannot be fathomed. They are vulgar not only because they are out of place, but because they represent the very idea of out-of-placeness: the engagement with the outside world in all its uncontrolledness that Cranford gentility rejects. Men are acceptable, as Signor Brunoni's magic tricks and Peter Jenkyns's romanticized tales of Indian adventure suggest, only if they organize their identities around fictions: fictions that obscure and mystify the origins of things.

The rules of Cranford and the Cranford sense of propriety thus display a rigidity that belies oft-made critical claims for the narrative's essential humor and good-naturedness. The village's violent rejection of Matty's brother Peter, for instance, showcases Cranford's ambivalent attitude toward men. Peter is a storyteller, an actor, and above all a practical joker; he "seemed to think that the Cranford people might be joked about, and made fun of, and they did not like it; nobody does" (C, 6:50). But his joking takes shape as an oblique expression of anger at the community's dislike and fear of men, bringing to the surface preoccupations that, its own form suggests, can be raised only in disguise. Peter's joke, which becomes *Cranford*'s chief concern (and has long been the chief interest of much *Cranford* criticism) speaks to the story's and the town's central area of conflict: the question of how, in Cranford, vulgarity is to be avoided; the impossibility of isolating one sex from the other, and, in general, the community's simultaneous need for and denial of men and the knowledge they represent. Done, Peter says, to give "the old ladies in the town ... something to talk about," the joke addresses precisely that of which they will not talk: what Peter does more than once is to dress as a woman, and what he does in this instance is to wear his sister Deborah's clothing and walk through the town cuddling a little pillow meant to represent a baby (C, 6:51). Literally taking the woman's place, he inhabits both her clothing and her most routinized function. This pointed bringing to attention of Cranford's trouble with men may account for the violent anger visited upon him by his father, who beats him, after which Peter disappears and is for some time thought to be dead. As the fantasy takes shape, and as the case of Captain Brown had already suggested, the town's exclusionary politics results in the imagining of the violent deaths of men, as if, unable to imagine any permissible role for them in Cranford society, the Cranford imagination simply kills them off – subsequently, in its ambivalence, joking about the episode and bringing them back to life.

The violence that greets Peter's joke, as well as the seriousness of its long-term consequences, allude to what might be called the "terror of manners" in Cranford: a desperate attachment to manners and habits defined by the ladies' willful blindness, the anxiety they betray about what are perceived as the mysterious rules and violent tendencies of the larger world.[5] The depth of anxiety exposed by a failure to follow the rules, as in Peter's case, as well as the perpetual appearance of men where none "ought" to be, reveals Cranford isolationism not as a solution to the problem of separate spheres but rather as a continuation of it, in which men are aligned with the real and women with the unreal, the fictional, the delusional. In her attempt to foresee, decipher, and thereby demystify the rules of masculine behavior, then, Miss Pole represents a deviation from the model of charming but self-destructive femininity that appears both here and in *Ruth*. For as turns out to be the case with the mysterious Signor Brunoni, knowing the nature of the thing in advance – however vulgar it might turn out to be – might avert the misery that arises from the deceptively pleasant condition of not knowing.

* * *

Ruth tells the story of an orphaned dressmaker's apprentice who is seduced and abandoned by a wealthy young man. Distraught and seeking suicide, Ruth Hilton is distracted by the apparently similarly self-destructive intentions of an elderly deformed man, who turns out to be the minister Thurstan Benson. After she comes to his aid, Benson persuades his sister Faith of Ruth's essential good nature and the two take her into their home, which includes along with them their servant Sally. In order to render Ruth acceptable to the community, especially to their strict and upright neighbor Mr. Bradshaw and his family, Faith provides her with a new identity as a visiting widow, Mrs. Denbigh, a detail that picks up the tie between women and fictionality so prominent in *Cranford*. Mrs. Denbigh's exemplary character and friendship with the Bradshaws' daughter Jemima enable her to live comfortably among them, to bear her child, and at the same time to become a model of rectitude for others, notably Jemima. After a long period of repentance during which she becomes a nurse, Ruth encounters her seducer once again, and while tending to his illness catches an infection that leads to her death.

Despite its focus on a single character, *Ruth* exists within the rubric of the social-problem novel; it is directed at contemporary discussion of whether fallen women could be "rescued" or reformed. Rescue work of this kind was very much a topic of the day, with projects such as "Homes for Homeless Women" being promoted by Angela Burdett-Coutts and Dickens; Gaskell's intervention focuses particularly on the double standard that censures the woman while exonerating the man. *Ruth* proposes, however, not exactly or not only that fallen women can be saved, but that women who appear fallen in the eyes of society may in fact be virtuous. The story draws on Gaskell's interest in an actual dressmaker's apprentice whose seduction by a doctor was encouraged by her employer. The entrapment device survives – Ruth's employer somewhat inexplicably insists that she attend the ball where she meets Bellingham – and this fact, along with Ruth's naivety seems to mitigate her responsibility for her situation. But the force of these details is countered by the story's reproduction of the familiar cultural narrative in which a sexual transgression results in the woman's punishment.

Like *Cranford*, *Ruth* focuses initially on the presence of men where, from the position of the novel's female-centered ideology, no men should be: in the familial circle represented by Ruth's mother, who died when Ruth was young, and its secondary manifestation in the group of dress-maker's assistants headed by the cruel stepmother-figure Mrs. Mason. Like *Cranford*, *Ruth* evokes a promise of feminine community, a world owned or at least governed by women, in which any men who remain have (as if Peter's disguise represents the fulfillment of a feminine wish) been transformed into members of the opposite sex. Thus the only man sanctioned within the novel's imaginative universe is Benson, whose gentleness of manner and physical deformity exempt him from the demands of conventional masculinity. But the novel never frees itself from an ima-gined audience of men, especially with respect to the character and appearance of Ruth. It begins with a scene that depicts the dressmaker's assistants alone, voyeuristically showcasing a group of young women ostensibly behaving as they might when no men are there to see them. Ruth is distinguished from the others not only by her beauty, but also by her ignorance of conventional behavior, particularly behavior that would suggest a knowledge of men. Unaware of social niceties such as modesty, for instance, she acknowledges that "she knows she is pretty" because "many people have told me so" (R, 2:12). But such naivety, oriented toward a phantasmic male gaze (the other girls find it incomprehensible) and charming and "natural" as it may be, accounts ultimately for Ruth's inability to anticipate (perhaps with "scientific explanations," as Miss Pole hopes to do) the social and physical consequences of her relationship with Mr. Bellingham.

The novel's masculine disruption begins as a welcome relief from this all-female realm, presented to some extent as the lair of a wicked stepmother. Ruth's only escape from the daily drudgery of dressmaker's work and the cold, rigid mistress who presides over it is the glittering society ball to which, Cinderella-like, she is sent, and where her beauty and her absorption in her work – and momentary lapse from it – catch the attention of Bellingham, the wealthy young man who becomes her lover. The novel's sorest point is the apparent innocence with which Ruth enters into the relationship. Ignorant of the social meaning of the thing she does, she is, as Gaskell writes of herself in a letter, "an improper woman without knowing it," or in the novel's words, "a beautiful ignoramus," not responsible for her actions because she is unaware of their meaning (*L*, 223; *R*, 6:75). Far from being unusual, however, Ruth in her ignorance exemplifies the "conspiracy of silence" within which Victorian girls were generally raised: the "state of repressed consciousness" identified by the critic Martha Vicinus that rendered it effectively impossible for women to act as responsible agents with regard to sexual behavior.[6] But her innocence/ignorance largely accounts for her appeal, both to Mr. Bellingham and, presumably, to many of the novel's readers.

A fallen woman without knowing it, Ruth is condemned by those who do not know her but wins over those who do, revealing a personality that is meant to belie the one-dimensionality of the type. Gaskell wishes to present in Ruth a breaking away from habit and convention, an "independent individual action ... superior to all outward conventionalities" (*R*, 1:2). But the scene in which Faith Benson sees her for the first time suggests that this breaking away leaves her with no place to go. Having passed judgment on Ruth before meeting her, wondering at how her brother could bring such a creature to their home, Faith's opinion changes entirely when she glimpses Ruth asleep:

> Mrs. Hughes had pinned up a piece of green calico, by way of a Venetian blind, to shut out the afternoon sun; and in the light thus shaded lay Ruth, still, and wan, and white. Even with her brother's account of Ruth's state, such deathlike quietness startled Miss Benson – startled her into pity for the poor lovely creature who lay thus stricken and felled. When she saw her, she could no longer imagine her to be an impostor, or a hardened sinner; such prostration of woe belonged to neither. (*R*, 11:114)

The effect is as problematic as it is peaceful: Ruth asleep is Ruth absorbed in another world, innocent by virtue of being unconscious, felled but presumably not fallen. Indeed, the image underscores the extent to which the novel is a study in the compelling quality of absorption, since Ruth's attention, presumably at the (unrepresented) moment of her fall as well as beyond, is always directed toward something other than herself. She focuses on nature, on the other women with whom she works, on Bellingham, on Thurstan Benson, and eventually on her own child, whose function in the novel is less to stand as evidence of her fallenness as to provide a morally appropriate site for her attention (as Benson says, "If her life has hitherto been self-seeking, and wickedly thoughtless, here is the very instrument to make her forget herself, and be thoughtful for another" [R, 11:119]). It is as if any response other than stock unhappiness and guilt would conjure an idiosyncratic identity that might then prove antithetical to Gaskell's sympathetic project. As a character, Ruth is imprisoned in Gaskell's prescriptive vision of female innocence.

Ruth attempts to elicit sympathy for a generally unsympathetic Victorian type by exploring the intricacies of individual motive and character, but the techniques required to neutralize the issue of Ruth's sexuality are finally inconsistent with those of characterological realism. Ruth's lack of introspection has the effect that, as Victorian critics noted, she seems less a fully realized character than the vehicle of a moral message, and a somewhat unclear one at that. Gaskell seeks to counter the stereotypical narrative of the woman's fall with a personal story in which a fall is somehow not a fall: unaware of the consequences of her actions, and thus supposedly not responsible for them, Ruth can earn the trust of those around her. But as it engages in a series of complex and contradictory negotiations with the issue of fallenness, the novel is also unable to escape the ideological contradictions in which the term is enmeshed. Ruth's sexual fall is in fact oddly parallel to Miss Matty's economic one: both are ascribed to lack of knowledge; both require lengthy periods of penitential activity once the relevant knowledge is revealed. Thus if Ruth's innocence and goodness and in particular her role as healer are meant to counter conventional representations of fallen women (details drawn from the original story are reversed in Gaskell's treatment, in which Ruth nurses Bellingham and is at the same time, in a metaphorical reenactment of their sexual relationship, "infected" by him), her fate reinforces such representations: in the most conventional of narrative fulfillments she atones for, and dies as a result of, her seduction by Bellingham. The novel cannot escape the contradictory status of its claim for Ruth's innocence, never quite managing to say that if fallenness is a societal construction, virtue must be as well.

The novel's effort to counter the prevailing influence of types and to resist the dominant narrative of the fallen woman thus pulls uncomfortably in several directions at once. Just as Gaskell's town dominated by women takes men as one of its chief concerns, so, too, does her insistence on Ruth's purity result in an idealized and conflicted representation. Perhaps most troublesome in this context is the dependence of Ruth's rescue on the construction of a "new," and false, identity. Gaskell has been criticized for omitting from the novel any scene of Ruth's fall, but the case can be made that her fall consists not in the sexual encounter with Bellingham, which takes place in the context of unconsciousness and innocence, but rather in the lie, executed with deliberateness and calculation.[7] Yet even in this interpretation, Ruth's fall both is and is not her own: it is a displaced but also shared, because gendered, guilt.

Both narratives rely heavily on characters who do in fact fail to conform to types – not only because they are thus able to cross boundaries of place (by way of Mary Smith) and gender (by way of Faith Benson, who possesses "masculine" qualities), but also because their characters display an awareness of the fictive nature of cultural and social identities, an awareness that distances both texts from conventional realism. Rejecting the terms of dominant cultural narratives in their rejection of men and masculinity, *Cranford* and *Ruth* seem at the same time unable to imagine an alternative that does not render their female characters susceptible to fantasy and self-delusion. Such an alternative may, however, lie both in the nature of these characters and in the generic peculiarities that link the texts together: a sense that only an awareness of the artificiality of social structures, including literary ones, may provide an escape from the claustrophobic gender binary within which these works (no less than the culture they describe) seem to be caught. For even as she lovingly describes the eccentricities of Cranford's inhabitants, Mary Smith – a name whose refusal to play the character game encloses it in invisible quotation marks – points toward an artificiality evident elsewhere in her text: in Peter's disguise, in Brown/Brunoni, in the generic instability of *Cranford* itself. In *Ruth* Faith Benson's invention of a fictional identity similarly bespeaks a distance from the rules that govern the larger community as well as the realist genre: rules that lend authority and consistency to the very structures that Gaskell here wishes to contest. Putting to work a belief in the efficacy of fictions to paper over, if not overcome, ideological stalemates, Faith's device suggests that the alternative to masculine rule is not feminine rule but rather a more profound destabilization of categories: a refusal to play by the rules that perpetuate such oppositional logic.

Notes

1 See for instance Nina Auerbach, *Communities of Women: An Idea in Fiction* (Cambridge, MA: Harvard University Press, 1978).
2 On the comic and caring aspects of the Cranford ladies' lives, see Hilary Schor, *Scheherezade in the Marketplace: Elizabeth Gaskell and the Victorian Novel* (New York: Oxford University Press, 1992). For the alternative view, see Patsy Stoneman, *Elizabeth Gaskell* (Brighton: Harvester, 1987).
3 Stoneman, *Elizabeth Gaskell*, 93.
4 John Gray, *Men Are From Mars, Women Are From Venus: A Practical Guide for Improving Communication and Getting What You Want in Your Relationships* (New York: HarperCollins, 1992).
5 For "terror of manners," see Mary Ann O'Farrell, "Jane Austen's Mafia," Conference on Narrative Literature, Berkeley, 2003.
6 Martha Vicinus, *Suffer and Be Still: Women in the Victorian Age* (Bloomington: Indiana University Press, 1972), 161, quoted in Stoneman, *Elizabeth Gaskell*, 103.
7 See Amanda Anderson, *Tainted Souls and Painted Faces: The Rhetoric of Fallenness in Victorian Culture* (Ithaca: Cornell University Press, 1993), and Audrey Jaffe, *Scenes of Sympathy: Identity and Representation in Victorian Fiction* (Ithaca: Cornell University Press, 2000).

5

LINDA H. PETERSON

Elizabeth Gaskell's
The Life of Charlotte Brontë

Before *The Life*: nineteenth-century women's biography

Charlotte Brontë died on March 31, 1855, and when Elizabeth Gaskell learned of her death, she resolved to write a memoir of her friend and fellow-novelist. On May 31, 1855, she wrote to Brontë's publisher, George Smith of Smith, Elder: "if I live long enough, and no one is living whom such a publication would hurt, I will publish what I know of her, and make the world (if I am but strong enough in expression,) honour the woman as much as they have admired the writer" (*L*, 345). The opportunity came sooner than Gaskell expected. On June 16, 1855, the Reverend Patrick Brontë, Charlotte's father, addressed a letter to Gaskell, with a request for her "to write a brief account of her life and to make some remarks on her works"; he added: "You seem to me to be the best qualified for doing what I wish should be done."[1]

When Gaskell agreed to write a biography of Brontë, the models for a woman author's life were few, and none distinguished. Alexander Dyce had published *Specimens of British Poetesses* (1825) and Anne Katherine Elwood *Memoirs of the Literary Ladies of England* (1843), the first an anthology of representative poems with biographical headnotes, the second a collection of short biographies describing each author's life circumstances and chief literary works.[2] Both were informational, the second inspirational to aspiring young women. As Elwood acknowledged in her preface, her *Memoirs* were for the amateur, "intended only for such of her own sex, who, not feeling themselves equal to profound and abstract subjects, can derive amusement and information from what is professedly too light for the learned, and too simple for the studious."[3]

The authorized biographies of nineteenth-century women writers were not much superior, though they set the agenda for subsequent women's life writing. After Laetitia Landon's death in 1838, Emma Roberts, a friend and minor writer, prefixed an account of the poetess's career to *The Zenana and*

Minor Poems (1839), testifying to Landon's domesticity and countering claims that she had committed suicide after an ill-advised marriage to George MacLean, governor of Cape Coast, Africa.[4] Laman Blanchard, another literary friend, then issued his *Life and Literary Remains of L. E. L.* (1841), amplifying the account with further instances of Landon's talent, achievement, and tragic death.[5] In the same decade, Henry F. Chorley published *Memorials of Mrs. Hemans* (1836), a personal reminiscence with a selection of literary letters, and the sister of Felicia Hemans followed with a hagiographic account of the poetess's life in her *Memoir* (1840), assuring the public of the domestic woman behind the literary author and revealing the dutiful daughter, affectionate sister, and solicitous mother who, more than any individual, "would have shrunk more sensitively from the idea of being made the subject of a biographical memoir."[6] At mid-century, however, no biography of a woman writer had realized a noteworthy form or achieved literary distinction; certainly, nothing approached the accomplishment of James Boswell's *Life of Samuel Johnson* (1791) or John Gibson Lockhart's *Memoirs of the Life of Sir Walter Scott, Bart.* (1837–8).

Nineteenth-century fictional accounts of the woman artist were better as literary productions, but equally discouraging as models, whether hagiographic or scandalous. Following Madame de Staël's *Corinne* (1807), women novelists and poets presented the artistic woman as distinctly different from the domestic daughter, wife, and mother. Indeed, *Corinne*, with its Scottish hero attracted to the dark half-Italian, half-English poetess but committed to marrying his fair, pure English betrothed, taught the lesson of their incompatibility and the fate of the artistic woman as decline and death. Laetitia Landon promulgated the Corinne myth in many poems, most notably "A History of the Lyre" (1829), where Eulalie, a poetess, wastes away after her English lover returns to his Emily and, in the final scene, erects "a sculptured form" that is both her grave marker and a monument to fame.[7] Gaskell's Mancunian counterpart, Geraldine Jewsbury, modified the Corinne tradition in *The Half Sisters* (1847) to proclaim the lesson of the complementarity of the two female types, the artistic and domestic, as two "sisters," but Jewsbury's novel did not suggest a wholly satisfactory course for her heroine. When Bianca, the actress-protagonist of *The Half Sisters*, finally decides to marry "Viscount Melton, of Melton Hall, in Staffordshire, and of Fort Vernon, in Scotland," she gives up her career; the final chapter tells of the "bitter lamentations for the irreparable loss the stage had sustained from the abdication of its high-priestess," and Bianca appears instead in a cosy domestic scene, "working a cushion in crochet for Lady Vernon."[8] While Bianca assures us that "genius" can be shown in more than "one special mode of manifestation," it is hard to believe that Jewsbury meant this scene unironically. Clearly, it does not present a model for the sustained achievement of the woman writer.

These early nineteenth-century examples of women's life writing nonetheless left their influence on Gaskell as she contemplated a *Life of Charlotte Brontë*. In their focus on an author's domestic life and circumstances, and in their concern with characteristics of the woman of genius, such memoirs and novels raised questions that Victorian biographers (and their readers) felt the need to address: questions about the relationship of the private woman and the public author, the domestic and the literary, and the compatibility (or incompatibility) of the two.

As Gaskell addresses these enduring questions in *The Life of Charlotte Brontë*, she also anticipates new forms of women's biography. For the year 1855, in which Brontë died and Gaskell began research on her memoir, was a year of new directions. In 1855 Elizabeth Barrett Browning began writing her groundbreaking poem *Aurora Leigh*, a *Künstlerroman* (account of artistic development) that envisions the woman poet as both woman *and* artist, forging a new identity to achieve social good and reform the world's ills. In 1855, too, the essayist, historian, and novelist Harriet Martineau was diagnosed with a mortal illness, and decided to compose an autobiography; although she lived for another twenty years and the work was not published until 1877, a year after her death, this *Autobiography* charts the development of a professional woman of letters, revealing a career of intense involvement in the important social, political, and economic issues of the day. These new examples of life writing thus reformulated the question of the private woman and the professional author, suggesting different possibilities and new models. It was left to Gaskell to compose the most important nineteenth-century biography of a woman writer, by consolidating strands of earlier forms of life writing, responding to contemporary work, addressing key questions about the relation of a woman's life to her art, and creating a distinctive form of women's biography that would exert enormous influence for the rest of the century – and into the next.

The woman writer and exemplary domesticity

In an oft-quoted passage of *The Life*, Gaskell takes up the issue of authorship and domesticity:

> When a man becomes an author, it is probably merely a change of employ-
> ment to him. He takes a portion of that time which has hitherto been devoted
> to some other study or pursuit; ... But no other can take up the quiet, regular
> duties of the daughter, the wife, or the mother, as well as she whom God has

appointed to fill that particular place: a woman's principal work in life is hardly left to her own choice; nor can she drop the domestic charges devolving on her as an individual, for the exercise of the most splendid talents that were ever bestowed. (*LCB*, II, 2:259)

For Gaskell, domestic work is a duty which every woman must fulfil as daughter, sister, wife, or mother. This is a theme she inherited from prior women's life writing, but also one she deeply felt. As she explained to a young mother with literary ambitions, "When I had *little* children I do not think I could have written stories, because I should have become too much absorbed in my *fictitious* people to attend to my *real* ones. ... [Y]et ... every one, who tries to write stories *must* become absorbed in them, (fictitious though they be,) if they are to interest their readers in them." She advised the young woman to attend to her children and husband first, and wait for later years when "you will write ten times as good a novel as you could do now, just because you will have gone through so much more of the interests of a wife and a mother" (*L*, 695). In *The Life* Gaskell maintains this emphasis on a woman's duty: in the first volume she selects from Brontë's letters to show her subject fulfilling "woman's principal work," even as she reveals the "splendid talents" that are simultaneously developing.

The emphasis on duty emerges forcefully in the letters that Charlotte Brontë wrote to Ellen Nussey and Mary Taylor, her friends from Roe Head School, with whom she kept up a lifelong correspondence. Nussey provided Gaskell with approximately 350 letters, written between May 1831, when she and Brontë were schoolgirls, to March 1855, just before Brontë's death. The first letter Gaskell quotes depicts Brontë and her sisters at the Haworth parsonage reading, writing, drawing, walking, sewing, and doing "a little fancy work" (July 21, 1832) – all exemplary feminine activities (*LCB*, I, 7:91). Other early letters reveal Brontë analyzing novels, plays, biographies, and history books (July 4, 1834); moralizing on the temptations of London (June 19, 1834); confessing her spiritual faults (May 10, 1836); and submitting to "duty–necessity ... stern mistresses, who will not be disobeyed," as she leaves for a position as governess at Roe Head School (July 6, 1835) (*LCB*, I, 7:103). As Rosemarie Bodenheimer has noted, "Charlotte's first letters to Ellen Nussey might have been conduct-book models of an 'improving' correspondence."[9]

Although the Brontë-Nussey letters became more intimate, witty, and ironical as their friendship progressed, Gaskell selects extracts that emphasize Brontë's serious desire to improve her education and to become financially independent, and that show her deep commitment to her ailing father and dying siblings. The theme of familial duty begins in volume one, chapter eight, as Gaskell shows Brontë leaving home for a life of school-teaching "as monotonously and unbroken as ever" (early June 1837), returning to care for their servant Tabby who has broken a leg (December 29, 1837), and serving as housemaid at Haworth by "cleaning, sweeping up hearths, dusting rooms, making beds, etc." (April 15, 1839) (*LCB*, I, 8:110, 128). Gaskell reinforces Brontë's exemplary character by quoting an exchange with the poet laureate Robert Southey, who advised that "Literature cannot be the business of a woman's life, and it ought not to be. The more she is engaged in her proper duties, the less leisure will she have for it" – to which Brontë replied, "I have endeavoured not only attentively to observe all the duties a woman ought to fulfil, but to feel deeply interested in them" (*LCB*, I, 8:117, 119).

The opening chapter of volume two underscores the theme of womanly duty, as Brontë nurses her aged father through cataract surgery, even as she receives publishers' letters rejecting *The Professor* (written 1846) and attempts composing the opening chapters of *Jane Eyre* (1847). The final chapter of *The Life* concludes with a character analysis offered by Mary Taylor, also on this theme: "She thought much of her duty, and had loftier and clearer notions of it than most people, and held fast to them with more success" (II, 14:429). We know that this passage was important to Gaskell's conception of Brontë because the manuscript of *The Life* shows that she relocated it from an earlier place to the final chapter; as Angus Easson has noted, "this last extract from Mary Taylor's letter allows E[lizabeth] G[askell] to emphasize the heroic and tragic nature of C[harlotte] B[rontë] (stressed in the biblical phrasing and rhythms)."[10]

Gaskell emphasizes duty not only because it was an esteemed Victorian virtue, but also because it helped to disprove charges that the author of *Jane Eyre* was "unwomanly" and "unchristian." These accusations had surfaced in reviews of Brontë's novel in 1848. The *Christian Remembrancer* had observed, "a book more unfeminine, both in its excellences and defects . . . would be hard to find in the annals of female authorship. Throughout there is masculine power, breadth, and shrewdness, combined with masculine hardness, coarseness, and freedom of expression." The *North American Review* had noted the rise of "Jane Eyre fever" and its influence on "ladies' men" who, imitating Mr. Rochester, "began to swagger and swear in the presence of the gentler sex, and to allude darkly to events in their lives which excused imprudence and profanity." The harshest attack came in the *Quarterly Review*, in a review written anonymously by Elizabeth Rigby, later Lady Eastlake, who declared that "the autobiography of Jane Eyre is pre-eminently an anti-christian composition" and that "almost every word she utters offends us."[11] These criticisms of Brontë might have been laid to rest had not *Sharpe's London Magazine* revived them in June 1855, less than three months after her death, with "A Few Words about 'Jane Eyre.'" Written anonymously, the article revived the hurtful rumors about "Currer Bell" that had circulated at the publication of *Jane Eyre*, including suggestions of impropriety and coarseness, based on the character of Mr. Rochester who used "real wicked oaths, like a bold, bad, live man" and repeating the *Quarterly* speculation that the novel was written by a "strange man" or, if by a woman, by someone who had "long forfeited the society of her own sex."[12]

It was Gaskell's determination to refute these charges. In a letter to George Smith, publisher of *The Life*, she warned that she planned a "tirade against Lady Eastlake," the worst of the reviewers; "whatever Miss Brontë wrote Lady E. had no right to make such offensive conjectures" (L, 404). This "tirade" appears in opening paragraphs of volume two, chapter three, after Gaskell narrates the deaths of Branwell and Emily Brontë and as Anne, Charlotte's last surviving sister, goes into a fatal decline from consumption. Gaskell first quotes "the chivalrous spirit of the good and noble Southey" on issues of anonymity and then chastises the *Quarterly* reviewer, who went "into gossiping conjectures" about the real-life circumstances of "Currer Bell": "I protest with my whole soul against such want of Christian charity. Not even the desire to write a 'smart article' ... can excuse the stabbing cruelty of the judgment" (*LCB*, II, 3:281–2). *The Life* was written, as Gaskell concludes, for a different kind of reader, for a "more solemn public" "who know how to look with tender humility at faults and errors, how to admire generously extraordinary genius, and how to reverence with warm, full hearts all noble virtue" (*LCB*, II, 14:429).

The woman writer and artistic genius

If Gaskell wrote *The Life* to defend Brontë's domestic character, she also intended to display her literary genius and claim this trait for women authors. In the early nineteenth century, following Isaac Disraeli's *The Literary Character; or, The History of Men of Genius* (1795), literary biographers compiled anecdotes to demonstrate the evidence of genius in their subjects.[13] John Lockhart, for example, notes characteristics of Sir Walter Scott that fulfil common myths of literary genius, such as that Scott learned more as a boy by lying about the fields than he did by studying his Latin grammar, that he devoured old ballads and could recite them at length, or that early "vicissitude," his ill-health and lameness in childhood, caused the growth of genius of a benignant character.[14] Chorley similarly notes traits of genius in the young Hemans: her ability as a child to memorize quickly and recite long poems, her juvenile verse "prophetic of the style in which the poetess was on a future day so signally to excel," and two prize poems, "Wallace" and "Dartmoor," awarded top honours by the Royal Society of Literature in 1821 when Hemans was under thirty.[15] Indeed, Chorley makes female genius a key theme of his biography, prefacing his narrative of her life with the assertion that "genius is of no sex" and that, despite prejudice, women writers "are winning day by day, in addition to the justice of head commanded by their high and varied powers, the justice of heart which is so eminently their due."[16]

The word "genius" appears sixteen times in Gaskell's *Life*. Half of the uses occur in Brontë's letters, in references to other artists and authors, from William Makepeace Thackeray (whom she much admired), to James Hogg and Sydney Dobell, to her sister Emily, to the French actress Rachel; in these cases "genius" emerges as a key term in Brontë's lexicon, revealing her immersion in Romantic literature and culture. Gaskell's uses of the word cluster in two distinct places: in her description of Brontë's juvenilia in volume one and as she discusses the publication of *Jane Eyre*, *Wuthering Heights* (1847), and *Agnes Grey* (1847) in volume two.

In volume one, following the conventions of Romantic biography, Gaskell demonstrates the Brontë siblings' youthful genius and gives "curious proof how early the rage for literary composition had seized upon her [Charlotte]" (I, 5:62). She reproduces the fourteen-year-old Charlotte's "Catalogue of my Books, with the period of their completion up to August 3rd, 1830," quotes from her diaries and tales, and provides a facsimile of the juvenilia with "the extreme minuteness of the writing" (I, 5:64, 62). In volume two Gaskell narrates the story of the extraordinary publication of *Jane Eyre* and the revelation of its success to Brontë's father, noting that no friend or acquaintance had guessed its authorship: "No one knew they had genius enough to be the author" (II, 2:251). In these key places *The Life* confirms the genius of its subject, thus implicitly furthering Chorley's claim that "genius is of no sex."

Even so, Gaskell treats the concept of genius ambivalently, wary of its possible connotations of waywardness or imaginative extremity. In a letter to George Smith, written just after (with the help of Sir James Kay-Shuttleworth) she had taken the juvenilia from Haworth parsonage, Gaskell describes Brontë's Angrian tales as "the wildest & most incoherent things, ... *all* purporting to be written, or addressed to some member of the Wellesley family"; she adds, "They give one the idea of creative power carried to the verge of insanity" (L, 398). In another instance, when she writes of Brontë's experience at the Cowan Bridge School and her depiction of its founder, William Carus Wilson, as the Reverend Brocklehurst in *Jane Eyre*, she comments, "I cannot help feeling sorry that, in his old age and declining health, the errors, which he certainly committed, should have been brought up against him in a form which received such wonderful force from the touch of Miss Brontë's great genius" (*LCB*, I, 4:52). These instances reveal Gaskell's fear that genius might take an author in a wrong direction and that Brontë's habit of "making out" might (and did) lead to unfortunate consequences. More often, however, Gaskell tames the concept of genius by associating it with other virtues – as in the "brave genius" with which Brontë faced her sisters' ill-health, her father's blindness, and the rejection of her manuscript of *The Professor* (*LCB*, II, 1:232). Similarly, in a letter to Charlotte Froude, Gaskell described Brontë's "strong feeling of responsibility for the Gift, which she has [been] given" (*L*, 128).

Gaskell's association of "genius" with "duty" or "responsibility" is a classic Victorian gesture, one that has drawn sharp criticism from modern scholars. Deirdre d'Albertis has argued, for example, that Gaskell substitutes her own conception of duty with its "unambiguously public values" for Brontë's different conception of genius as "a responsibility only to realize the individual's full artistic potential."[17] Yet the concepts were intertwined in both writers' work. Duty was crucial to Gaskell's understanding of women's authorship and her conception of the relationship between the domestic and literary life. As she understood Brontë's life, it produced "two parallel currents": "her life as Currer Bell, the author; her life as Charlotte Brontë, the woman." Gaskell suggests that there are "separate duties belonging to each character – not opposing each other; not impossible, but difficult to be reconciled." Perhaps speaking for herself as much as for her subject, Gaskell attempts to reconcile these "separate duties" through a rewriting of the New Testament parable of the talents: the gifted writer "who possess[es] such talents, ... must not hide her gift in a napkin; it was meant for the use and service of others" (*LCB*, II, 2:258–9).

In this allusion to a Christian parable, Gaskell conveys her sense that artistic genius is a God-given gift and her belief that it must serve a purpose beyond the self. As she wrote to Eliza Fox in 1850, just after she had published *Mary Barton* (1848), "I do believe that we have all some appointed work to do, wh[ic]h no one else can do so well; Wh[ich] is *our* work; what *we* have to do in advancing the Kingdom of God; and that first we must find out what we are sent into the world to do, and define it and make it clear to ourselves" (*L*, 107). Easson has noted that in Gaskell's early novels "moral and aesthetic feeling" are closely linked.[18] This linkage of the moral and the aesthetic underlies her representation of Brontë's literary career – just as it influenced the careers of most other Victorian women writers.

Brontë, Gaskell, and the professional woman writer

In the mid-1850s, when Gaskell wrote her biography, young women artists and authors had begun pressing for a professional view of women's work in the public sphere. Barbara Leigh Smith, Bessie Rayner Parkes, Anna Mary Howitt, and others later called the "Langham Place group" (for their headquarters at 19 Langham Place, London) urged the improvement of education for women, professional training for women artists, and access to forms of employment reserved for men. In *Essays on Woman's Work* (1865), an expansion on her ideas in *Remarks on the Education of Girls* (1854), Parkes advanced six fundamental propositions: "Let women be thoroughly developed, thoroughly rational, pious and charitable, properly protected by law, have a fair chance of a livelihood, and have ample access to all stores of learning."[19] While Parkes and her circle concurred with Gaskell in treating women's work as a contribution to the social good, they nonetheless took a more professional approach to matters of employment – from training to payment to public recognition. In this sense they followed the lead of George Henry Lewes, who had articulated a case for the professionalization of literature in an unsigned essay for *Fraser's Magazine* in 1847, where he declared, "Literature has become a profession. It is a means of subsistence, almost as certain as the bar or the church."[20]

The term "professional" appears in *The Life* in only four instances, all references to male employment. Gaskell refers to the dwellings of lawyers and doctors, the "professional middle-class" who live in "our old cathedral towns"; she describes the local curates in "their professional character"; she mentions the Brontë sisters' training in French by "professional masters"; and she quotes "professional critics" in their estimates of *Jane Eyre*.[21] Gaskell associates professionalism, in other words, with the traditional male professions of the Church, medicine, law, and literature. Nowhere does she claim professional status for "Currer Bell," despite Brontë's keen interest, expressed in numerous letters to her publisher George Smith, in the professional practices of authors, editors, and publishers. Brontë further stated her desire to be treated not as a female authoress, but as "Currer Bell." As she wrote to Lewes, in a letter quoted partially in *The Life*: "I wish all reviewers believed 'Currer Bell' to be a man; they would be more just to him." That is, Brontë desired gender-neutral treatment, not judgment by "some standard of what you deem becoming of my sex" (*LCB*, II, 4:305).

Gaskell respects Brontë's distinction between "Currer Bell" and "Charlotte Brontë' in her formulation of the "two parallel currents," but does not associate the former with professional authorship. It is unclear whether Gaskell avoided the mid-nineteenth-century discourse of professionalism because she felt it inappropriate for women or because she felt that Brontë's character might be injured by the association. After all, reviewers had criticized *Jane Eyre*, along with Emily Brontë's *Wuthering Heights* (1847), as "coarse" and "unfeminine," and they might find further ammunition in a construction of Brontë's authorial self as "professional" and thus implicitly "masculine." Perhaps, too, Gaskell recognized in Brontë's letters an association of authorship with Romantic claims of genius, inspiration, and self-expression, rather than with mid-Victorian interests in professional status and gender equality. Whatever the motivation, Gaskell's *Life* projects a different view of the woman author from that presented in Harriet Martineau's *Autobiography*. Martineau traces her professional progress as "a solitary authoress, who has had no pioneer in her literary path," and revels in charting the steady accumulation of her earnings, noting in her *Autobiography* that she had been paid about ten thousand pounds for her essays and books.[22] In contrast, Gaskell minimizes the professional aspects of Brontë's career, excludes financial details from Brontë's letters to her publisher, and shows her subject as much more interested in ideas than in profits. The letters Brontë wrote to W. S. Williams, frequently quoted in *The Life*, are noteworthy in this regard as they express Brontë's opinions of canonical and contemporary literature, and steer clear of mundane details of book production.

The afterlife of *The Life of Charlotte Brontë*

Gaskell's presentation of Brontë as a gifted writer, plagued by poverty and ill health, but faithful to both her womanly duty and her literary gift, achieved immediate success. Patrick Brontë wrote on April 2, 1857, a week after *The Life*'s publication, "You have not only given a picture of my Dear Daughter Charlotte, but of my Dear Wife, and all my Dear Children, and such a picture too, as is full of truth and life"; he added on July 30, 1857, "the 'Memoir' is ... in every way worthy of what one Great Woman, should have written of Another, and ... it ought to stand, and will stand, in the first rank of Biographies, till the end of time" (*CH*, 373–4). Other private letters were equally glowing in their praise. Lewes, who had contributed his correspondence, wrote from the Scilly Isles, where he and George Eliot were staying, to say that the book was deeply moving and that he believed it would "create a deep and permanent impression; for it ... presents a vivid picture of a life noble and sad, full of encouragement and healthy teaching, a lesson in duty and self-reliance" (*CH*, 386). Charles Kingsley assured Gaskell, "Be sure that the book will do good. It will shame literary people into some stronger belief that a simple, virtuous, practical home life is consistent with high, imaginative genius."[23]

The periodical reviews similarly recognized Gaskell's literary achievement and reinforced her themes of duty and genius. Chorley, author of the biography of Felicia Hemans, declared in the *Athenaeum*, "As a work of Art, we do not recollect a life of a woman by a woman so well executed" (*CH*, 375). Like many others, the *Saturday Review* highlighted the theme of duty: "We see the woman, not the authoress, in these annals of Haworth parsonage; and as a woman Charlotte Brontë was in every way remarkable. She clung to duty with a most unselfish completeness, and an utter abnegation of all that makes a woman's life happy." But the reviewer also reinforced the vision of Brontë as a literary genius:

> We may accept it as an undoubted psychological fact that, by mere force of genius, a young woman really did apprehend a phase of the human heart of the most complex and subtle kind ... It was by instinct or insight that she knew how a rude, strong, generous man, maddened by the desperation of a forlorn middle age, would clutch at a stray hope of love. So far her genius was wholly creative.   (*CH*, 378)

With greater succinctness, the *Spectator* echoed: "it is impossible to read through Mrs. Gaskell's two volumes without a strong conviction that Charlotte Brontë was a woman as extraordinary by her character as by her genius" (*CH*, 379).

The Life of Charlotte Brontë sold quickly, so that in April 1857 Smith, Elder issued a second edition.[24] That edition sold just as quickly, until all unsold copies were recalled on May 26, 1857, when a threat of legal action from the solicitors of Lady Scott (the former Mrs. Robinson) required a revision of volume one, chapter thirteen. Gaskell had depicted the unnamed Mrs. Robinson as the seducer of Branwell Brontë (following the accounts she had heard from Charlotte and Patrick Brontë) and had castigated her for the pain and suffering that her dalliance had caused the Brontë sisters. Mrs. Robinson, who had remarried to become Lady Scott and now circulated in London society, was not the only figure who objected to her representation in *The Life*. The relatives of William Carus Wilson, founder of the Clergyman's Daughters School at Cowan Bridge, charged Gaskell with factual errors. Several literary figures objected to details of their lives or works. (For example, Harriet Martineau objected to the suggestion that she and Brontë fell out over Martineau's publication of *Letters on the Laws of Man's Nature and Development*, which many readers considered an avowal of atheism. John Stuart Mill pointed out that an article on women's emancipation in the *Westminster Review* was written not by himself, but by his late wife, Harriet Taylor, and objected to Gaskell's characterization of its author as "derogatory" and thus hurtful to himself.) And then the Reverend Arthur Nicholls, Charlotte's widower, began to ask for revisions in the portrait of Patrick Brontë.

When Gaskell returned home from a holiday abroad in June 1857, she set to work at revisions, a task that quickly became a burden. She wrote wearily to her publisher George Smith, for example, to "take out the pistol shooting" (one of several objections to the depiction of Patrick Brontë), as "I am willing to 'do anything for a quiet life'" (*L*, 467–8). But the heaviest rewriting involved tempering the sharp melodrama of Branwell's guilty passion for his employer's wife, and his subsequent dismissal from his tutorship at Thorp Green and descent into alcoholism and opium addiction. In a letter to Smith of October 2, 1856, Gaskell had referred to Lydia Robinson as "that bad woman who corrupted Branwell Brontë" and asked him, "Do you mind the law of libel[?]" (*L*, 418). Whether or not she intended libel, Gaskell certainly intended melodrama with its sharp contrast between good and evil, the sinned against and the sinning. In the first edition of *The Life*, she introduces the episode of Branwell's affair dramatically with the phrase "The story must be told," and ends even more dramatically with Patrick's nightly guarding of his son with pistols and Branwell's drinking himself to death and whimpering "with a drunkard's incontinence of speech," "[I]t's all over with me" (*LCB*, I, 13:204, 214). In the third edition she retains Branwell's descent into addiction, but simply states, "In fact, all their latter days blighted with the presence of cruel, shameful suffering – the premature deaths of two at least of the sisters – all the possibilities of their earthly lives snapped short – may be dated from Midsummer 1845."[25] There is no explanation for Branwell's addiction or reason given for the "cruel, shameful suffering."

The alterations to *The Life* provoked significant debate, then and now. Mary Taylor, Brontë's lifelong friend, called it a "mutilated edition."[26] Mary Mohl, Gaskell's friend, sent an ironic preface to pass on to her publisher: "If anybody is displeased with any statement or words in the following pages I beg leave to with-draw it, and to express my deep regret for having offered so expensive an article as truth to the Public" (*L*, 455). Elisabeth Jay, a distinguished editor of *The Life*, suggests that the revisions for the third edition improve the work aesthetically, in that the new text "produce[s] an ever-tightening circle of gloom, now unalleviated by passionate outbursts" (*LCB*, xxxviii). Angus Easson, another distinguished editor of *The Life*, argues for the greater truth of the third: "There is truth in tone, ... as well as in fact and the truth of the third edition is often more persuasive than the truth of the first."[27] Yet those passionate outbursts are fundamental to the story of *The Life* and to Gaskell's motivation for its composition, as her letters to Smith attest.

Whether or not one prefers the more melodramatic first edition or the more moderate third (and the modern reader may choose between Jay's first in Penguin and Easson's third in Oxford World's Classics), *The Life* has had significant influence on women writers from Gaskell's day to our own. Her contemporaries reviewed the biography publicly and commented privately. Martineau, who privately requested that Gaskell alter specific details of her domestic routine, publicly praised *The Life* as a modern equivalent of Plutarch's biographies and medieval saints' lives: "These forms have passed away, but the substance remains; and, little as Charlotte Brontë knew it, she was earning for herself a better title than many a St. Catherine or St. Bridget, for a place among those noble ones whose virtues are carved out of rock, and will endure to the end" (*CH*, 426–7). The novelist Margaret Oliphant publicly lamented the exposure of Brontë's private life in her assessment of "The Brontë Sisters" (1897), but in her journal she noted after reading Gaskell's *Life* in 1864, "I don't suppose my powers are equal to hers – my work to myself looks perfectly pale and colourless besides hers – but yet I have had far more experience and, I think, a fuller conception of life."[28] George Eliot defended *The Life* against critics who thought "its revelations in bad taste – making money out of the dead – wounding the feelings of the living etc. etc.," adding that she and Lewes "thought it admirable – cried over it – and felt better for it."[29] Bodenheimer further notes that Eliot read this biography, along with Margaret Fuller's journals and Lockhart's *Life of Sir Walter Scott*, for "glimpses into hidden emotional lives and sources of inspiration."[30]

Inspiration and imitation were primary effects of *The Life* on younger, aspiring writers. The "New Woman" novelist Mary Cholmondeley recalls in her memoir, *Under One Roof: A Family Record* (1918), "we four sisters" racing "up and down the old schoolroom to get warm," having "long discussions on books and people and Life" – in effect becoming a reincarnation of the Brontës; "later on when I read Mrs. Gaskell's *Life of the Brontës* [*sic*]," she adds, "I realized with surprise that other eager young women had walked up and down their old schoolroom just as we had done, before we were born."[31] The novelist Charlotte Riddell took Brontë's life more fully as a model for her own. In her autobiographical fiction, *A Struggle for Fame* (1883), the heroine Glenarva Westley writes to help her impoverished family, nurses her ailing father, surprises him with a manuscript of a novel, suffers a round of publishers' rejections, eventually finds a sympathetic editor, achieves literary fame, and even marries a faithful, if dull suitor – all episodes modeled on *The Life of Charlotte Brontë*. But Riddell recognized, as did many later Victorian novelists, the need to write beyond the ending of *The Life*. Her novel questions the model of "two parallel currents " and the equation of literary fame and domestic tragedy that marked Brontë's life (or, as Riddell puts it, when her heroine sells a novel but loses her father, "Once again FAME had crossed the threshold hand-in-hand with DEATH!)."[32] Glenarva Westley's life course, based on Riddell's own, demonstrates that the parallel currents – of the woman and the author, the domestic and the professional – are impossible, not just difficult, to negotiate. By the time Emily Morse Symonds published *A Writer of Books* (1898), a "New Woman" novel with a writer-heroine, she still imitated aspects of Brontë's fiction but left behind the mid-Victorian model of authorship for a more professional life that, as Margaret Stetz puts it, "follows from resisting and breaking the laws imposed upon women, including those upon women fiction-writers."[33]

Gaskell helped to create the model of the woman novelist as a dutiful daughter, inspired writer, and tragic heroine – or, as we call it today, the "myth": a myth of genius and martyrdom, of solitude and loneliness, of domesticity and inspiration, of fame and death.[34] Elaine Showalter has argued that "as Charlotte Brontë and George Eliot increasingly came to dominate their period and to represent the models against which other novelists were measured, they became objects of both feminine adulation and resentment."[35] Whether women writers admired or resented Brontë, whether they imitated her exemplary character or shunned it for a more rebellious persona, they nonetheless had to reckon with the questions about women's authorship that Gaskell formulated in her monumental *Life of Charlotte Brontë*.

Notes

1 Patrick Brontë to Elizabeth Gaskell, June 16, 1855, quoted in Angus Easson, *Elizabeth Gaskell* (London: Routledge & Kegan Paul, 1979), 134.
2 Alexander Dyce, *Specimens of British Poetesses* (London: T. Rodd, 1825); Mrs. [Anne Katherine] Elwood, *Memoirs of the Literary Ladies of England*, 2 vols. (London: Henry Colburn, 1843).
3 Elwood, *Memoirs*, I, v–vi.
4 Emma Roberts, "Memoir of L. E. L.," in *The Zenana and Minor Poems of L. E. L.* (London: Fisher, 1839).
5 Laman Blanchard, *Life and Literary Remains of L. E. L.*, 2 vols. (London: Henry Colburn, 1841).

6 Henry F. Chorley, *Memorials of Mrs. Hemans, with Illustrations of her Literary Character from her Private Correspondence*, 2 vols. (London: Saunders and Otley, 1836); *Memoir of the Life and Writings of Mrs. Hemans, by her sister* (Edinburgh: William Blackwood and Sons, 1840), I:1.

7 Laetitia Elizabeth Landon, "A History of the Lyre," in *Selected Writings*, ed. Jerome McGann and Daniel Riess (Peterborough: Broadview Press, 1997), l. 432.

8 Geraldine Jewsbury, *The Half Sisters*, ed. Joanne Wilkes (1847; Oxford: World's Classics, 1994), 27:390–1.

9 Rosemarie Bodenheimer, *The Real Life of Mary Ann Evans: George Eliot, Her Letters and Fiction* (Ithaca: Cornell University Press, 1994), 33.

10 Elizabeth Gaskell, *The Life of Charlotte Brontë*, ed., intro., and notes Angus Easson (Oxford: World's Classics, 1996), 568, n. 457.

11 *Christian Remembrancer* 15 (April 1848), 396–409; *North American Review* 141 (October 1848), 354–69; and *Quarterly Review* 84 (December 1848), 153–85; in Miriam Allott, ed., *The Brontës: The Critical Heritage* (London: Routledge & Kegan Paul, 1974), 89, 98, 107, 109.

12 All phrases but the penultimate come from "A Few Words about 'Jane Eyre,'" *Sharpe's London Magazine*, 6 n.s. (June 1855), 339–42. The expression who had "long forfeited the society of her sex" is Elizabeth Rigby's in the *Quarterly Review*, which the reviewer for *Sharpe's* elsewhere paraphrases. For a useful discussion of Gaskell's role in this unfortunate transmission, see Linda K. Hughes and Michael Lund, *Victorian Publishing and Mrs. Gaskell's Work* (Charlottesville: University of Virginia Press, 1999), 124–40.

13 Isaac Disraeli, *The Literary Character; or, The History of Men of Genius, Drawn from their own Feelings and Confessions* (1795), ed. Benjamin Disraeli (London: Frederick Warne, 1840). From 1791 to 1834 Isaac Disraeli also issued six volumes of *Curiosities of Literature*, biographical anecdotes about (male) authors that gave evidence of their unique character.

14 John Gibson Lockhart, *Memoirs of the Life of Sir Walter Scott, Bart.* (Boston: Otis, Broaders, and Company, 1837–8), 11–30, 95–104.

15 Chorley, *Memorials of Mrs. Hemans*, I:11–12, 31, 39.

16 *Ibid.*, I:6–7.

17 Deirdre d'Albertis, "'Bookmaking out of the Remains of the Dead': Elizabeth Gaskell's *The Life of Charlotte Brontë*," *Victorian Studies* 39 (1995), 1–31, 12–13. See also Donald Stone, *The Romantic Impulse in Victorian Fiction* (Cambridge, MA: Harvard University Press, 1980).

18 Easson, *Elizabeth Gaskell*, 109.

19 Bessie Rayner Parkes, *Essays on Woman's Work* (London: Alexander Strahan, 1865), 6.

20 George Henry Lewes, unsigned article, "The Condition of Authors in England, Germany, and France," *Fraser's Magazine* 35 (March 1847), 285–95. According to Lewes, "able literary men in England mak[e] incomes *averaging* 300£ a-year," and "the real cause we attribute to be the excellence and abundance of periodical literature" (286, 288).

21 *LCB*, I, 1:11; I, 9:142; I, 10:156; II, 2:247.

22 Harriet Martineau to Lord Brougham, October 10, 1832, in *Harriet Martineau: Selected Letters*, ed. Valerie Sanders (Oxford: Clarendon Press, 1990), 32; Harriet Martineau, *Autobiography*, 2 vols. (London: Smith, Elder, 1877), I:268.

23 Charles Kingsley to Elizabeth Gaskell, May 14, 1857, in Allott, ed., *The Brontës*, 343.

24 A first edition of 2,021 copies was released in March 1857. On April 22, 1857, 1,500 copies of the second edition were issued, and another 700 on May 4, 1857.

25 *LCB*, Appendix I, 13:447.

26 Mary Taylor to Ellen Nussey, January 28, 1858, in Joan Stevens, ed., *Mary Taylor, Friend of Charlotte Brontë* (Oxford: Oxford University Press, 1972), 134.

27 Easson, *Elizabeth Gaskell*, 150.

28 Margaret Oliphant, "The Brontë Sisters," in Oliphant, *Women Novelists in Queen Victoria's Reign: A Book of Appreciations* (London: Hurst & Blackett, 1897), 25–26, and *The Autobiography of Margaret Oliphant*, ed. Elisabeth Jay (1899; Peterborough: Broadview Press, 2002), 43.

29 George Eliot to Sara Sophia Hennell, May 22, 1857, in *The George Eliot Letters*, ed. Gordon S. Haight, 9 vols. (New Haven: Yale University Press, 1954), II:330.

30 Bodenheimer, *The Real Life of Mary Ann Evans*, 234–5.

31 Mary Cholmondeley, *Under One Roof: A Family Record* (London: John Murray, 1918), 102–3.

32 Mrs. J. H. [Charlotte] Riddell, *A Struggle for Fame* (London: Richard Bentley, 1883), 3:346.

33 Margaret Stetz, introduction to George Paston [Emily Morse Symonds], *A Writer of Books* (1898) (Chicago: Academy Publishers, 1998), xiv.

34 See Lucasta Miller, *The Brontë Myth* (London: Jonathan Cape, 2001).

35 Elaine Showalter, *A Literature of Their Own: British Women Novelists from Brontë to Lessing* (Princeton: Princeton University Press, 1977), 105.

6

MARION SHAW

Sylvia's Lovers and other historical fiction

"But history, real solemn history, I cannot be interested in ... The quarrels of popes and kings, with wars or pestilence, in every page; the men all so good-for-nothing, and hardly any women at all – it is very tiresome: and yet I often think it odd that it should be so dull, for a great deal of it must be invention. The speeches that are put into the heroes' mouths, their thoughts and designs – the chief of all this must be invention, and invention is what delights me in other books."

> – Jane Austen, *Northanger Abbey* (1818)

"[T]he novel is history. That is the only general description (which does it justice) that we may give to the novel."

> – Henry James, "The Art of Fiction" (1888)

Between 1818 and 1888 historical study and the writing of realist fiction are in the ascendancy. The novel becomes respectable and its claim to respectability rests on its proximity to history, its likeness to life: as Henry James says, "In proportion as in what [fiction] offers we see life *without* rearrangement do we feel that we are touching truth."[1] At the same time, the study of history becomes self-conscious, reflective, and increasingly concerned with the lives of common people; this growth of modern historicism owes much to its competitive proximity to the novel. Each discourse is implicated in the other. In terms which could apply equally to the realist-historical novel, outgrowing its Gothic and picaresque ancestry, Thomas Carlyle noted a new era for historians as early as 1830: whereas history was once concerned to gratify "our common appetite for the wonderful, for the unknown," modern history is now no longer to do with battlefields, senate houses, and kings' antechambers but with "the dark untenanted places of the Past, where, in formless oblivion, our chief benefactors ... lie entombed." Social life, he writes, "is the aggregate of all the individual men's lives ... History is the essence of innumerable Biographies."[2]

This radical break with earlier historiographical models and standards was developed by two of the most progressive historians of the time. In an

1842 article entitled "The Modern Art and Science of History," Philip Harwood asserted that history should provide "a genuine transcript of an era or an event." He claimed that "Nothing is too lowly to furnish data for historical science ... Modern history knows the historical value of the little facts that make the common life of little men."[3] Henry Buckle, the first volume of whose *The History of Civilisation in England* was published in 1857, carried the argument forward in stating that historical detail was good in itself but not sufficient for a modern science, where a connecting narrative was required:

> the unfortunate peculiarity of history is that although its separate parts have been examined with considerable ability, hardly anyone has attempted to combine them into a whole, and ascertain the way in which they are connected with each other ... [Therefore] for all the higher purposes of human thought history is still miserably deficient and presents that confused and anarchical appearance natural to a subject of which the laws are unknown and even the foundation unsettled.[4]

As if in answer to this complaint, two years later the greatest historian of the age, Charles Darwin, published *On the Origin of Species* (1859), a model of the new historical method, whereby scattered facts are brought together into a whole and the laws of evolution are given a settled foundation. The fact that the book's content had such a momentous impact was due in no small measure to its calm, relentless use of such a historical method. Darwin's famous concluding paragraph seemed to offer a metaphor for what historical study was seeking to achieve. The "entangled bank" is alive with "elaborately constructed forms, so different from each other, and dependent on each other in so complex a manner, [which] have all been produced by laws acting around us."[5]

The serious historical novel flourished in the middle decades of the nineteenth century – for example, William Makepeace Thackeray's *Henry Esmond* (1852), Charles Dickens's *A Tale of Two Cities* (1859), Charles Reade's *The Cloister and the Hearth* (1861) – and as *Sylvia's Lovers* was published in 1863, George Eliot's *Romola* was completing its serialization in the *Cornhill Magazine*. In spite of Eliot's caution against what she called "the *modern-antique* species [which] have a ponderous, a leaden kind of fatuity," most of the major novelists wrote at least one historical novel, encouraged by the great outpouring of books and articles on the importance, and the changing nature, of historical research.[6] The Victorians believed in history as a means to progress and knowledge; the lives of the dead could teach them how to live and the sufferings and triumphs of history could mirror their own.

The task facing the historical novelists was to give the appearance of truthfulness, what James calls life without arrangement, while also imposing a pattern on the randomness of life and the arbitrariness of events. Without pattern, or what might be called the laws of fiction, the novel would be formless, indeterminate and inconclusive. James acknowledges this conflict in his comment that "Art is essentially selection, but it is a selection whose main care is to be typical, to be inclusive."[7] The model for this was set by the writer whom all regarded as the progenitor of serious historical fiction, Sir Walter Scott. Truth to real life was Scott's aim in his most famous and hugely successful novel, *Waverley* (1814), where he says in the preface that he will reject the kind of Gothic novel in which "the owl would have shrieked and the cricket cried in my very title-page"; instead, "the force of my narrative [will be thrown] upon the characters and passions of the actors; – those passions common to all men in all stages of society [though upon them] the state of manners and laws casts a necessary colouring."[8] The eponymous hero of *Waverley* is a rather nondescript young man whose fictional purpose is selectively to record the opposing factions involved in the Jacobite rebellion of 1745. Characters around him typify the extremes of the conflict and he himself represents the compromise that Scott believed the historical process had brought about. This is a model that Gaskell will follow in her historical fiction, where opposing forces in times of turmoil and change are represented by "typical" characters. Scott also set the terms for classifying a novel as historical. His novel's full title is *Waverley; or 'Tis Sixty Years Since*, which establishes a limit in time past, later than which a novel would not subsequently be classed as historical. It becomes a convention that the majority of historical novels follow, including *Sylvia's Lovers*, which has a present-day narrator describing events of sixty years earlier.

Gaskell's fiction is everywhere obsessed by history. The three fictions focused on in this chapter, *My Lady Ludlow* (1858), *Lois the Witch* (1859), and *Sylvia's Lovers* (1863), are obviously historical but several of her shorter fictions could have been included. "The Poor Clare" (1858), for example, takes up a vantage point in 1747 to tell of events "a long way back," and "The Old Nurse's Story" (1852) roves back over several generations to the time of the war with America.[9] Just as interesting, Gaskell's nonhistorical stories begin with a sense of the forces and events that have shaped the present. Most famously, *The Life of Charlotte Brontë* (1857) begins with a description of Keighley as a town "in process of transformation" because without that sense of process it would be impossible to arrive at "a right understanding of my dear friend Charlotte Brontë" (*LCB*, I, 1:11, 2:17). *Wives and Daughters* (1866) openly admits that it must start with personal history, "with the old rigmarole of childhood" (*WD*, 1:1). Memory in many of her greatest stories is the key to personal history: "I see her now," says the narrator of *Cousin Phillis* (1864) repeatedly, as he summons the "remembrance of many a happy day, and of several little scenes [. . . that] rise like pictures to my memory" (*CP*, III, 267). *Cranford* (1853) remembers the past of its aging inhabitants, which rises like the "faint, white, ghostly semblance" of Miss Matty's parents' letters of 1774, which she has to burn, because "No-one will care for them when I am gone" (*C*, 5:44). The rejoinder to Miss Matty's comment, of course, is that it is the writer's responsibility to care for what is gone, "to record the history of innumerable biographies." As William Wordsworth, one of Gaskell's favorite poets, writes in 1802 in the preface to *Lyrical Ballads*, "in spite of difference of soil and climate, of language and manners, in spite of things silently gone out of mind and things violently destroyed, the Poet binds together by passion and knowledge the vast empire of human society, as it is spread over the whole earth and over all time."[10]

The very contemporary task of writing *The Life of Charlotte Brontë* left Gaskell much troubled by the hostile response it received: "I *did so try* to *tell the truth*," she wrote to Ellen Nussey in 1857, but "for the future I intend to confine myself to lies (i.e. fiction). It is safer," she wrote to William Fairbairn (*L*, 454, 458). In the years to follow, a kind of compromise was reached in which she was to keep to fiction, but fiction spliced with historical events of sixty years or more ago. *Lois the Witch* and *Sylvia's Lovers* are based on the Salem witch trials of 1692 and the press-gang activities of the late eighteenth century respectively. *My Lady Ludlow* is different in that its narrative is fictional but the context is highly attentive to historical detail. It was first published in *Household Words* from June 19 to September 25, 1858. The following year it was published in volume one of the two-volume *Round the Sofa*, a collection of stories with an introductory narrative by an unidentified girl who, along with "a few old fogies . . . and one or two good sweet young women," gather round the sofa of an elderly invalid, Margaret Dawson, every Monday evening.[11] The narrator recalls that these evenings happened long ago, when Margaret was sixty, and the account Margaret gives is of a time when she was a girl living in Lady Ludlow's household. The figure of Lady Ludlow is positioned, therefore, in the early years of the nineteenth century (the Battle of Trafalgar is mentioned as a recent event, and she dies in 1814) but because history in Gaskell is never an abrupt beginning or end, but an unfolding of layer upon layer, the stories that Lady Ludlow and other characters tell also reach back in time, to a period some twenty years earlier and beyond. In this loosely structured text, history is gossip and digression rather than linear. In fact, as

Margaret says, "It is no story: it has neither beginning, middle, nor end," and although she is the framing narrator, the story has many voices, which complement each other and give a prismatic view of the truth of events. The great historical event, the "real solemn history" that is embedded in these receding and interweaving narratives, is the French Revolution but, typically for Gaskell, this is personalized into the story that Lady Ludlow tells of the lovers Virginie and Clément, who are caught up in the persecutions following the French Revolution and are guillotined.

As a cripple and a dependant, Margaret features as the narrative device of one who is compelled to listen and watch rather than act, and thus become the repository of all the news and gossip of the parish of Hanbury. Lady Ludlow is from an ancient aristocratic family and embodies the traditionalist values that, in an age of revolution, are being swept away. A staunch royalist, opposed to all that is new and modern, or that in any way breaches class distinctions or moves toward a more egalitarian society, she is introduced into the story as a historical curiosity, an image held up to Gaskell's readership of what society may have been like sixty years ago, and further back than that, for Lady Ludlow is, even in her own time, a relic of bygone ages. "[M]ost of her opinions," Margaret comments, "when I knew her in later life, were singular enough then but had been universally prevalent fifty years ago."[12] Lady Ludlow, as a historical focus, then, reaches back to the middle of the eighteenth century, and in her resistance to change reaches forward to the middle of the nineteenth century when many of the things she has opposed have either happened or are imminent.

There is an insistence throughout the text that history lies around us in the litter of everyday life. In helping Lady Ludlow to clear out the drawers of a bureau, Margaret wonders over "the meaning of many of the things we turned out ... I was puzzled to know why some were kept at all" (3:36). Some, like the scraps of paper or a bit of a broken riding whip, do not give up their history, but the stones she finds are read in a multidimensional way. They had come from the palaces of the Roman emperors, been turned up by farmers preparing the ground for onion-sowing, and been picked up by Lady Ludlow when a girl, with the intention of making a table from them. But the plan had failed and now they lie in the drawer "with all the dirt out of the onion-field upon them." Lady Ludlow forbids Margaret to wash them, "for it was Roman dirt – earth I think she called it – but it was dirt all the same"(3:36). The play of difference between "dirt" and "earth" subtly conveys the difference between discarded history, detritus, and preserved history, which still has life and growth in it. They are the same but the perception of what is precious alters according to the historian.

If this is the history that lies around in daily life, there is also chronicled history, and *My Lady Ludlow* very skillfully picks up on all the controversial issues and events of turn-of-the century Britain. Lady Ludlow's comment, "When I was a girl, one never heard of the rights of men, one only heard of the duties," briefly evokes not just the controversy over Tom Paine's inflammatory *The Rights of Man* (1791–2) but the whole revolutionary fervour of that time (4:51). There is also a glancing reference to Jean Jacques Rousseau, whose writings, particularly *Du Contrat Social* (1762), on the natural goodness and equality of men, had influenced the ideas of the French Revolution. The gossipy comments of Miss Galindo on that "invention of the enemy," the spinning-jenny, summarizes the coming of "iron and steel ... to do the work ordained to man at the Fall" (14:201). The young evangelical clergyman, Mr. Gray, who opposes the slave trade, will not take sugar in his tea because "he thinks he sees spots of blood in it," and he "leaves little pictures of negroes about, with the question printed below, 'Am I not a man and a brother?'" (10:136–7). New agricultural methods are being practiced by a retired Birmingham baker, Mr. Brooke, a man despised because he is a Dissenter and has made his money in trade but who nevertheless has taken farming lessons from the modernizing pioneer landowner Thomas Coke of Holkham in Norfolk. The agrarian and industrial revolutions and the anti-slavery movement are all captured in the *Cranford*-like world of Hanbury.

Historical process in *My Lady Ludlow*, however, particularly focuses on the question of education for the working classes. Mr. Gray wishes to start a Sunday school; Mr. Horner, the estate manager, wishes to teach a tinker boy to read and write and do accounts, and hopes for a day school at some future time. Lady Ludlow opposes both of these on the grounds that education is dangerous: "it was levelling and revolutionary, she said" (1:11). By the end of the story, Lady Ludlow has been defeated, Sunday school and day school exist, and the tinker boy has become a clergyman. The story is viewed from a perspective of the rapidly increasing provision of education for the working classes, culminating in W. E. Forster's Education Act of 1870, which provided for education to be available for everyone under the age of thirteen, although it was years before it could be fully implemented. A. N. Wilson has argued that the Victorians "invented the concept of education as we now understand it; ... it is from them that we derive our axiomatic assumption that learning should be formalised learning, education institutionalised, the imparting of knowledge the duty of society and the state to every citizen."[13] It is an axiomatic assumption in *My Lady Ludlow* that it is a good thing that the tinker-boy has gone to school and then to college to become a parson. His education represents metaphorically a measure of control over the wilder elements of society – the thieves, poachers, gypsies, and blasphemers exemplified by his father. Ironically, Lady Ludlow, in opposing this benign form of control, is on the side of anarchy and revolution, though her chief reason for opposition is the fear of revolution. The microcosm of Hanbury typifies a half-century-long class struggle, and in its reconciliation of opposing forces suggests that a combination of evangelical Christianity and mercantile shrewdness may have been the reason that Britain did not slide into revolution in 1842 or 1848, as other countries did. Mr. Gray, with his passion for saving the souls of the parish children, and Mr. Horner, who has worked in Birmingham, and has acquired "a kind of worldly wisdom [with] maxims [that] savoured of commerce and trade," typify that formidable combination (1:6).

By the end of the story, barriers of class and gender have been breached: not only is a vagabond boy the parson and the illegitimate Miss Bessy respectably married, but the gentleman Captain James marries the Dissenting baker's daughter, and Miss Galindo can show that she can be as good a clerk and accountant as any man. The edifice of privilege and hierarchy surrounding Lady Ludlow is crumbling, and the text signals this while paying tribute to the graciousness, generosity, and *noblesse oblige* of a bygone age and mode of life. The story succeeds in celebrating change: the old is revered but is recognized as needing to give way to the new. Pattern is discernible; Gaskell is inclusive as well as selective in the manner of Scott, and her progressive evolutionary narrative shows society moving toward greater heterogeneity and freedom. It is a dialectical process which Darwin was describing in the same year as *My Lady Ludlow* was published. It is necessary, he says, "to keep steadily in mind that each organic being is striving to increase ...; that each at some period of its life, during some season of the year, during each generation or at intervals, has to struggle for life, and to suffer great destruction ... and that the vigorous, the healthy, and the happy survive and multiply."[14]

Although there is progression toward reconciliation of a kind at the end of *Lois the Witch*, it is much more painfully and doubtfully achieved. The story was published in *All the Year Round* in 1859, Gaskell becoming so absorbed in it that what should have been forty pages became two hundred: "But it is not very good; too melodramatic a plot; only I have grown interested in it, and cannot put it aside" (*L*, 535). Unlike *My Lady Ludlow*, this narrative draws on actual events, for *Lois the Witch* shows how the town of Salem in New England was overwhelmed in 1692 by religious hysteria, with widespread charges of witchcraft given credibility by elders of the church and by the judiciary. By the following year, when the episode ended, "at least 156 people had been imprisoned, including nineteen who hanged, one who was pressed to death, and at least four who died in prison."[15] The history of Salem had intrigued Gaskell for many years. In 1847–8, at the beginning of her writing career, she had submitted stories to *Howitt's Journal* under the pseudonym "Cotton Mather Mills," a joke from a writer among the cotton mills of Lancashire but a strange choice nevertheless, as Cotton Mather was one of the Puritan divines prominent in the Salem trials.

Gaskell was probably influenced in her complex treatment of the Salem hysteria, and its roots in sexual repression and religious mania, by Nathaniel Hawthorne's *The Scarlet Letter* (1850). The troubled, frustrated Pastor Nolan in *Lois the Witch* has affinities with Hawthorne's Arthur Dimmesdale, whose elfin child Pearl foreshadows the restless, malicious Prudence in Gaskell's tale. Justice Hathorn, who condemns Lois, is mentioned in the Custom-House introduction to *The Scarlet Letter*, and acknowledged as Hawthorne's ancestor. Most notably, however, both fictions have at their center a woman alone and persecuted, yet possessed of an integrity and courage which withstands authority and dominance.

If the Hawthorne connection was probably a stimulus to write of the subject, Gaskell's main factual source seems to have been Charles Upham's *Lectures on Witchcraft, Comprising a History of the Delusions in Salem* (1831). *Lois the Witch* follows Upham in many respects, quoting him almost verbatim at times, and the story is peopled with the characters and the landscape he describes, using his details of how the tragedy began, the afflictions of those believed to be bewitched, the activities of the accusers, and the sufferings and deaths of those accused.[16] Gaskell also seems to take suggestion from Upham in ascribing motives to the accusers beyond the general hysteria and fear of the devil; there were those, Upham says, who "were willing to abuse the opportunities offered by the general excitement" to be revenged on those they believed had injured them, or to advance their own status, as in the case of Cotton Mather.[17] This is echoed in the actions of Grace, Faith, and Prudence, who have their own reasons beyond the charge of witchcraft for condemning Lois. Upham also suggestively gives the many meanings that the word "witch" can carry, such as "diviner, enchanter, charmer, conjuror," and these are developed by Gaskell into the fateful conversation in Widow Smith's house in which Lois's bewitching charms are playfully evoked.[18] As in *Ruth* (1853) and *Sylvia's Lovers*, a woman's beauty is a snare that can lead men into wrong or desperate actions. Gaskell's great achievement in this story is the interpolation of the invented heroine-victim into historical data. She also asks and answers the question usually left out of historical records: what was it like to be an ordinary, "little" individual caught up in these events?

Gaskell asks this question on behalf of the victim, and also on behalf of the New Englanders who become her persecutors. The terrifying landscape they inhabit, their fear of Indians and the French, and their uncompromising religion, born of privation and persecution, are understood as causes, if not excuses, for their behavior. The text subtly cautions against judgment, with Gaskell reminding her readers on several occasions that England has its own history of superstitious persecutions. Such hysteria is always dangerously close, and the narrative voice stands clear of the action at the beginning of chapter three to warn against unsubstantiated claims: "Where evidence takes a supernatural character, there is no disproving it ... You hardly know the limits of the natural powers; how then can you define the supernatural?"[19] This modern, positivist analysis of the psychology of belief in witchcraft is endorsed later by Lois in her recognition of the physical reality of her situation in the shape of a heavy chain round her ankle: "They feared, then, that even in that cell she would find a way to escape. Why, the utter, ridiculous impossibility of the thing convinced her of her own innocence, and ignorance of all supernatural power; and the heavy iron brought her strangely round from the delusions that seemed to be gathering about her."[20] Lois steps out of her time into an Enlightenment state of mind at this crucial point in her life, but not far enough to dispense entirely with a Christian ending to the story. Lois comforts the Indian woman who will be hanged alongside her with stories of Christ's life and "holy fragments of the Psalms," but her last cry is the human one of "Mother!"

Historical records come to the rescue of this disconcerting and subversive story, because there exists irrefutably the written confession of the persecutors, given verbatim in Gaskell's text, asking for forgiveness, "first of God for Christ's sake [and] by the living sufferers." But Lois's English lover cannot accept this: "All their repentance will avail nothing to my Lois, nor will it bring back her life."[21] Although he finally agrees to join his prayers with those of the repentant Judge Sewall, the story ends equivocally. The essentially optimistic synthesis that emerges at the end of *My Lady Ludlow* is not repeated in *Lois the Witch*. "Was it, indeed, true that she was to die? She, Lois Barclay, only eighteen, so well, so young, so full of love and hope ... ?"[22] Darwin's prescription of who will survive does not prevail here; rather, the story confirms his earlier comment that the struggle for existence is "generally more severe between species of the same genus, when they come into contact with each other, than between species of distinct genera."[23] Why this should be so is only "dimly" understood, he says, and it is Gaskell's achievement to help us to clarify the reasons why the Salem community turns upon one who is an incomer but is still of the same genus.

The ending of *Sylvia's Lovers*, though free of historical constraints, is as darkly equivocal as *Lois the Witch*, and suggests that Gaskell's view of how history evolves is now no longer optimistic. Published in 1863, the novel is set in 1793 in Monkshaven, based on Whitby on the northeast Yorkshire coast, at that time a successful whaling port. Sylvia Robson is a farmer's daughter who is loved by two men, Kinraid, the handsome harpooner on a whale ship, whom she loves, and her cousin Philip Hepburn, the "plain" shopman who sells general haberdashery down in the town. The background to the story is the war with France and a consequent use of impressment, whereby sailors are taken into naval service against their will. Whalemen were protected but Charley Kinraid is captured nonetheless when he is alone on the beach, walking back to Newcastle to join his ship. This deed is witnessed by Hepburn, who does not tell Sylvia but allows her to think that Kinraid is dead. There is a riot against the press gang in Monkshaven, instigated by Sylvia's father Daniel, who is arrested and hanged. Impoverished as a result, Sylvia marries Hepburn, moves into the shop in the town, and gives birth to their daughter. After about three years, Kinraid, now in the Royal Navy, returns to claim Sylvia but she will not go with him, though she says she will never live with Hepburn as his wife again. Hepburn leaves Monkshaven and joins the army, and at the Battle of Acre he sees and rescues Kinraid, but is badly disfigured soon afterwards. He makes a painful journey home, rescues his daughter from drowning, and is finally reconciled with Sylvia, just before his death.

Gaskell constantly reminds the reader of the gap between then and now, the historical changes that have taken and are taking place. Not only is England no longer in fear of invasion, and the practice of impressment fallen into disuse, but other customs and habits of thought are recalled, sometimes with regret, sometimes with gratification, as bygones. Describing the haggling over butter and eggs at the market cross, she writes, "There was leisure for all this kind of work in those days" (*SL*, 2:16), and "those days" chimes repeatedly throughout the novel to emphasize the passage of time and the differences that history brings. One of the most interesting tensions between past and present is in the lives of women at the turn of the century and their expectations and status at the time Gaskell was writing. Although the feminist movement in the late 1850s was still in its infancy, with some years to go before women could own their own wages and property, and still longer before they could vote (1918), petitions had been presented to parliament to enfranchise women, such as that put forward by John Stuart Mill in 1857. It is with wry amusement that Gaskell notes the low estimation of women in the rural community of her novel; for example, that men would rather talk to their dogs than their wives, "when the first blush and hurry of youth is over" (*SL*, 8:84). Women accept this subordination, as in the case of Sylvia's mother Bell, who is better educated and more sensible than her husband, but believes, against all the evidence, that he has "the superior intellect of the masculine gender" (*SL*, 11:118). Illiterate Sylvia is trapped in a world of dependency on men: unequipped to earn her own living, her beauty is her only asset and it leads to the fatal obsession and desire for ownership of her cousin. Gaskell perhaps points to an alternative though austere future for women in the figure of Hester Rose, the shop assistant who secretly loves Philip. She earns her keep, refuses to marry a man she does not love, and gives her life to duty and service to others.

Gaskell did extensive research for the novel, consulting Whitby residents, the Annual Register, and books on whaling, the press gang, and the history of Whitby. There is a palpable feel of actuality to the story, aided by Gaskell's extensive use of dialect. Like Scott, she anchors her story in actual events, embedding in it biography (Sylvia's father is based on William Atkinson, the man hanged at York for incitement to riot, and uses Atkinson's actual words as he urges the rioters forward) and the "big solemn history" of the Battle of Acre and the wars with France. But the emotional charge of the novel is carried by fictional characters, particularly Sylvia and Hepburn. Although Napoleon is glimpsed – "a little man" at the center of a circle of French generals – and Sir Sidney Smith, the admiral in charge of British forces, speaks a few sentences, they are no more than historical markers. The noise of actual events is in the background but the foreground is occupied by the unhistorical – in two senses: that which is both unimportant and invented. Gaskell takes the historical detail of a man hanged in 1796 and develops it into a story of how the "little lives of little men" – and, particularly, women – are affected by events over which they have no control. This leads to a central concern in the novel with the collision between individual and corporate will, between private and national history. It is dramatized in the conversation between Hepburn and Daniel Robson in which they discuss the rights and wrongs of impressment, the need for national security against personal liberty. Hepburn reminds Robson that "laws is made for the good of the nation, not for your good or mine" (*SL*, 4:40). Robson's irascible reply – "I'm a man and yo're another, but nation's nowhere ... [N]ation! nation, go hang!" – is a futile assertion of individual rights (*SL*, 4:41). When he enacts these in the public arena, in his own version of justice on behalf of pressed seamen, he is arrested and executed. Sylvia's own desire to help the whalers escape the press gang is similarly helpless: "It's the law," Hepburn tells her, "and no one can do aught against it, least of all women and lasses" (*SL*, 3:28).

Like Lois, Sylvia must die young; the vibrant, vital creature in a red cloak of the early part of the novel becomes "a pale, sad woman, allays dressed in black [who] died before her daughter was well grown up" (SL, 45:502). The only positive earthly outcome is the emigration of Sylvia's daughter to America, having married a cousin, as her mother did, but that lies outside the novel's scope and is no more than a gesture toward an optimistic future. As far as the main protagonists are concerned, the conclusion is a dissolution into Christian abstraction, in which "All will be right in heaven – in the light of God's mercy" (SL, 45:499). The novel has been structured around opposites, which Sylvia's two lovers embody: the sea and the land, orality and literacy, legend and history, attraction and repulsion, loss and recovery. But in the final stages, as if the task of reconciling these oppositions, or finding a synthesis deriving from them, is proving too much, there is resignation in the face of futility and frailty and the only resolution that can be found is outside the flow of history. What seem to remain of an earthly record are Hepburn's initials, P. H., above the almshouses and the legend of his martyrdom at the hands of a hard-hearted wife. But this is not quite all, for the "lady" who visits the public baths and talks with the bathing woman picks up the strands of a story that has been molded out of "popular feeling, and ignorance of the real facts" and asks the questions that have been left out of it: " 'What became of the wife?' ... 'And the daughter?' " (SL, 502). The lady – the lady novelist, Gaskell the historian-novelist – will write the "real facts" of Sylvia's story but it will be fiction; she will take the oral tradition and give it the permanence of the written word. This will instate Sylvia in history, rescue her from "formless oblivion" and give her a biography. It is, however, thin compensation. The "grandeur" in a view of life that could see infinite variety and struggle governed by laws seems to have deserted Gaskell in this novel.

Why her mood darkened at this time is perhaps related to the distress in the Lancashire cotton towns caused by the American Civil War. It certainly slowed down the completion of Sylvia's Lovers, and is echoed in the novel's theme that far-off events cause local, personal suffering. Other contemporary issues seem to have preyed on her mind, some of them surfacing in historical guise. As George Eliot pointed out, "The finest effort to re-animate the past is of course only approximate – it is always more or less an infusion of the modern spirit into the ancient form."[24] In this respect each of the three fictions shows a preoccupation with outbursts of public disorder: the reign of terror in My Lady Ludlow, the witch hunts in Lois the Witch, and the riots against the press gang in Sylvia's Lovers. All three are "real solemn history," and they resonate with events in Gaskell's "time of the now," perhaps particularly with the Indian Mutiny of 1857, in which

Indian regiments rebelled against their employers in the East India Company, leading to the transfer of the administration of India from the Company to the British crown.

Gaskell was certainly very concerned on a personal level because her daughter was engaged to a soldier involved in the action, and on a general level because of the shocking nature of the conflict: "From the depths of ignorance I am roused up to the most vivid & intense interest" (*L*, 463). Like that of many contemporary novelists, her fiction does not directly reflect the mutiny but enacts a displacement of mutiny anxiety onto other sites and times. The mutiny, which raged from May 1857 to 1859, and involved great brutality on both sides, shook British confidence in a benign partnership between the East India Company and the Mughal emperors. Its abruptness and wildfire contagion resonate with the episode in *Sylvia's Lovers* where Sylvia's father unleashes a riot, which he cannot control and which brings harsh reprisals: "men's not to be stopped wi' a straw when their blood is up," he says, "tho', mebbe, a wouldn't do it again" (*SL*, 24:271; 25:277).

Underlying the representation of conflict and struggle in the novel is the increasing impact of *On the Origin of Species*. It is significant that the epigraph to *Sylvia's Lovers* is from section fifty-six of Alfred, Lord Tennyson's *In Memoriam*, a poem Gaskell much admired, itself a product of the same intellectual climate that produced *Origin of Species*. The group of sections fifty to fifty-six are the most "Darwinian" of the poem in which a violent, lawless evolutionary struggle, "nature red in tooth and claw," seems to prevail, and any purpose to life is hidden, "Behind the veil! Behind the veil!"[25] The "truth of the universal struggle for life" should not, Darwin says, be other than "thoroughly engrained in the mind" and from this conviction arises an appreciation of why species slaughter other species and sometimes their own kind.[26] In one of the most memorable passages in *Origin of Species*, Darwin discusses the life cycle of various species of ants, and in their slave-making, murderous, territorial, and pupae-protecting behavior he implicitly describes human behavior.[27] By analogy, all too easily drawn in the years after the publication of *Origin of Species* and in the furore that greeted it, human destiny is no more than to be "blown about the desert dust,/Or seal'd within the iron hills."[28] If *My Lady Ludlow* is an ameliorative evolutionary narrative, by the time of *Sylvia's Lovers* the Darwinian message has been fully absorbed. "Big, solemn history," as a public manifestation of the struggle for existence, sweeps away the lives of "little men." In June 1857 Gaskell had written of the duty of a writer to tell painful truths: "Like all pieces of human life, faithfully told there must be some great lesson to be learnt" (*L*, 449). The great lesson of *Sylvia's Lovers* is the painful truth of history that there is not necessarily a purposeful, progressive narrative of human life, or only, perhaps, in a heaven that lies outside the remit of the historical novel.

Notes

1 Henry James, "The Art of Fiction" (1888), in *The Art of Fiction and Other Essays by Henry James*, ed. Morris Roberts (London: Oxford University Press, 1948), 3–23, 16.

2 Thomas Carlyle, "On History" (1830), in Carlyle, *Selected Writings*, ed. Alan Shelston (London: Penguin, 1971), 51–8.

3 Philip Harwood, "The Modern Art and Science of History," *Westminster Review* 38 (October 1842), 337–71, 357.

4 Thomas Henry Buckle, *History of Civilisation in England*, 2 vols., quoted in Franz Boas, "Historians in the Sixties," in John Drinkwater, ed., *The Eighteen Sixties: Essays by Fellows of the Royal Society of Literature* (Cambridge: Cambridge University Press, 1932), 177–9.

5 Charles Darwin, *On the Origin of Species by Means of Natural Selection or The Preservation of Favoured Races in the Struggle for Life* (1859) (London: Penguin, 1968), 459.

6 George Eliot, "Silly Novels by Lady Novelists" (1856), in Eliot, *Selected Essays, Poems and Other Writings*, ed. A. S. Byatt and Nicholas Warren (London: Penguin, 1990), 159.

7 James, "The Art of Fiction," 17.

8 Walter Scott, *Waverley; or, 'Tis Sixty Years Since* (1814), ed. Claire Lamont (Oxford: World's Classics, 1986), 1:3–5.

9 Elizabeth Gaskell, "The Poor Clare," in Gaskell, *My Lady Ludlow and Other Stories*, ed. Edgar Wright (Oxford: World's Classics, 1989), 271.

10 William Wordsworth, "Preface to *Lyrical Ballads*," in Wordsworth and Samuel Coleridge, *Lyrical Ballads*, ed. R. L . Brett and A. R. Jones (London: Methuen, 1965), 259.

11 Elizabeth Gaskell, *Round the Sofa*, in Gaskell, *My Lady Ludlow and Other Stories*, 437.

12 Gaskell, "*My Lady Ludlow*," in Gaskell, *My Lady Ludlow and Other Stories*, 1:11. Hereafter references are to this edition and are made parenthetically in the text.

13 A. N. Wilson, *The Victorians* (London: Hutchinson, 2002), 282.

14 Darwin, *Origin of Species*, 129.

15 Bernard Rosenthal, *Salem Story: Reading the Witch Trials of 1692* (Cambridge: Cambridge University Press, 1993), 3.

16 Charles Upham, *Lectures on Witchcraft, Comprising a History of the Delusions in Salem* (Boston, 1831), 16.

17 *Ibid.*, 106.

18 *Ibid.*, 17.

19 Elizabeth Gaskell, *Lois the Witch*, in Elizabeth Gaskell, *Cousin Phillis and Other Tales*, ed. Angus Easson (Oxford: World's Classics, 1981), 152.

20 *Ibid.*, 178.

21 *Ibid.*, 191–2.
22 *Ibid.*, 181.
23 Darwin, *Origin of Species*, 127.
24 Eliot, "Silly Novels by Lady Novelists," 159.
25 Alfred, Lord Tennyson, *In Memoriam*, ll. 56:15, 28. Published in 1850, *In Memoriam* predated *On the Origin of Species* but drew on previous evolutionary theories, such as Charles Lyell's *Elements of Geology* (1838).
26 Darwin, *Origin of Species*, 115–16.
27 *Ibid.*, 243–7.
28 Tennyson, *In Memoriam*, ll. 56:19–20.

7

LINDA K. HUGHES

Cousin Phillis, *Wives and Daughters*, and modernity

In 1906 A. W. Ward pronounced *Cousin Phillis*, first serialized in the *Cornhill Magazine* from November 1863 to February 1864, "one of the loveliest prose idylls in our literature" (*W*, VII, xiv); in 1977 John Lucas questioned the pastoralism of *Cousin Phillis* but deemed *Cranford* (1853) and *Wives and Daughters*, serialized in the *Cornhill* from August 1864 to January 1866, "beautiful idylls."[1] Pastoral idyll unquestionably forms an element of both *Cornhill* serials. Paul Manning, the young engineer who narrates *Cousin Phillis*, emphasizes the quietude of Hope Farm, where time passes so slowly that individual seconds can be marked: "The tranquil monotony of that hour made me feel as if I had lived for ever ... with my two quiet hearers, and the curled-up pussy cat sleeping on the hearth-rug, and the clock on the house-stairs perpetually clicking out the passage of the moments" (*CP*, II, 242). Part three of *Cousin Phillis* is structured by the timeless cycles of rural life and the "little pictures" (as the Greek *eidyllion* is often translated) intrinsic to idyll: "several little scenes, [come] back upon me ... like pictures to my memory ... corn harvest must have come after hay-making, apple-gathering after corn-harvest" (*CP*, III, 267). *Wives and Daughters* begins in the suspended time of childhood and nursery rhymes ("To begin with the old rigmarole of childhood. In a country there was a shire"), as twelve-year-old Molly Gibson awakens in wonder at the new attire she will don to visit The Towers, home to Lord and Lady Cumnor (*WD*, 1:1). In the pages that Gaskell completed before her death abruptly terminated the novel's measured pace, Molly traverses a circuit that encompasses only her village, The Towers, Hamley Hall, Ashcombe, and the fields between.

Gaskell's scenes of radiant tranquility ensured continued scrutiny of her work in an era that prized "timeless" values and literary form – though the idyllic Gaskell was usually considered a minor or feminine talent

("Mrs. Gaskell"), for example, by Lord David Cecil.[2] With the revaluation of her work begun in the 1970s, quickened by feminist theory, materialist analysis, and new historicism, Gaskell's idylls have been increasingly repositioned as highly complex, multivalent narratives that address fundamental social conflicts and that, like the fiction of George Eliot and Thomas Hardy which followed (and learned from) the mature Gaskell, reveal a deep awareness of historical change. As the political scientist and philosopher Marshall Berman comments, "To be modern is to find ourselves in an environment that promises us adventure, power, joy, growth, transformation of ourselves and the world – and, at the same time, that threatens to destroy everything we have, everything we know, everything we are."[3] Gaskell's pastoralism in *Cousin Phillis* and *Wives and Daughters* is inseparable from her representation of modernity and its solvent effects; the encroachment of modernity is especially apparent in her depiction of agricultural change, the city's impingement upon the country, new intellectual structures effected by science and technology, and resulting changes in social and gender relations.

Some distinctions need to be made between the two fictions. As a shorter tale or *nouvelle*, *Cousin Phillis* can be read at a sitting, its structure discerned all at once, and its focus is also immediately clear: "It is about Cousin Phillis that I am going to write" (*CP*, I, 221). The focus of *Wives and Daughters* is not so apparent in the opening account of Molly's disastrous visit to The Towers, nor, though its design is carefully laid – the unreliable Hyacinth Kirkpatrick resurfaces as Molly's stepmother; Molly's return visit to The Towers in chapter fifty-eight as an intelligent, attractive woman in command of herself marks her recovered physical, emotional, and erotic vitality – can readers immediately discern it. The beginnings of Gaskell's novels typically forecast little. The first chapters of *North and South* (1855) led Charlotte Brontë to infer that it was a novel of religious doubt rather than industrial relations. After the first part of *Wives and Daughters* appeared, the Church of England *Guardian* could be forgiven for sniffing that "the new tale which holds the first place in the *Cornhill Magazine*, does not promise much. It deals with lords and ladies, but their language and conversation are rather those of rich *parvenus* than of well-born and well-bred people."[4] Narrative swerves are possible only in full-length novels and, in Gaskell's hands, register a philosophical vision. For her full-length narrative structures, like her Unitarian beliefs, refuse a teleology that ordains an end implicit in the beginning. Rather, both narratively and philosophically, Gaskell privileges induction and evolutionary development.

Cousin Phillis and *Wives and Daughters* also diverge in narrative strategy. Phillis's inward experience is largely opaque, filtered only through Paul Manning's first-hand account. If this narrative overlay suggests the silencing of women, Paul is in other ways an eminently suitable narrator. That he, too, is unformed at the outset makes him an apt conduit for introducing elements of modernity to Hope Farm; still open to influence himself, Paul has not learned to impose a cautionary filter on his actions – hence his "hero-worship" of Edward Holdsworth and introduction of him to his kin (*CP*, II, 254). First an awkward boy intimidated by the tall, learned, beautiful Phillis, then an empathic bystander, and ultimately the mature narrator who comprehends that his desire to comfort his cousin unleashes suffering and conflict, Paul obliquely mirrors in his development the deepening significance of the tale and Phillis's own trajectory of growth.

Gaskell's female narrator in *Wives and Daughters* blends easily with the central consciousness of the novel, Molly Gibson, a strategy evident in the opening "rigmarole of childhood" as the narrator participates in the language, wonder, and play of the tale's young protagonist (*WD*, 1:1). Molly is sometimes deemed the bland norm of Victorian girlhood against which the far more interesting Cynthia Kirkpatrick kicks – and sparkles. But Molly's modes of knowing, which are predicated on curiosity, fierce commitment to justice, and penetrating observation born of sympathetic affection, are largely those of the narrative itself. Her fury at Betty's mistreatment of the governess, Miss Eyre, metamorphoses into the fury encouraged in readers by Hyacinth's injustices to Molly; Molly's possession of secrets that allow her to see and know more than other characters in unfolding situations also aligns her with the superior knowledge of the narrator, as does her habit of quietly standing to the side and "reading" others: "her observant eyes" are "the first to discover the nature of Roger Hamley's attraction" to Cynthia, and she later watches Roger's face "and read something of his feelings" when he calls on the young women (*WD*, 28:325, 332). The narrator of *Wives and Daughters* is mobile and certainly knows more about Molly's sexual development than Molly does. Yet the customary blend of narrative perspective with the central character's consciousness helps to enact an ethic of sympathetic observation that is crucial to *Wives and Daughters* and looks ahead to George Eliot's *Middlemarch* (1872), in which sympathetic observation is also an ethical imperative. Gaskell's narrative strategy, moreover, anticipates Henry James's commitment to a central filtering consciousness as part of his novels' design, especially that of *Portrait of a Lady* (1881).

If they differ in structure and narrative strategy, however, *Cousin Phillis* and *Wives and Daughters* both trace a girl's arrival at erotic self-awareness as she pursues a quiet life in a rural community that, like the girl, is undergoing subtle but relentless change. The compression of *Cousin Phillis* enables readers to mark the exact point at which erotic desire makes itself known to the Holman daughter. In part one the seventeen-year-old Phillis still wears the pinafore of childhood despite her womanly attractions: "She was a stately, gracious young woman, in the dress and with the simplicity of a child" (*CP*, I, 228). In part two Paul gives "cousin Phillis a wide berth" after discovering her intimidating command of languages yet still notes that "her hair was looking more golden, her dark eyelashes longer, her round pillar of a throat whiter than ever" (*CP*, II, 235). The significance of these markers of sexual fecundity in Phillis is not lost on the more eligible Holdsworth, and Phillis's first response to Holdsworth is a blush, a signal at once of modesty and of physical awareness that she is being looked at with the eyes of desire. In part three the moment of sexual awakening comes when Phillis, her father, Holdsworth, and Paul are caught in a thunder-shower and huddle together for shelter; Holdsworth has immediately wrapped his coat "round her neck and shoulders," and Phillis, concerned that Holdsworth has suffered a recent attack of fever, attempts to place the coat on him and "[i]n doing so she touched his shirt" that clings to his wet skin (*CP*, III, 269). Her body's knowledge completes in an instant the sexual maturation toward which Phillis has been moving all along, and after Holdsworth's sudden departure for Canada she is driven by desire so insistent, so raw, that Paul discovers her hiding beneath a woodstack, where "[s]he was making a low moan, like an animal in pain, or perhaps more like the sobbing of the wind" (*CP*, III, 283). Told by Paul that Holdsworth loves her, she is "warbling" in tune with birds' mating calls by the following spring and hence is all the more devastated when Holdsworth marries a young woman who vaguely resembles Phillis in French Canada (*CP*, IV, 289).

Both her anguish and her eroticized body are underlined in the powerful scene in which Phillis, "half undressed" but covered "with a dark winter cloak, which fell in long folds to her white, naked, noiseless feet," her face "strangely pale" and her "eyes heavy in the black circles round them," speaks out her love and humiliation before collapsing (*CP*, IV, 308). In nearly dying of brain fever she loses her erotic markers of golden hair (which is shorn) and beseeching eyes; when she recovers, her blush is asexual, born of self-knowledge that the old ways no longer suffice for her: "Phillis asked me ... if I thought my father and mother would allow her to go and stay with them for a couple of months. She blushed a little as she faltered out her wish for change of thought and scene" (*CP*, IV, 316–17). The ascetic final words of the tale ("we will go back to the peace of the old days. I know we shall; I can, and I will!") are open-ended, for Phillis's physical and erotic changes effect a corresponding literary change: her story can no longer conform to a courtship plot and its predictable closure in marriage (*CP*, IV, 317).

It is difficult to identify a single moment in which Molly acquires sexual awareness and self-knowledge in *Wives and Daughters*; within an expanded narrative Gaskell could place greater reliance on subtle, intermittent hints of Molly's development. But Gaskell foregrounds Molly's sexual development in so far as the novel's entire plot is driven by it. Mr. Coxe's love letter to Molly prompts not only her removal to Hamley Hall for an extended visit but also her father's remarriage to Hyacinth Kirkpatrick, which in turn brings both Cynthia Kirkpatrick and Mr. Preston into Molly's life. Ironically, all these stratagems are unnecessary: Molly is oblivious of Mr. Coxe (and her own sexuality) at the time; Mr. Coxe is soon removed when he inherits a handsome legacy; the second Mrs. Gibson lowers rather than maintains or raises the moral tone of the household; and Molly is precipitated into rather than saved from scandal as a result of having the companionship of a sister. Molly's physical maturation is in any case unstoppable, as her physician father ought to know, and culminates in the rich beauty that Osborne Hamley had predicted all along. Although Gaskell's death prevented full closure of her courtship plot, she had already indicated the final outcome by including Roger's recognition that Molly, "and she alone, could make him happy" and Mr. Gibson's wry conclusion after seeing Molly distressed at Roger's departure for a six-month voyage: "Lover *versus* father! ... Lover wins" (*WD*, 60:670, 679).

The narratives of sexual selection and physiological change in *Cousin Phillis* and *Wives and Daughters*, however, are inseparable from larger cultural narratives of rural encounters with modernity, even in the depths of the countryside. The Reverend Holman still relies on traditional agricultural practices that he recognizes in the *Georgics* of his beloved Virgil, still ends work by singing a hymn. Yet the minister's intellectual curiosity and consumption of books not only make him a lively companion to men of the world, especially Mr. Manning (Paul's father) and Holdsworth, but also give him a scientific bent of mind that marks him with the impress of modernity. On the day Phillis makes erotic contact with Holdsworth by touching him, they are caught in a thunderstorm because they are experimenting with a theodolite, the surveying tool that Holdsworth is teaching the Holmans to use, and that imposes abstract grids onto natural contours to map their farm in terms quite foreign to Virgil. The farm itself remains traditional, but the guiding intelligence behind it has encountered, and embraced, key aspects of modernity.

Agricultural change is more central to *Wives and Daughters*. What the cultural critic Raymond Williams observes of Thomas Hardy's work is true as well of the rural economy that shapes a key encounter in Gaskell's last novel:

> the market forces which moved and worked at a distance were also deeply based in the rural economy itself: in the system of rent and trade; in the hazards of ownership and tenancy; in the differing conditions of labour on good and bad land, or in socially different villages . . . ; and in what happened to people and to families in the interaction between general forces and personal histories.[5]

The principal exponent of changing farm, labor, and market conditions is Preston, who conducts himself as a free agent in a competitive social and economic arena rather than as a traditional steward consigned by birth and obligations to a given place in a rural hierarchy. Trading (in a metaphoric and literal sense) on his good looks and the fine figure he has fashioned by subjecting his body to disciplined athletic development, as well as his expertise in law and land, Preston advances in influence, replacing the old-fashioned farm agent Mr. Sheepshanks in the oversight of Lord and Lady Cumnor's Hollingford property, and in popularity, quickly forming a social network among villagers. He is also the embodiment of rude aggression and narcissism, indifferent to the claims of anything but his economic, social, and erotic self-interest. His social and erotic pursuits take place mostly offstage, but chapter thirty, entitled "Old Ways and New Ways," brings him and Squire Hamley, and the orders of life they represent, into direct conflict.

Tellingly, the Squire encounters Preston supervising modern farm improvements because Hamley is fulfilling a traditional role of the squirearchy, visiting a dying servant and tenant, his former gamekeeper. Although Hamley can no longer afford a game preserve, the loyal servant relays alarm at gorse covers being pulled up by Preston's workers, whom (since they now occupy an alien order of things) the gamekeeper terms "strangers, though some on 'em is th' men as was turned off your own works, squire" (*WD*, 30:351). The encounter is more complex than the clash of old and new, however, for the squire who glories in a name dating back to Anglo-Saxon times had begun the same improving drainage of farm land before his neighbors had, studying the topic intensively and urged on by his metropolitan-born wife to take advantage of a central government grant program. He, too, has embraced modernity. But he has been balked in his plans by the need to repay the debts of his son and heir, Osborne Hamley – debts which have forced him to lay off some of the men now working for Preston – and by the death of his wife, who is no longer there to encourage him.

The clash between Preston, who insists on legal and scientific proof that some of his workers are destroying Hamley's property, and Hamley, who having just left a dying retainer assumes that he will receive the same respect he met with there, quickly escalates into the competing claims of class and of feudal versus democratic virtues, which pit traditional courtesy against the rights of the self-made man. Gaskell, however, makes it clear that these clashes play out at the surface, for what are really at stake are, in Williams's terms, "hazards of ownership and tenancy" and "what happened to people and to families in the interaction between general forces and personal histories." Squire Hamley is galled by his son's failure to distinguish himself at Cambridge University, galled by having the son's creditors come to value the timber on the property, conscience-stricken at having laid off men who needed the work to live, and anguished over the loss of his wife and his son's estrangement, and he uses the trivial matter of gorse plucked up to vent his distress. But Preston, the good economic man, can see only the trifling value of the gorse ("it may probably amount to half-a-crown," he sneers as the squire turns away) and the squire's steady refusal to recognize him as a fellow man of worth (*WD*, 30:354).

Williams mentions Gaskell only as a novelist of urban industrialism in *The Country and the City*, his study of changing relations between country and city in literature. Yet *Cousin Phillis* and *Wives and Daughters* also exemplify another point he makes of Hardy's work: "The pressures to which ... characters are subjected are then pressures from within a system of living, itself now thoroughly part of a wider system. There is no simple case of an internal ruralism and an external urbanism."[6] In Gaskell's narratives the country and the city are defined by their shifting exchanges and by a cosmopolitan internationalism fostered by circulating print culture and transport systems. The very premise of *Cousin Phillis* is the railroad's reach into the countryside. Paul Manning is the transitional character who, in Williams's terms, has "become in some degree separated from [country living] yet who remain[s] by some tie of family inescapably involved," just as Roger Hamley is in *Wives and Daughters*.[7] And like Eliot in *Middlemarch*, Gaskell uses the coming of the railroad to mark a changing era. The railroad embodies modernity not merely because it is a new technology but also because it is part of a rationalized system of interconnection within a nation and requires a new way of seeing that ignores traditions and local, even national boundaries. To a railroad engineer, land comprises data and a problem to be solved, not a site of cultural memory or the slow process of crop yields; the engineer thus perceives land as does a mobile modern subject, as a place to reside in, work in, and move on from – which is why Holdsworth shifts so easily from the Italian Piedmont to Eltham and Hornby to French Canada. And like the railroad as well, Holdsworth's advent at Hope Farm has a solvent effect on the past. He transmits the excitement, pulse, and color of modernity, turning Virgil into virtual cinema rather than venerable text for Reverend Holman: "He makes Horace and Virgil living, instead of dead, by the stories he tells me of his sojourn in the very countries where they lived" (*CP*, II, 266). After he leaves, Phillis is infected with the twin ills of urban modernity, ennui and restlessness: "there had been a new, sharp, discordant sound to me in her voice, a sort of jangle in her tone; and her restless eyes had no quietness in them" (*CP*, IV, 296). Her solution is to participate in a defining act of modernity – to move on, though only (she thinks) temporarily.

Gaskell never shifts the scene of *Wives and Daughters* to London in her completed chapters because Molly stays in Hollingford. Yet London plays a surprisingly active role in the novel's events, a means by which Gaskell can unobtrusively register the conduits of change, and exchange, in the world she represents. Not only Cynthia Kirkpatrick (another exemplar, like Holdsworth, of deracinated modernity) but also Squire Hamley and Osborne find their mates in London. Hamley, who represents the best of the old squirearchy, refuses to visit London, but his daily life is shaped by it since Mrs. Hamley has imported the London custom of dressing for dinner into the household. Moreover, although Gaskell veils the fact until midway through the novel, Mrs. Hamley is a merchant's daughter, which means that for all his talk of Osborne's marrying an heiress as befits his rank, the old squire has himself inaugurated the practice of marrying down. Mrs. Hamley can also be said to insert the marketplace into Hamley Hall, and Roger's use of talent as capital to make his way in the world marks him as his grandfather's heir. But of course Osborne goes much further, marrying not only a servant but also a French Catholic. Osborne meets Marie-Aimée Scherer in Hyde Park, that most cosmopolitan of sites where classes promiscuously mingle along with residents and visitors. As early as 1800 the poet Mary Robinson commented of London parks, "The public promenades, particularly on the sabbath, are thronged with pedestrians of all classes, and the different ranks of people are scarcely distinguishable either by their dress or their manners."[8] If Osborne does not long survive his marriage, he nonetheless produces an heir who will inherit the Hall – especially since Roger concludes that "it is not likely I shall ever make it my home again" (*WD*, 58:653). Roger's destiny is an international career; the Hall's is to be owned by the offspring of an international and cross-class union.

For Cynthia, London is a safety valve, a means of escaping the stultifying company of her mother, the harassment of Preston, and the limited happiness she foresees in marriage to Roger. Hyacinth circulates second-hand London gossip in order to appear fashionable. But London influences life in Hollingford in other ways, in part through its print culture. Molly is given the most recent issue of the *Quarterly Review* with which to amuse herself when she visits The Towers in lieu of traveling to London for Cynthia's wedding; Roger reads about the wedding in *The Times*. More tellingly, perhaps, the Hollingford Book Society orders its books from London, and their display in Grinstead's book shop creates a rural counterpart to Hyde Park, where men and women of varying status encounter each other and where Molly becomes the supposed participant in a sexual intrigue when she is seen giving Preston an envelope. If, finally, Gaskell begins chapter twenty-six, "A Charity Ball," by underscoring how rare it was to see duchesses and diamonds "before railroads were, and before their consequences, the excursion-trains, which take every one up to London now-a-days, there to see their fill of gay crowds and fine dresses," by chapter fifty-seven Lady Cumnor has just returned from taking her daughter to the station on the new London-Birmingham line (*WD*, 26:294; 57:638). Hollingford, like Hope Farm, has become a node in a communication network that quickens interchanges between the country and the city.

Not only technology but also the natural sciences inform Gaskell's late work, not surprisingly given her distant kinship to the Darwins and the deliberateness with which she patterned elements of Roger Hamley's early career after Charles Darwin's. If modern science maps knowledge in ways that can fortify dominant power structures, its methods and institutions also loosen constraints. In *Cousin Phillis* Mr. Manning, Paul's father, signifies the rising importance in capitalist societies of a meritocracy built on talent, invention, and inductive knowledge all ranged in opposition to *a priori* judgments. Science in this sense promotes democracy, since scientists' interaction relies on exchanges of knowledge more than on social status; mobility, since innovation is rewarded with increased wealth and new career opportunities; and urbanization, since the pursuit of science requires metropolitan centers where the like-minded can gather and build upon prior work (a different model from the older amateur naturalist or botanist, like Gaskell's Job Legh in *Mary Barton* or Eliot's Reverend Farebrother in *Middlemarch*, who acquire knowledge in isolation from others). Nineteenth-century science, then, both produces ideas and technologies that change life and thought, and in its social practice embodies key features of modernity. Paul's father is a transitional figure. He has begun as a working-class mechanic, but newspapers announce his "discovery of a new method of shunting," and by the time he visits Hope Farm he has been offered a partnership in a manufacturing enterprise that will permanently alter his social standing (*CP*, I, 236; II, 250). Holdsworth, possessed of middle-class privileges, pays tribute to what a keen intellect can do in this newer era: "Here's a Birmingham workman, self-educated, one may say – having never associated with stimulating minds, or had what advantages travel and contact with the world may be supposed to afford – working out his own thoughts into steel and iron, making a scientific name for himself – a fortune, if it pleases him to work for money" (*CP*, II, 254). Since Paul later marries the daughter of his father's new partner, Mr. Manning passes on his social ascent to his son – a form of social rather than biological evolution. The knowledge of science that affords Mr. Manning mobility and opportunity in an urban environment also serves as a shared discourse among similarly educated men in the country and city, hence Mr. Manning's animated conversations with both the Reverend Holman and Holdsworth.

As *Wives and Daughters* opens, Mr. Gibson is the traditional country physician, if an improved version thanks to his acute mind and up-to-date scientific training. When Lord Hollingford, who has acquired "much reputation in the European republic of learned men," begins to reside for extended periods at The Towers, he imports this "republicanism" and invites "all sorts of people to The Towers," which "meant really those who were distinguished for science and learning, without regard to rank" (*WD*, 4:35–6). Thus Mr. Gibson, rather than pursuing the solitary researches of an amateur, is drawn into a rural scientific network that ignores boundaries of class, just as he enters into intellectual exchanges afforded by his publications in "the more scientific of the medical journals" (*WD*, 4:37). Roger Hamley first achieves notice as senior wrangler, the highest-ranking mathematics student at Cambridge University, and his scientific article on comparative anatomy quickly confers international standing on him. This recognition has local effects when he is invited to The Towers not because he is (as his father assumes) a Hamley of Hamley but because a visiting French scientist wants to meet him. In turn he wins appointment as the naturalist on an expedition, and his letters from Africa are read at the Royal Geographical Society, turning him into a London celebrity. From being the stolid second son of a local squire, he transforms himself into a cosmopolitan intellectual whose discoveries will profoundly alter the outlook of his generation, a peculiarly modern narrative of historical change bound up with the story of a country village.

Gaskell's unobtrusive yet finely realized depiction of deep historical change is inseparable from her attention to gender relations, which perforce alter in response to changing conditions. Gaskell takes care to couple positive and negative exemplars of modernity, particularly among her male characters. In *Cousin Phillis* Holdsworth suggests the price to be paid by mobility: although he does nothing improper and is genuinely attractive to everyone he meets, his deracination in conjunction with his careerist ambition incline him toward superficial commitments and eager adaptation to whatever lies at hand. Women are to him types, accordingly. He wishes to sketch Phillis as Ceres, the goddess of agriculture and fertility, and the French Canadian woman he eventually marries is, he tells Paul in a letter, "curiously like Phillis Holman" (*CP*, IV, 291). But modernity is equally expressed in Mr. Manning, who is nurturing and kind. As Paul remarks:

> I was an only child; and though my father's spoken maxim had been, "Spare the rod and spoil the child," yet, unconsciously, his heart had yearned after me, and his ways towards me were more tender than he knew, or would have approved of in himself could he have known. My mother, who never professed sternness, was far more severe than my father. (*CP*, I, 220)

A similar pairing occurs in *Wives and Daughters*, with Preston embodying the rapaciousness of modernity, his "grey, roving, well-shaped eyes" signifying both his masculine beauty and a man on the make (*WD*, 13:158). Roger Hamley, in contrast, exemplifies like Mr. Manning the hopeful possibilities of modern masculinity, even some elements of the "New Man" sought at the century's end. For Roger does not separate but rather conjoins science and nurturing as well as companionate relationships. He befriends Molly and becomes her mentor while conducting research in the ponds and fields surrounding Hamley Hall, when he hears the miserable girl who has just quarreled with her father over his remarriage and displays equal tenderness for fauna and human vulnerability:

> He had been out dredging in ponds and ditches, and had his wet sling-net, with its imprisoned treasures of nastiness, over his shoulder ... He did not see Molly ... when, looking among the grass and wild plants under the trees, he spied out one which was rare, one which he had been long wishing to find in flower, and saw it at last, with those bright keen eyes of his. Down went his net, skilfully twisted so as to retain its contents, while it lay amid the herbage, and he himself went with light and well-planted footsteps in search of the treasure. He was so great a lover of nature that, without any thought, but habitually, he always avoided treading unnecessarily on any plant; who knew what long-sought growth or insect might develop itself in what now appeared but insignificant? ... He stopped; he saw a light-coloured dress on the ground ... For a minute or two he thought it would be kinder to leave her believing herself unobserved ... However, whether it was right or wrong, delicate or obtrusive, when he heard the sad voice talking again, in such tones

of uncomforted, lonely misery, he turned back, and went to the green tent
under the ash-tree.   (*WD*, 10:117–18)

Rather than merely consoling her, he seeks to still her anguish by awakening her curiosity and so invites her to look at his collected specimens
under a microscope; in this case (in contrast to Holdsworth's theodolite), an
impersonal scientific apparatus becomes a medium of male nurturance:
"[he] cherished her first little morsel of curiosity, and nursed it into a very
proper desire for further information" (*WD*, 10:124). He similarly draws
on science, and his willingness to assume his mother's role of comforter and
conciliator, to nurse his father back into emotional wellbeing when he
applies the salaries of his Cambridge fellowship and expedition appointment to resuming drainage work on his father's land – and to supporting, in
secret, Osborne's wife and heir.

But in one respect Roger is a transitional figure himself, while Mr. Gibson
is positively stranded in the old order: their attitudes toward women.
Mr. Gibson loves his young daughter deeply but thinks she need be only
minimally literate. He instructs her governess, Miss Eyre, "Don't teach
Molly too much" (*WD*, 3:32). As a corollary he also defines science and
knowledge in gendered terms, and the narrator slyly hints at his fallacy:

> He had rather a contempt for demonstrative people, arising from his medical
> insight into the consequences to health of uncontrolled feeling. He deceived
> himself into believing that still his reason was lord of all, because he had
> never fallen into the habit of expression on any other than purely intellectual
> subjects. Molly, however, had her own intuitions to guide her.   (*WD*, 3:30)

Unused to examining his feelings or to expecting much from women's
intellect, he is impelled into marriage by his possessive alarm at a prospective
suitor for Molly, by Hyacinth's conventional expressions of sentimental (and
hypocritical) interest in his young daughter, and above all by the aesthetic
surface appeal of the widow: "her voice was so soft, her accent so pleasant,
that it struck him as particularly agreeable after the broad country accent he
was perpetually hearing. Then the harmonious colours of her dress, and her
slow and graceful movements, had something of the same soothing effect
upon his nerves that a cat's purring has upon some people's" (*WD*, 10:107).
The result is not merely fallacious logic (since in the end Molly needs no
protection from Mr. Coxe) but considerable pain to his daughter. And even
after the marriage, he is no wiser. When Cynthia manages her mother by
feigning indifference to an invitation from Hamley Hall that she fully
intends to accept, "Mr. Gibson, ... who, surgeon though he was, had never
learnt to anatomize a woman's heart, took it all literally, and was

excessively angry both with Cynthia and her mother; so angry that he did not dare to trust himself to speak" (*WD*, 36:416). Later still, he exclaims to Molly in another fit of exasperation with Cynthia, "I think the world would get on tolerably well, if there were no women in it," by which point his blind spot is tantamount to inept reproductive medicine (*WD*, 48:547). The precedent of Gaskell's keen-minded provincial doctor who pursues scientific research yet is deluded into an imprudent marriage by a socially adept, winningly attractive, but superficial and egocentric woman, may have influenced Eliot when she came to fashion the narrative of Tertius Lydgate in *Middlemarch*.

Roger is another scientist initially swayed by the surface appeal of a beautiful woman, and he, too, inflicts pain on Molly accordingly. When at one of Hyacinth's dinners Roger abruptly ignores Molly – she who has stood as spiritual daughter to his mother – as "he feasted his eyes" on Cynthia, "Molly suddenly felt as if she could scarcely keep from crying – a minute ago he had been so near to her, and talking so pleasantly and confidentially; and now he almost seemed as if he had forgotten her existence" (*WD*, 24:278, 282). The character modeled after Darwin is, ironically, subject to the biological determinism of sexual selection where she is concerned, driven by her brilliant "plumage" to instinctual rather than reasoned response: "It was only the thought of Cynthia that threw Roger off balance. A strong man in everything else, about her he was as a child" (*WD*, 31:364). His suspension of intellect is evident even in the empty clichés with which he surrounds her: "[Cynthia] would know at any rate how dearly she was beloved by one who was absent; how in all difficulties or dangers the thought of her would be a polar star, high up in the heavens, and so on, and so on" (*WD*, 33:388). Eventually, of course, he learns to value the companionate love, as well as rich beauty, offered by Molly. In this expanding concept of womanhood, as in the brilliance of his scientific career, Roger surpasses Mr. Gibson; together the two men suggest yet another of the novel's historical changes over time.

But Roger requires help to broaden his views, for when he returns from Africa he has otherwise matured but is still in hot pursuit of Cynthia. She saves Roger – by choosing another mate herself, appropriating the agency of selection that Darwin would later reserve for males. In many ways a product of modernity herself, Cynthia reads Voltaire as easily as English authors and has no identity rooted in place or persons, having spent her childhood in boarding schools (mostly in France) because a child would have hampered her mother's efforts to sustain gentility through schoolteaching and invitations to country houses between terms. Taught neither the customary domestic affections associated with marriage and motherhood nor the professional skills that would support an independent single life, Cynthia instead learns her mother's lesson of the crucial need to please others (and is better at it, given her superior skill in hiding inner thoughts and her more brilliant beauty). If Cynthia harbors no malice, she has no sense of purpose in life; if she wants to be possessed by no one, she cannot support herself. In the end she chooses wisely: Mr. Henderson sparkles but is not too deep, and his pursuit of fashion fits him, like Cynthia, to make the most of urban consumer culture in London. As Molly concludes on meeting Cynthia's future husband, "he wanted something in Molly's eyes . . . , and in her heart of hearts she thought him rather commonplace" (*WD*, 56:634). Cynthia most overtly resists the patriarchal sway of Mr. Gibson, Roger, and their ilk, but Cynthia's is ultimately the everyday story of the novel, for she wants nothing from life beyond the common middle-class goals of affluence, security, admiration, and fashionable pleasures.

Molly (as her proximity to the narrator might suggest) is instead the "unique and very remarkable young woman" of the novel.[9] She considers herself so rooted in village life that on her return to Hollingford after Osborne's death she inwardly comments, "There's Hollingford church-spire . . . I think I never wish to go out of sight of it again" (*WD*, 52:592). Yet her customary condition throughout the novel is being out of place, as when she first visits The Towers as a child; when her father's remarriage destroys their intimate companionship and leaves her no clear-cut role in the household; when she inadvertently overhears the secret of Osborne's marriage while at Hamley Hall; whenever Cynthia's more evident attractions leave Molly little to do in the company of men; and when she meets Preston in order to help extricate Cynthia from an unfortunate engagement and ends up being ostracized by acquaintances as a scandalous flirt. Squire Hamley finds Molly's presence at Hamley Hall essential after Aimée's arrival, but Molly still is not "at home" there and begins to sink under a steady accumulation of burdens: the ruptured intimacy with her father, her pain over Cynthia's contracting and then breaking an engagement to Roger, secrets long suppressed and the social shunning they have exacted, the death of Osborne, sheer overwork and exhaustion, and depression over Roger's continued absence and the possibility that he will die from the fever he has reported months earlier. That a young woman at the end of her teens has been able to endure so much for so long alone suggests Molly's complexity and strength of character.

Coping with these challenges, however, requires apparent passivity, as does her quiet submission to the experience of displacement. Yet Molly also possesses active qualities that make possible the social and intellectual mobility associated with modernity. Molly's loyalty, sincerity, and commitment to speaking the truth, for example, win her a friend in Lady Harriet, who is bored by the bland clichés and supine deference of most villagers and welcomes Molly's refreshing, assertive candor when she refuses to hear her friends the Miss Brownings mocked by the local aristocrat. Molly's interactions with Lady Harriet parallel those of Mr. Gibson with Lord Hollingford in so far as both result from intellectual merit and unembarrassed directness of manner. Molly's ability to keep secrets (which she shares with Cynthia) no matter what the consequences also fosters greater independence of character, which surfaces when she goes directly to Hamley Hall on hearing of Osborne's death, leaving Hyacinth spluttering remonstrances behind her. Because she need not worry about always pleasing others, furthermore, she can carry herself with equanimity even amid unfamiliar settings, as her final visit to The Towers demonstrates. Above all, Molly's intellectual curiosity and lifelong habit of reading equip her for life beyond the limited circuit of village life. She has had to win the right to further study "by fighting and struggling hard" against her father's prejudices, becoming in the process a voracious reader of "every book that came in her way, almost with as much delight as if it had been forbidden" (WD, 3:32).

By the end of the novel, the little girl who mumbles her ignorance of French during her earliest visit to The Towers has become the young woman sufficiently schooled in that tongue to mediate between Squire Hamley and Aimée. Nor does she ever abandon the interest in science that Roger first nurtures in her, as she demonstrates in her conversation with Lord Hollingford at the charity ball. Her joy in the subject as an end in itself and as the arena within which Roger triumphs, as well as her increasing physical grace, designate her as one fitted for companionate marriage with a man soon to become a leading intellectual. The significance of her provincial girlhood and the mobility afforded by her character and intellectual attainments is nicely played out near the end when Lord Hollingford scoffs at Molly's suitability for Roger, "a man who will soon have an European reputation," since she is only "a very pretty, good little country-girl." But as his sister Lady Harriet rejoins, Hollingford has himself pronounced her "unusually intelligent," and, more tellingly, "Molly Gibson is capable of appreciating him" (WD, 58:653–4). Roger, unlike his father and brother, will take his wife from the countryside.

If Frederick Greenwood's editorial postscript to the novel, which purported to convey plans for the ending that Gaskell discussed with him, is to be believed, Molly herself ends up in London:

> [Roger] becomes professor at some great scientific institution, and wins his way in the world handsomely. The squire is almost as happy in this marriage

as his son. If any one suffers for it, it is Mr Gibson. But he takes a partner, so as to get a chance of running up to London to stay with Molly for a few days now and then and "to get a little rest from Mrs Gibson."   (*WD*, 58:684)

By a rigorous logic that he himself might well endorse, Mr. Gibson is still to suffer the consequences of his ill-considered marriage. But Molly moves from a quiet provincial town to London as the wife of a leading scientist, a narrative not only of courtship and good character triumphant but of modernity.

Greenwood's editorial note, of course, lacks full authority, and Molly's future, like Phillis Holman's, is left satisfyingly open-ended. Yet both the *nouvelle* and the novel terminate as they do partly because of their modern mode of production, that is, magazine serialization and the mass production and distribution of an author's writings. Gaskell's novel had run for so long in the *Cornhill* by the time she died on November 12, 1865, that simply leaving the story where the manuscript broke off was unthinkable – hence Greenwood's postscript and its tantalizing hints. But Gaskell did not give *Cornhill* readers the ending of *Cousin Phillis* she envisioned, either. *Cornhill* proprietor George Smith sought to end the *nouvelle* after the third part, and to dissuade him from this decision (presumably occasioned by shortage of space) Gaskell provided a sketch of the complete tale, including a fifth installment never finished. Had *Cousin Phillis* terminated with part three, Paul would have baldly announced the marriage of Holdsworth and expressed inability to narrate the consequences. Had the story terminated with part five, Paul would have returned to Hope Farm after Reverend Holman died to find Phillis "making practical use of the knowledge she had learnt from Holdsworth and, with the help of common labourers, levelling & draining the undrained village – a child (orphaned by the fever) in her arms, another plucking at her gown – we hear afterwards that she has adopted these to be her own" (*FL*, 259–60). The endings of *Cousin Phillis* and *Wives and Daughters*, then, resulted not merely from Gaskell's guiding artistic vision but also from the impersonal business interests of modernity.

Nor is this the only way in which Gaskell's *Cornhill* work engaged the modern literary marketplace. The 1860s market was dominated by sensation fiction, which was designed to boost circulation by leaving readers breathless for the next magazine installment and a further glimpse of the secret driving the plot. In her shorter tales of 1859–64, including *Cousin Phillis*, Gaskell shrewdly adapted elements of sensation fiction to probe complex human and cultural conditions. *Cousin Phillis* involves a woman's secret passion and its disruptive effects on the household, and Holdsworth is even more clearly associated with sensation fiction, since Reverend Holman compares his electrifying stories to "dram-drinking" – the term that H. M. Mansel applied to the effects of sensation fiction in an unsigned article in the *Quarterly Review*, mere months before *Cousin Phillis* began its serial run in the *Cornhill* (CP, II, 266).[10] Similarly, Jenny Uglow has argued of *Wives and Daughters* that "concealment starts to shape the plot itself, like a contemporary sensation novel, hanging on sexual and financial misdemeanour."[11] Cynthia and Molly represent, as it were, the alternate attractions of sensation fiction and realism. Cynthia exerts a "power of fascination" on others and injects a series of exciting incidents into the plot (WD, 19:225). While conceding that she cannot master "steady every-day goodness," Cynthia is "capable of a great jerk, an effort, and then a relaxation" (which sounds curiously akin to weekly installments of sensation fiction). She offers in addition the attractions of "fun," "charm," and the utterance of "startling things" (WD, 19:229–30). If Molly presents fewer dramatic shows to onlookers, she and Cynthia are frequently mistaken for each other; and eventually Molly becomes Cynthia's double, sharing Cynthia's secrets and undertaking clandestine meetings with Preston. The distinction between them is that Molly is more closely associated with ethical sympathy than with fascination: "Molly's was the interest of affection, not the coarser desire of knowing everything for a little excitement" (WD, 38:435). Although Molly seems so "every-day" compared to the more glamorous Cynthia, she is the rarer being who can sustain "steady every-day goodness." And she has attractions of her own, if they are less readily apparent. As the aesthetic connoisseur Osborne remarks, in five years Cynthia is likely to appear a bit "coarse" while Molly's "more perfect grace" will have become ever more apparent (WD, 29:335–6).

The same can be said of Gaskell's novel. On the surface it is so quiet a story that during its serialization the weekly magazines' most common remark (when they noticed unfolding parts at all) was that the serial "continued" or was "an every-day story" or was "readable as ever."[12] But underneath the placid, even idyllic, surface, Gaskell layers a complex tale of physiological, individual, and steady cultural change. Gaskell's novels, of course, had always engaged modernity in one form or another. *Mary Barton* (1848) and *North and South* (1855) pair crises in industrialism and in personal relations while incorporating Mary and Jem Wilson's emigration to Canada and the international marriage of Frederick Hale. *Cranford* could not be narrated without the intrusion of Mary Smith from industrialized Drumble, and the fates of Peter Jenkyns and the Brown family reveal the pressures exerted on provincial life by the British Empire. What distinguishes the late novels is Gaskell's diminished reliance on structural dyads (worker and owner, north and south) and her increasingly sophisticated ability to create a world embedded in an intricate matrix of ongoing social and historical change. The turning point for this new development can be located in *The Life of Charlotte Brontë* (1857), which demanded that Gaskell place a writer in a fully imagined world within which multiple interactive influences – personal, familial, geographical, historical, cultural, international – shaped Brontë's complex life and works. A crucial part of this story was the interchange of rural Yorkshire with the London publishing world, which acted in concert to change literary history. Gaskell remains an accomplished idyllist, but her delineation of deep agricultural and historical change in *Cousin Phillis* and *Wives and Daughters* underscores her modernity and the importance of these late works as a context and, at times, as precedents for *Middlemarch* and Hardy's Wessex fiction.

Notes

1 John Lucas, *The Literature of Change: Studies in the Nineteenth-Century Provincial Novel* (Brighton: Harvester, 1977), 2.
2 Lord David Cecil, *Early Victorian Novelists: Essays in Revaluation* (London: Constable, 1934), 199.
3 Marshall Berman, *All That Is Solid Melts Into Air: The Experience of Modernity* (New York: Penguin, 1988), 15.
4 "Table-Talk," [Church of England] *Guardian* 3 (August 1864), 770.
5 Raymond Williams, *The Country and the City* (Oxford: Oxford University Press, 1973), 209.
6 *Ibid.*, 209.
7 *Ibid.*, 200.
8 Mary Robinson, "Present State of the Manners, Society, Etc. of the Metropolis of England," [1800] intro. Adriana Craciun, *PMLA* 119 (2004), 103–19, 111.
9 Coral Lansbury, *Elizabeth Gaskell: The Novel of Social Crisis* (London: Paul Elek, 1975), 197.
10 H. L. Mansel, unsigned article, "Sensation Novels," *Quarterly Review* 113 (April 1863), 251–67, 253.
11 Jenny Uglow, *Elizabeth Gaskell: A Habit of Stories* (London: Faber and Faber, 1993), 581.
12 *Weekly Dispatch*, November 6, 1864, 6; January 1, 1865, 6.

8

SHIRLEY FOSTER

Elizabeth Gaskell's shorter pieces

Elizabeth Gaskell's fiction is beginning to receive the attention it deserves; her novels are widely available in paperback editions, several have been adapted for radio and television, and recent critical studies have helped to establish her as one of the important novelists of the Victorian period. But, curiously, her shorter pieces have been largely disregarded by publishers and critics alike, perhaps because until now many have been difficult for modern readers to access[1], though both T. A. Ward and Clement Shorter included most of them in their respective Knutsford (1906) and World's Classics (1906–19) editions. Gaskell's shorter works make up a considerable portion of her oeuvre: alongside her seven full-length novels and four novellas, she published more than forty short pieces, including stories, essays, autobiographical reminiscences, and travelogues.[2] Wide-ranging in content and technique, these show Gaskell at her most original and inventive, experimenting with genre and narrative methodology, and dealing with topics which, though also explored in her novels, often have a sharper impact in the more restricted space. One reason for the relative obscurity of these pieces may be their resistance to easy grouping or classification. Their variety makes it difficult to place them in obvious generic categories – usually a publishing desideratum – and their transgressive characteristics represent a kind of literary hybridization which prevents easy definition. Yet it is this variety and originality which makes them so fascinating and so deserving of critical consideration.

"Storytelling" – one of the most popular forms of domestic entertainment in the Victorian period – was one of Gaskell's acknowledged strengths, as noted by Charles Dickens, who published so many of her shorter fictions, when he referred to her as his "dear Scheherezade" who could enthrall an audience for at least a thousand and one nights.[3] Gaskell's delight in and talent for telling stories is attested to by various of her contemporaries. An 1859 letter to her from William Wetmore Story, her friend in Rome, for example, recalls nostalgically how she had entertained them on a visit: "let us see your face and hear your voice again ... Will you not tell us more of your charming stories – and give us some more living sketches of character."[4] Indeed, when in "Company Manners" (1854), her light-hearted comparison of French and English social habits, Gaskell writes, "The art of telling a story is born with some people, and these have it to perfection," she could well have been describing herself (W, III, 508). Ghost stories seem to have been her particular forte. An early biographer reports that she was famed as "an excellent narrator of stories ... A gentleman in Manchester, who was a frequent visitor at the house, told me how Mrs. Gaskell had once kept him up through many a night while she told ghost stories, of which she possessed a goodly store."[5] Gaskell herself recounts how, when Charlotte Brontë was staying with the Gaskells in April 1853, she had to stop telling "some dismal ghost story" because the younger woman was afraid of being kept awake all night by it (LCB, II, 12:406).

Gaskell wrote only one specific ghost story, but the elements intrinsic to the genre – creation of atmosphere, building of suspense, the ability to shock – were put to good use in all her stories. Her love of myth, legends, and folktales also feeds into her shorter pieces. Her school music books contain ballads dealing with the kinds of themes and events that she replicates later in her writing. Visits to relatives in North Wales, both before and after her marriage in 1832, supplied her with tales about a wild and semi-barbaric people and dramatic happenings; when she took her friend Emily Winkworth to stay there in 1848, her Uncle Sam poured a "brimful of Welsh stories ... into [Emily's] not unwilling ears" (L, 61). She was also interested in local traditions, as is indicated by two early letters to the Howitts in which she describes the customs which pertain in rural Cheshire, where she grew up; notably, one of these refers to the "old solitary manor-houses ... with their painted windows, from which one may in fancy catch a glimpse of the inhabitants of former days walking through long dark avenues" (L, 14). Such material was to provide the inspiration for several of her shorter pieces. Her letters are full of recalled stories, anecdotes, and gossip, all grist for her literary mill and showing that she was, in Henry James's phrase, someone "on whom nothing is lost."[6]

As was common in the period, most of Gaskell's shorter pieces first appeared in journals, this to some extent determining their nature and format. Her earliest productions were issued in Howitt's Journal, a short-lived periodical with an earnestly moral and reformist purpose, founded and run by William and Mary Howitt. At this time Gaskell also published (probably at Mary Howitt's instigation) in Sartain's Union Magazine, an American periodical which contained sentimental and moral tales and light sketches, as well as essays on literary subjects. In 1850 she started writing for Dickens's newly established *Household Words*, a publication designed to appeal to a family readership, to be morally beneficial, and "[t]o show to all, that in all familiar things, even in those which are repellent on the surface, there is Romance enough, if we will find it out ... to bring the greater and the lesser in degree, together, and mutually dispose them to a better acquaintance and a kinder understanding."[7] Gaskell continued to write for Dickens through the 1850s and into the early 1860s, after he had launched his *All the Year Round* in 1859, but as her own ideas about what a short story should be became more defined and assured, she increasingly felt the constraints of his editorship. Their literary relationship grew more and more strained, as they argued about matters such as length, narrative divisions, and even plotting, and it was with some relief that Gaskell accepted George Smith's invitation to become a contributor to his *Cornhill Magazine* in 1860. In the last year of her life, too, she wrote a few pieces for his newly founded *Pall Mall Gazette*.

For all their disagreements, however, Gaskell's employment by Dickens gave her the opportunity to develop her skills as an essayist and short story writer. One of the arguments he used to persuade her to become a contributor to *Household Words* was that the shorter form of the story would suit her domestic lifestyle better than longer works, and in some ways he was right – Gaskell always found the demands of a full-length novel somewhat burdensome and worrying. The more frequent financial returns from this mode of writing were also welcome, as family needs increased. But it was undoubtedly a mode that particularly suited her talents, allowing her to exploit her imaginative resources in inventive and innovative ways.

These talents are evident in the range, of both subject matter and technique, of Gaskell's shorter pieces. They implement vivid description of place, autobiographical reminiscence, historical investigation and speculation, and exciting and melodramatic events; they experiment with form, using multilayered and multivocal narration, mingling past and present, and exploiting a central voice which is both observer and participator. Especially notable is their generic indeterminacy. Although, in a letter to a novice writer, Gaskell makes a clear distinction between the essay form, where the narrative must "introduce certain opinions and thoughts" with "neatness pithiness, & conciseness of expression," and the novel, for which a "good plot" is essential, many of her shorter pieces deliberately and effectively blur the boundaries between "fact" and "fiction" (*L*, 541). By suggesting ways in which the imagination can stimulate reflection on a historical moment, using memory to capture the past and then recreating it as a new, quasi-invented, formulation, these pieces foreground the act of creativity itself.

Because of this complexity, grouping Gaskell's short works for discussion is not easy. Merely to treat them chronologically is to obscure the common elements that link them over a period of nearly twenty years. They can most usefully be analyzed under broad, though not exclusive, headings: those that focus on the relationship between character and environment; those that are primarily social satire; Gothic and melodramatic tales; historical tales; and the hybrid pieces which come closest to what Gaskell herself defined as an essay. As a prelude to considering these groups, it is useful to glance briefly at Gaskell's first prose publication, "Clopton Hall," since it encapsulates many of the concerns and narrative techniques of her later work. Gaskell offered this short article, about a visit she made to Clopton Hall in Warwickshire while she was at school near Stratford-upon-Avon, to William Howitt for inclusion in his *Visits to Remarkable Places* (1840). At the heart of the piece is the story of Charlotte Clopton, a former inhabitant of the hall who, assumed dead from the plague, was buried in the vault of Stratford church; a few days later, her self-mutilated body was found outside the tomb, the ghastly evidence of her attempt to survive. The story is cast as personal reminiscence, with Gaskell building up the atmosphere by visually detailing the approach to the hall: "desolate, half-cultivated fields" and pillars "surmounted with two grim monsters" (W, I, 505). An actual portrait of Charlotte herself, found during the narrator's ramblings through empty and reputedly haunted rooms, inspires the recreation of the dreadful encounter with the dead girl: "they saw by the torchlight, Charlotte Clopton in her grave clothes, leaning against the wall; and when they looked nearer, she was indeed dead, but not before, in the agonies of despair and hunger, she had bitten a piece from her white shoulder! Of course, she had *walked* ever since" (W, I, 506). The relish for grisly detail, the fascination with morbid or melodramatic family history, and the way in which avowedly personal recall slips readily into imaginative invention all make this short piece precursive of Gaskell's later writings.

Character and environment

Gaskell's real entrée into the literary world came with her three stories for *Howitt's Journal*: "Libbie Marsh's Three Eras" (June 1847), "The Sexton's Hero" (September 1847), and "Christmas Storms and Sunshine" (January 1848). In the first two she established a characteristic mode – the exploration of the relationship between character and environment, usually drawing a moral message from it. The third, a slightly unconvincing tale dealing with the reconciliation between two antagonistic married couples, precipitated by the sickness of a child, contains some humorous social observations but otherwise warrants little attention. "The Sexton's Hero" is a story that draws on Gaskell's own regional experience. Set in the area of Morecambe Bay, near Silverdale, a favorite holiday resort of the Gaskells, it opens with a lovingly remembered description of the view across the bay; then, in what was to become a common pattern in the stories, it takes the reader into the narrative via a second narrator, here the Sexton, who tells the tale of Gilbert Dawson, the eponymous hero, "dead and gone this many a year ago" (W, I, 491). It transpires that the Sexton is partly telling his own story – he is the man who married the girl loved by the quiet and reserved Dawson, and who, together with his young wife, was rescued from drowning in the bay sands by the rejected suitor. The ending is sombre, not triumphant: Dawson sacrifices himself and is lost in the swirling tide, while the Sexton himself has "never done mourning to this day" (W, I, 500). Simple in outline and message (it redefines "heroism"), the story exemplifies Gaskell's interest in the lives of apparently unremarkable people, refracted through the medium of imagined recall.

"Libbie Marsh's Three Eras" introduces Manchester into Gaskell's work, as well as themes and settings developed in her longer fiction. In three parts, it tells how the plain, shy seamstress, Libbie Marsh, befriends Franky Hall, the little crippled son of a neighbor, buying him a canary, helping to look after him, and finally, after his death, going to live with his mother. At one level it is a straightforward tale of self-sacrifice (Libbie purchases the canary with her hard-earned savings) and moral transformation (the crotchety Mrs. Hall becomes "a different woman to the scold of the neighbourhood she once was; touched and softened by the two purifying angels, Sorrow and Love" [W, I, 3:488]). More significantly, it skillfully shows how the environmental conditions of a large industrial city impinge upon the lives of the inhabitants. As in her two "Manchester novels," *Mary Barton* (1848) and *North and South* (1855), the topographical specificity (streets are named), local dialect, and careful social observation (the story is set in the relatively prosperous 1830s and the financial extravagance of the mill-workers is noted) not only give authenticity but are also linked to the psychological implications of the story. Thus Libbie's feeling of "otherness" among the well-meaning but insensitive people around her compounds her sense of loneliness and uselessness; conversely, it is the cramped habitations of the "courts" which makes her aware of Franky's plight, as she see him at the window in a neighboring dwelling. The second part of the story, which describes the Whitsun outing to Dunham Park (interestingly, an early outline of *Mary Barton* includes this as an element in its plot), is notable for its portrayal of the rural surroundings in contrast to distant Manchester with its "motionless cloud of smoke" hanging over it (W, I, 2:477). The Wordsworthian resonances of this section, with its insistence on the power of natural beauty to heal discord and promote love, not only articulate Gaskell's own deep affiliations with the countryside, but also – like the opening scene in *Mary Barton* – vividly image the joy of such rare snatched pleasures in the harshness of working-class life.

Gaskell returns, more centrally and urgently, to the rural/urban contrast in her more extended study of the effects of city living, "Lizzie Leigh," a tale which deals with the "fall" of a young woman who leaves her farm home in Rochdale to find work in Manchester. Although it was the first of Gaskell's pieces which Dickens published in *Household Words*, in March–April 1850, it was probably written earlier. As well as looking back to "Libbie Marsh" and *Mary Barton*, it also prefigures themes of later works – the fallen woman, child/parent relationships, and the redemptive power of female love. Again, its use of dialect and its topographical detail give regional authenticity. It opens with the death of James Leigh, and hints at "the family's disgrace" (W, II, 1:208), but it is several pages before the facts are revealed about his daughter, Lizzie. Mrs. Leigh resolves to leave the farm and take her two sons to live in Manchester, a place "where there was no garden or outbuilding, no fresh breezy outlet, no far-stretching view, over moor and hollow," in order to find the lost Lizzie (W, II, 1:213). The subject of prostitution and how to remedy its evils was close to Gaskell's heart; her acquaintance with Dickens was initiated when she wrote to him about a young dressmaker's apprentice turned prostitute, then in prison in Manchester, and Esther in *Mary Barton* and the eponymous heroine of *Ruth* (1853), as well as Lizzie, are examples of her literary treatment of the topic. The literary prototype of the Prodigal's return is also embedded in the story, as, by a series of slightly unlikely coincidences, Lizzie is eventually found, is restored to her mother, and, her child having died, returns with her to Rochdale.[8] Here she leads a life of isolation and self-abnegation with her mother, devoting herself to others: "every call of suffering or of sickness for help is listened to by a sad, gentle-looking woman, who rarely smiles ... but who comes out of her seclusion whenever there is a shadow in any household" (W, II, 4:241). The emphasis on moral redemption through suffering and self-sacrifice is of course a familiar trope in the period, but the story moves beyond the conventional in its reformulation of gender types and roles. At the beginning we are told that for the past three years Mrs. Leigh has "rebelled against her husband as against a tyrant, with a hidden, sullen rebellion, which tore up the old landmarks of wifely duty and affection," because he will not forgive his daughter nor allow his wife to go to look for her (W, II, 1:207). Throughout, harshness and lack of compassion are associated with the male characters: Lizzie's older brother, Will, only slowly relents toward her, and the father of the woman who looks after Lizzie's child remains unsympathetic to her. As in so many of Gaskell's works, female love and forgiveness here challenge a male-centered view of sin and retribution.

Gaskell's concern for both the moral and physical plight of the urban poor does not feature in her stories after this point (though of course she takes it up again in *North and South*), but themes of hardship, personal sacrifice, and individual isolation feature constantly in her shorter pieces. Many of these center on women and their difficult negotiations with the outside world. Two other stories of 1850, "Martha Preston" (*Sartain's Union Magazine*, February 1850) and "The Well of Pen-Morfa" (*Household Words*, November 1850), deal with this topic. The latter frames its narrative with personally authenticated reminiscence. Set in North Wales, it opens with a first-person narrator who gives an account of the region and inserts herself into the story: "I have received great, true, beautiful kindness from one of the members of the family of whom I just now spoke as living at Pen-Morfa" (W, II, 1:243). Having established this tone of familiarity, the narrative moves to the main tale of Nest Gwyn, but prefaces it with a brief reference to a "stern and severe-looking" woman, a local beekeeper who lives in gloomy isolation (W, II, 1:243). Her history – like Lizzie Leigh she is a "fallen woman" – is a fitting prologue to a story which foregrounds female endurance in adversity. Nest's story, orally transmitted to the narrator, tells of the pretty and vain village girl who is seriously injured when she slips on ice at the well, having put on fine but impractical clothes to impress her lover. Rejected by this lover after he learns that she will be crippled for life, Nest is finally turned from her bitterness by the teachings of an old Methodist minister; as a kind of perpetual penance (though her "sin" is far less morally reprehensible than that of Lizzie), she takes a half-witted woman to live with her until her own death some years later. Although in some ways this story may be seen as reinforcing Victorian orthodoxies of female self-abnegation, it also valorizes a woman's self-construction: Nest's burden is harsh but it is a role which she, and not an external authority, has chosen for herself.

"Martha Preston" similarly explores female independence operating beyond the hegemony of patriarchal structures. Originally published in *Sartain's*, it was rewritten for *Household Words*, where it was published in October 1855 as "Half a Lifetime Ago"; it was slightly revised again to form one of the linked stories in *Round the Sofa* (1859). The progressive versions illustrate Gaskell's tendency to reuse material, and also her fascination with certain themes. In the course of the revisions, characters' names were changed, the setting was moved from the original Loughrigg Fell to a few miles further south, near Coniston, and alterations were made to the plot. Taken together, the differing versions also show one of Gaskell's most interesting narrative innovations – the constant slippage between real and invented, present and past, effected by the juxtaposition of historically authenticated detail and imaginative reconstruction, with the narrator as both observer and creator. "Martha Preston" is cast as an extended reminiscence in which the teller, recalling nostalgically the area in which Martha lives, recounts "what I heard of the inhabitants of that cottage during the last thirty years."[9] The chronological specificity (the date of Martha's engagement is given as 1818) encourages readers to accept the story as historically and socially "true," while the telling itself exploits fictional modes.

Martha Preston is a young farm woman, who, engaged to be married, gives up her fiancé when he tries to insist that her idiot brother, to whom she has devoted herself, should be placed in an asylum. Years later, she rescues this fiancé's son from a snowdrift and the boy becomes her adopted "nephew," later coming to live with her on the farm when he is grown and married. The conclusion envisions a present in which Martha herself still lives, happily surrounded by her surrogate grandchildren: "There will not be a grave in Grasmere churchyard, more decked with flowers ... than that of Martha Preston when she dies."[10] When Gaskell rewrote the tale, she made it much grimmer. "Half a Lifetime Ago" explores more deeply the psychological effects of betrayal: the lover's heartlessness and cruelty are foregrounded, as are the agonies of conscience and misery suffered by the heroine, Susan Dixon, faced with the choice between romantic love and familial duty. The ending also lacks the optimism of "Martha Preston." Susan becomes increasingly hardened and embittered, especially after her brother's death; years later, she finds her lover (not his son, as in the earlier version) dead in the snow, and eventually takes his widow and children to live with her, as a penance rather than a blessing. The image of the fulfilled maternal figure is replaced here by a bleaker vision of womanhood. Yet in portraying Susan as a successful farmer and respected local businesswoman, Gaskell suggests that successful and independent female activity should not be viewed only in terms of compensation for emotional impoverishment. Her portrayal also looks forward to later stories that depict women's insertion into the male realms of work and decision-making.

The last two stories which can be considered in this group both offer more traditional views of gender roles and relationships, though still dealing with themes of loss and extreme emotion in specific geographical locations. In "The Heart of John Middleton" (*Household Words*, December 1850), Nelly Hadfield is injured and subsequently invalided when she tries to protect her lover, John Middleton (the teller of the tale) by intercepting a stone aimed at him by his rival, Dick Jackson (foreshadowing a similar incident in *North and South*). She becomes the angelic influence who softens the morose and violent Middleton after their marriage, and dissuades him from his vengeful desire to turn Jackson over to the law when, many years later, the latter returns to the area as an escaped convict. Here female self-sacrifice leads to death: the saintly Nelly dies soon after. Despite its somewhat formulaic pattern, however, the story is remarkable for its portrayal of fierce and violent feeling, and, as Jenny Uglow points out, the language reaches an apocalyptic Old Testament intensity in its paralleling of the wild Lancashire environment and the raging emotions of the protagonist, with his "hating heart" (W, II, 385).[11] The story also anticipates other short pieces in which Gaskell works out themes of vengeance and fate. The narrator feels he is of a "doomed race," branded by the sins of his criminal father, and although he eventually comes to accept the New Testament creed of forgiveness, his dark passions take a terrible toll on all around him (W, II, 385).

"The Half Brothers," written in 1859 specifically for *Round the Sofa*, is another Lake District tale of contempt and dislike turning to remorse and love. A privileged younger son (the narrator) is allowed to lord it over his morose and apparently stupid half-brother, but the latter's worth is revealed when he rescues his sibling from a fierce snowstorm on the Fells. Reconciliation between them follows, but also death, as the rescuer finally succumbs to cold and exhaustion. The story has no particularly striking features, but it does once more highlight Gaskell's fascination with wild and remote landscapes in which the more savage side of human nature, fostered by such an environment, struggles with a better spirit of Christian benevolence.

Social satire

Many of the stories in the previous group could be said to exhibit a Romantic sensibility, a Wordsworthian emphasis on the close relationship between character and environment, albeit with both a darker coloring and more muted optimism. This next group, all in some ways generically linked to Gaskell's best-known work, *Cranford* (1853), and related to an earlier generation of writers, including Robert Southey, Mary Russell Mitford, Maria Edgeworth, and Jane Austen, employs a more satirical tone and tempers its observations of human psychology with humor, a trait largely absent from the previously discussed pieces. The episodic nature of *Cranford* itself – it began with a single contribution to *Household Words* in December 1851, "Our Society at Cranford," and continued as a serial until May 1853 – suggests the extent to which Gaskell was attracted to this form of social vignette. These shorter works also show the continuing hold which Knutsford material had over her imagination.

"The Last Generation in England" (July 1849) was the first of the two works which Gaskell published in *Sartain's Union Magazine*, and like its fellow, "Martha Preston," presented its material as more fact than fiction. In the opening section the unnamed narrator explains that a chance reading of Southey's *The Doctor* (1834–47) has inspired her to record some details of country town life, "either observed by myself, or handed down to me by older relations." She also makes it clear that her purpose is essentially that of a social historian: "even in small towns scarcely removed from villages, the phases of society are rapidly changing, and much will appear strange, which yet occurred only in the generation immediately preceding ours" (*C*, 161). This statement of course has special resonance for an American audience, unfamiliar with English social peculiarities, but it also articulates Gaskell's preoccupation with change and development. Dealing with the hierarchical layers of provincial society, from the landed gentry to the riffraff at its fringes, the piece is obviously based on her Knutsford experiences, including anecdotes told to her by her Holland cousins; some of its most amusing material is later incorporated into *Cranford* – the cow who wore a flannel waistcoat and drawers, the cat who swallowed the lace, and the teatray hidden under the sofa, for example. Curiously, however, in contrast to the note of nostalgic reminiscence which characterizes both *Cranford* and some of the pieces about rural life, the tone here is socio-scientific: the narrator separates herself from those she is describing – the local elderly ladies, for instance, are merely "living hoards of family tradition and old custom" – and only rarely links herself with a communal "we" (*C*, 166).

Mr Harrison's Confessions, generally categorized as one of Gaskell's novellas, is more obviously a work of fiction. It was published between February and April 1851 in *The Ladies' Companion*, a journal to which Gaskell contributed only once, and for which she seems to have had little regard.[12] The eponymous narrator tells his brother, Charles, the story of his early experiences as a doctor in Duncombe (Knutsford), focusing particularly on the absurd situation in which he apparently romantically engaged himself to three ladies at once. The approach is humorous, and, even more than in "The Last Generation," the narrator's ironic, dispassionate tone sets up a distance between him and his material, encouraging readerly amusement but not empathy. His mockery of the foibles of Duncombe society extends even to small details: on receiving inquiries about his health from a Mr. and Mrs. Bullock, he comments, "Who would have expected such kindness from such an unpromising name?" (*W*, V, 1:409). The narrative stimulates a subtextual reading, however: we are reminded throughout that these are the observations of a somewhat callow, self-confident young man who has, moreover, fairly conventional ideas about women (like Lydgate in George Eliot's *Middlemarch* [1872], he is also ready to patronize provincial society). The series of misapprehensions by which Harrison gets himself entangled in matrimonial futures, none of which he desires, creates comedy, but the text does establish an understanding of, if not deep sympathy for, the plight of single women, often impoverished, in a small-town community. Importantly, too, Harrison himself has to learn to appreciate people and customs toward which earlier he was condescending. The novella concludes happily with his marriage to Sophy, the vicar's daughter (the only tragic event in the tale is the death of Sophy's little brother, Walter), but its increasingly short and fragmented sections suggest Gaskell's inability to maintain interest in the work.

"The Cage at Cranford" (*All the Year Round*, November 1863) functions, as its title suggests, as a kind of addendum to the novel, returning to the familiar world of ten years earlier, with the same characters and the same social eccentricities. Comedy here, too, derives from elements such as verbal misunderstandings and absurd behavior. But overall it lacks the finesse of its predecessor, relying for its plot on a rather labored joke about a "cage" that Jessie Gordon sends from France to Miss Pole, "as cages were so much better made in Paris than anywhere else" (*C*, 170). Puzzlement and apprehension about the usefulness of such an item are finally dispelled when the present arrives – not a home for Miss Pole's parrot, but a "new and fashionable" structure made up of calico and hoops (*C*, 169). Mildly amusing, but generally inconsequential, the story suggests that Gaskell is no longer really engaged with this mode of social satire.

Gothic tales

In many ways the tales in this group represent the most striking of Gaskell's shorter pieces; exploiting narrative techniques of mystery, melodrama, and suspense, and treating subjects such as murder, revenge, sexual jealousy, and hatred, they are in marked contrast to both the satirical observation of the *Cranford* mode and the nostalgic reminiscence of some of her other pieces. Various critics have linked them to the Gothic genre: a recent collection, entitled *Gothic Tales*, classifies its contents as "pleasurably eerie short stories and novellas"; several of such stories are discussed in a chapter on the supernatural in a book dedicated to the "Gothic Tradition"; another modern collection classifies them as "Strange Tales."[13] While the Gothic nomenclature is not wholly apt, since the tales contain more psychological intensity and interest in abnormal states of mind than startling effects for their own sake, their fascination with the violent, shocking, and discordant, and their exploration of the paranormal invites classification of this kind. In these stories, as Laura Kranzler observes, the boundaries of history, gender, and textuality are crossed, as they juxtapose a known present with a disturbingly unfamiliar past.[14] They also problematize the distinction between fact and fiction, not, as in some other Gaskell stories, in order to reflect on the functions of memory, activated through telling, but in order to destabilize and disorient.

As in most of her shorter pieces, environmental influence and oral tradition are important sources of inspiration; here, however, Gaskell draws on tales of strange and wild behavior associated with often remote and mysterious places and legends about fate and doomed inheritance. The stories reflect Victorian preoccupations with mental states, especially those perceived as diseased or "unnatural," and with "development," both degenerative or regressive as well as progressive. Contemporary novelists such as Dickens and Wilkie Collins played on their readers' appetites for the grim and ghastly in their treatment of the underside of so-called civilized life. Gaskell herself enjoyed some of the sensation fiction of the 1860s, such as Caroline Clive's *Why Paul Ferroll Killed his Wife* (1860), Mary Elizabeth Braddon's *Aurora Floyd* (1863), and novels by Mrs. Henry Wood.[15] Significantly, however, she realized the potential of the short story form for the treatment of such material: while there are sudden deaths and highly dramatic moments in her novels, they are integrated into the wider whole, whereas the sparser structure of the shorter pieces allows for a starker and more shocking foregrounding of sensational material.

Gothic elements are not exclusive to this particular group of stories, of course. The live burial in "Clopton Hall" and the storm-like passions in "The Heart of John Middleton," as well as melodramatic sections in other pieces to be discussed below, indicate Gaskell's predilection for the extremes of human behavior. Her delight in the mysterious and uncanny is also revealed in an article she wrote for *Household Words* in 1851 entitled "Disappearances." This ostensibly nonfiction piece, a series of anecdotes about people who have disappeared under strange circumstances, is typical of the liberties Gaskell takes with the (his)stories she claims to have heard. This is especially so in her account of a young doctor's apprentice in North Shields who suddenly vanishes, and who, she suggests, was murdered. The theme of disappearance is taken up again in the short story "The Man-chester Marriage" (*Household Words*, December 1858), about a presumed-dead husband who returns after his wife has remarried. And of course it provides the key episode in Gaskell's later novel, *Sylvia's Lovers* (1863).

The range and variety of the short pieces which could be considered all or partly "Gothic" is noteworthy, especially from the 1850s onward. One of the earliest, written for the 1853 Christmas number of *Household Words*, is "The Squire's Story," a work typical in its exploitation of the borders between fact and fiction. It tells the story of Edward Higgins, a notorious eighteenth-century highwayman living in Knutsford (Barford in the tale) in the house next to the one in which Gaskell herself would grow up. The key event is approached obliquely as the main narrator hints at certain oddities about the apparently respectable gentleman who has taken the White House: "there was a sinister cold look in his quick-glancing, light blue eye, which a keen observer might not have liked" (W, II, 533). The story reaches its climax when, after news of the brutal murder of an old woman in Bath, Higgins, in a paranoid act of confession, made in the third person to avoid suspicion, unfolds to a naive and uncomprehending listener the gruesome details of the deed which he has himself committed. The compulsive act of storytelling itself is emphasized, as Higgins, horrifically trapped in his own guilty recollections, recreates the terrible sequence of events: "he cut her throat; and there she lies yet, in her quiet little parlour, with her face upturned and all ghastly white, in the middle of a pool of blood" (W, II, 546). The graphic detail here is echoed in a letter of 1855, in which Gaskell reports the self-abuse of a deranged Dissenting minister known to her: "He [said] 'Don't look at me. My nose was growing so large, I have pared it all round with my razor,' – and his face really was all blood!" (FL, 122).

Several other stories in this category foreground brutality and violent death, as well as physical and psychological aberration. "The Doom of the Griffiths" (*Harper's New Monthly Magazine*, January 1858) is a modern version of the Oedipus myth, recreating a (purportedly) old Welsh legend which states that because, centuries ago, one of the Griffiths collaborated in a plot to murder Owen Glendower, they were cursed by him: "when nine generations have passed from the face of the earth, thy blood shall no longer flow in the veins of any human being. In those days the last male of thy race shall avenge me. The son shall slay the father" (W, V, 1:238). The story skillfully portrays the working out of the curse, but not merely through the operation of fate. The characters are driven as much by their personal traits – uncontrollable emotions of hatred, jealousy, and despair – as by an external doom, and the narrative explores the force of such emotions in the context of dysfunctional family relationships. When the close bond between Owen Griffiths (the ninth-generation son) and his widowed father is disrupted by the latter's remarriage to an unsympathetic woman with a spoilt son of her own, the young man secretly marries a Welsh farmer's daughter, but dares not tell his father. The old squire's discovery of the situation not only initiates the chain of events which will culminate in the "doom," but also precipitates one of the most shocking acts of violence in all of Gaskell's fiction. In his "ungovernable rage," and "inarticulate with fury," the squire snatches Owen's child from its father's arms and hurls it toward its mother; failing to reach her, "the infant fell against the sharp edge of the dresser down on to the stone floor" (W, V, 2:261). After a series of subsequent events, Owen finally "murders" his father, when, during a furious tussle between them, the older man loses his balance and falls to his death. The violence and melodrama link to Gaskell's recognition of the terrible consequences of obsession – the idea of his fate has corrupted Owen's mind – and the conclusion, depicting Owen, his wife, and her father sailing away, presumably to their death, holds no hope of a redemptive future.

Two other stories of this period, "The Sin of a Father" (*Household Words*, November 1858) and "The Ghost in the Garden Room" (*All the Year Round*, Extra Christmas Number, 1859) – renamed, respectively, "Right at Last" and "The Crooked Branch" when they were reprinted in 1860 in *Right at Last, and Other Tales* – further explore the violent and irrational elements in human psychology. The former is a slight story that hinges on a secret which a young husband keeps from his wife – namely, that his father was a transported convict. The second story is altogether more disturbing (though it contains no ghost), portraying another grotesque subversion of familial relationships in which the son enacts murderous urges toward his parents. Dramatic excitement is provided by the scenes in which the lonely farm is attacked by robbers. The real horror, however, lies in the final scene, at the court trial, when the corrupted beloved son of the old couple is revealed as the leader of the robber gang, and, on his father's testimony, the one "who shouted out for to hold th'oud woman's throat if she did na stop her noise" (W, VII, 258).

This strain of physical and psychological melodrama is particularly noticeable in the productions of the last few years of Gaskell's life. Not all, however, are artistically successful. "Crowley Castle" (which first appeared in the 1863 Christmas number of *All the Year Round*, entitled "How the First Floor Went to Crowley Castle") is an example of a "Gothic" story which does not quite work. In a narrative formula which harks back to "Clopton Hall," a group of boarding-house lodgers visit the ruins of Crowley Castle, where the building's historical associations precipitate an account of the family and its tragic history of jealousy and hatred. In particular, Victorine, the passionate Frenchwoman with "deadly smile" and "furtive eyes" who poisons the rival of her adored childhood charge, Theresa, seems more caricature than villain (W, VII, 702, 708). "A Dark Night's Work," also in *All the Year Round* (January–March 1863) – Dickens added "Dark" to the title, probably to increase the melodramatic suggestiveness, though to Gaskell's displeasure –, more successfully blends psychological realism and heightened action. Themes of conscience and guilt, conflicting loyalties, and the struggle between love and duty echo those in Gaskell's longer fiction as well as some earlier stories; the link between the central dramatic event (Mr. Wilkins's unpremeditated murder of his business partner) and the subsequent effect on those involved is convincingly managed. Wilkins slips into alcoholism and loses control over his business, while his daughter, Ellinor, to whom he has revealed his guilty secret, is faced with the choice between telling the truth to her fiancé and protecting her father. Like Susan Dixon in "Half a Lifetime Ago," she chooses family loyalty over love, but the crushing result of her sacrifice is shown in her permanent loss of spirit and health. Although she finally marries the clergyman who has long loved her, this is a subdued and essentially passionless closure. The tale also exemplifies the problems over methods of publication which Gaskell often faced with her shorter pieces. Originally intended as a single unit, it did not easily fit into the number of installments that Dickens required for his periodical; yet when the publisher Verlag Tauchnitz was proposing to issue it in one volume, it seemed to Gaskell somewhat slight and she hastily concluded, "I am afraid that it is rather short for one volume. I am very sorry, but alas! I had no more to say about them" (*FL*, 254).[16]

"The Grey Woman" (*All the Year Round*, January 1861), another story notable for its effective dramatic writing, also suffers from a degree of flatness in the ending, but it is generally far more exciting and suspenseful than "A Dark Night's Work." It is also well suited to the serial form in which it was issued. Purportedly the Grey Woman's own autobiographical history, read in manuscript by an external narrator, it is in three parts, the first two ending at important moments in the narrative: Anna Scherer's first misgivings about her marriage, and her and her maid Amante's desperate attempts to escape capture by her pursuing husband, Monsieur de la Tourelle, after they have fled from him. Elements of terror, disguise, and perilous adventures – all the stuff of sensation fiction – are ably manipulated. Reminiscent of earlier Gothic fiction, too, especially the novels of Ann Radcliffe, it also focuses on buildings as sites of danger and mystery. Anna is a virtual prisoner in Tourelle's chateau, whose two parts "were joined into a whole by means of intricate passages and unexpected doors, the exact positions of which I never fully understood," but which she and Amante have to negotiate in order to make their escape when they discover that Tourelle is a member of a ruthless gang of outlaws (the analogy with Bluebeard's castle is also obvious here) (W, VII, 1:315). The narrative of part two is particularly dramatic, including Anna's discovery, while she is trapped in darkness in her husband's study, of "the clenched and chilly hand of a corpse"; the escape from the chateau in disguise; and the strategies they employ to avoid being caught by Tourelle (W, VII, 2:327). This story is not just a spine-chiller, however, and the psychological horrors of Anna's experiences are well documented. Its treatment of gender is also particularly interesting. Tourelle, a cruel and ruthless man, is described as having features "as delicate as a girl's" and his bedroom is filled with the perfume from "the scent-bottles of silver that decked his toilet-table" (W, VII, 1:309, 2:325). In a parallel gender subversion, Amante cuts her hair, puts on men's clothes, and acts out the role of male protector to Anna, disguised as a peasant woman. The cross-dressing foregrounds false assumptions about gendered roles and behavior, as well as stressing women's vulnerability in a world of male violence and treachery. The ending of the story, however, is both bleak and anticlimactic: the last view of Anna from the pages of the faded manuscript is of a ghost-like figure, grey-haired and ashen-complexioned, married to the doctor who has treated her in her breakdown, but permanently broken-spirited.

The most powerful story in the Gothic mode, which Gaskell wrote for *All the Year Round*, is *Lois the Witch* (October 1859), a recreation of the Salem witch trials in seventeenth-century New England, dramatized through the fortunes of Lois Barclay, a young English girl who goes to live with her Massachusetts relatives and is caught up in the terrible happenings. Gaskell's interest in America was longstanding – the pseudonym "Cotton Mather Mills," under which her first three stories were issued, suggests knowledge of the Puritan writer Cotton Mather, and she had certainly read Nathaniel Hawthorne's *The Scarlet Letter* (1850). Always interested in tales of mystery and magic, she consulted various accounts of the early American hysteria in order to authenticate her story. Lois's experiences in her Uncle Hickson's strictly Puritan household – with its cold and severe mother, its religious fanatic son, and its psychologically disturbed daughters – inexorably merge into the communal happenings, themselves instigated by obsession and frenzy. As Louise Henson points out, in the 1850s "superstition was regarded as both a factor contributing to, and a product of, the kind of mental derangement with which it was identified," and Gaskell's sophisticated narrative illustrates this view.[17]

Thus while the horrors of witch mania are skillfully depicted – the accusation by her young cousin Prudence Hickson that Lois has bewitched her, the latter's trial and imprisonment with the persecuted old Indian woman, Nattee, and their final executions – the moral and intellectual disorders of Salem society as a whole are microcosmically reflected in the dysfunctional Hickson family. The corrosive resentments and tensions here, exacerbated by the repressive nature of Puritan society, are, Gaskell makes clear, indicators of a fatal breakdown in the relationships between desire and love, spirituality and humanity. Her story brilliantly reconfigures the events of seventeenth-century America in the context of nineteenth-century scientific rationalism, showing not just that the personal is political but that monomania can fatally destroy natural human impulses (as indeed is shown in other Gaskell stories). Even Lois's final gesture of selfless sympathy, as she comforts the terrified Nattee, cannot protect her from a psychologically warped society.

Somewhat surprisingly, given her interest in ghost stories, Gaskell made little use of the supernatural in her work, even in those pieces which have been defined here as "Gothic." Her only specific venture into this genre is "The Old Nurse's Story," given to Dickens for the 1852 Christmas number of *Household Words*. There are reminders of *Wuthering Heights* (1847) here, both in its narrative strategy – the story is told by the old nurse, Hester, who, like Nelly Dean, relates the strange happenings years after they have occurred – and in its central event, the vision of the Phantom Child, excluded from the household, who taps at the window and tries to lure the young Rosamund out into the snow. The mysterious atmosphere is built up by further details: the setting of the isolated Northumberland manor house with its many wings and locked rooms; the portrait of Maude Furnivall turned to the wall; the organ music which emanates from an old, broken instrument. The final climactic scene, with the spectre-child, the apparition of the younger Furnivall sister, and the ghostly figure of the old lord "with grey hair and gleaming eyes," striking at the young mother and her child with his crutch, is a masterly piece of dramatic writing (W, II, 444). As with the other Gothic stories, too, the drama is heightened by being linked to extreme and obsessive human emotions – here female pride and jealousy, paternal tyranny, and male cruelty.

"The Poor Clare," written for *Household Words* four years later, is an equally powerful story, set in the eighteenth century, which deals with the paranormal and the uncanny, though it contains no actual ghosts. Again, the melodrama is enacted in the context of violent and destructive passions. When her daughter's dog is shot by the hot-tempered local squire, the old Irishwoman Bridget Fitzgerald curses him, predicting that the creature he loves best will come to be "a terror and a loathing to all" (*W*, V, 1:341). Her revenge rebounds on herself: the squire's greatest love is his daughter Lucy, the child of the woman he lured away many years ago who was, unknown to him, Bridget's daughter; the curse is the terrible double self which torments Lucy and isolates her from all around her. Lucy's destiny, presented through the eyes of the narrator, a young lawyer sent to investigate the Fitzgerald family business, becomes the signifier of a corrupt, deviant female sexuality, coexisting with her outward angelic femininity: "a ghastly resemblance ... with a loathsome demon soul looking out of the grey eyes, that were in turns mocking and voluptuous" (*W*, V, 2:362). The story includes the familiar tropes of penitence and redemption – the curse is lifted only after Bridget, a Roman Catholic, has sacrificed herself as a Poor Clare in revolution-torn Antwerp – but its most compelling feature is the way in which it implements its dramatic effects to explore divergent images of womanhood and the fatal split between inner and outer consciousness.

As a coda to this discussion of the Gothic tales, it is worth mentioning "Curious If True" (*Cornhill*, February 1860), which serves as a kind of parody of the genre. This time the mysterious castle in which the narrator is forced to seek shelter turns out to be peopled with bizarre rather than threatening figures: a man in boots who reminds him of a cat, a fat old lady who has ruined her feet by forcing them into little slippers, and a beautiful princess who sleeps all the time. These are of course all characters from Perrault's fairytales, reincarnated in a half-magical, half-realistic setting.[18] While the tale seems to be making a satirical point about the failure to distinguish between fact and fiction, it may also be a wry self-referential commentary on the absurdities of Gothic melodrama.

History and hybridity

Some of the most artistically interesting of Gaskell's shorter works are those which cross genres, often calling attention to storytelling itself as a medium of historical enlightenment and development. Combining elements of story, essay, and sketch (Charles Lamb's *Essays of Elia* [1820–3] and Mary Russell Mitford's *Our Village* [1819] may be prototypes here), such pieces explore the progression from past to present within a context of meditative and discursive analysis. "Cumberland Sheep-Shearers" (*Household Words*, January 1853), for example, a delightfully evocative vignette describing a hot July day in the Lakeland hills, is also a nostalgic reminder of a fast-disappearing way of life. Some of these hybrid pieces, like several of the short stories, are inspired by Gaskell's experiences of travel in Europe. "Six Weeks in Heppenheim" (*Cornhill Magazine*, May 1862), the fictional tale of a young German girl's dilemma about whom to marry, also voices Gaskell's memories of her holidays in Heidelberg and the Rhine region. More extensively, her deep interest in France and French culture also inspires a variety of linked literary modes. Thus the observations on French life and history in the primarily fictional "My French Master" (*Household Words*, December 1853), a gentle tale of a French émigré who settles in England and marries a local farmer's daughter, take a more obviously documentary form in "Traits and Stories of the Huguenots" (*Household Words*, December 1853), "Company Manners" (*Household Words*, May 1854), and "An Accursed Race" (*Household Words*, August 1855). The first of these details the background and traditions relating to the Huguenots in Europe and the New World in a series of vignettes, but complicates its factual narrative with metafictional elements. Implementing the kind of multiple narration characteristic of Gaskell's stories, it plays with the reader by not revealing until the end that the friend of the woman who relates the story – a descendant of the Huguenots who has provided her with some of her information – is actually related to the Norman farmer mentioned earlier in the piece. "Company Manners" begins as a discussion of a series of articles on the well-known seventeenth-century *salonnière* Madame de Sablé, and moves on to compare French and English social customs. "An Accursed Race," like the Gothic tales, is concerned with the darker side of history. Here Gaskell explores the more lurid aspects of French history, detailing (and deploring) the outrages suffered by the despised Cagots because of their supposed physical deformities – their grisly ears without lobes, their infectious odor, and their diseased skin.

"French Life" (*Fraser's Magazine*, April–June, 1864) is a much more substantial piece whose generic complexity well demonstrates Gaskell's skill in bringing together a variety of modes and material. Formulated as a series of purported journal entries, loosely based on a trip to Brittany in May 1862 and including other French experiences, it incorporates historical anecdote, French and English social history, travel writing, Gothic melo-drama, and personal reminiscence. The narrative weaves the past and present together by shifts in tense which establish the narrator as both commentator/observer and participant. Thus it opens with the recreative immediacy of travel discourse – "We went today along the Boulevard Sévastapol, Rive Gauche, to pay a call" (*W*, VII, 1:604) – then slips into the present tense as Madame A's house is described – "In the far corner [of the bedroom] is the bed: a grand four-post, with looped-up draperies of some warmer colour ... which look like a pictorial background to the rest of the room" (*W*, VII, 1:605–6). Details of French middle-class domestic life, and its differences from English life, move the piece into essay mode, the observations sharpened by the indication that these have been personally experienced and by the inclusion of direct conversation.

The two most interesting sections of "French Life" are the account of the narrator's researches in Brittany for her projected biography of Madame de Sévigné (Gaskell never actually wrote this biography), and the story of the Marquise de Gange. The first continues the informal, intimate discourse of travel writing: "I sank back in my [train] seat in a lazy, unobservant frame of mind, when Irene called out, 'Oh, look! there is a peasant in the goat-skin dress one read about; we must be in Brittany now'" (W, VII, 2:634–5). The description of the visit to Les Roches, Madame de Sévigné's farm, with its almost photographic topographical detail and acute sense of atmosphere, seamlessly merges visual recall with historical meditation. The second piece, a grim tale of the period of Louis XIV, tells the story of a beautiful and wealthy young woman married to the cruel Marquis de Gange, who tries to poison her and from whom she tries to escape. The narrative structure – a historical anecdote, deriving from a literary source discovered by the narrator, retold in quasi-fictional mode and inserted into the main narrative – replicates many of Gaskell's pieces, while the melodramatic details and shocking emphasis on bodily disintegration (the effects of the poison) also look back to earlier tales.

Two other substantial shorter pieces demonstrate the generic transgressiveness of much of Gaskell's work, too, this time with specific emphasis on historical change. "Morton Hall" (*Household Words*, November 1853), combining story and social commentary, interweaves history and legend, past and present. Set mainly in Lancashire, it also further illustrates the pervasive hold of Knutsford memories on Gaskell's imagination, especially in its concern with social and environmental development in a small provincial town. The story, in three parts, moves chronologically from the seventeenth century to the present. The sections are held together by the familiar technique of multiple narration: old Bridget Sidebotham both acts as the channel through which events are told and herself reports directly in the later period. Its main concern – history as progression and process – is presented through the key themes of marriage and the changing roles of women, and it describes the gradual shift from a hierarchical, restrictive society to one in which women are no longer constrained by subservience to male tyranny. So the first section, which portrays the violent and destructive marriage of the Cavalier Sir John Morton to the Puritan Alice Carr, with its Gothic elements of madness and imprisonment, gives way to the more subdued second section which describes the gradual demise of the Morton family over twenty years and shows the futility of prioritizing female self-sacrifice and social pride over genuine affection. Only in the last section, with its satirical portrayal of the absurdly conflicting theories of education enforced upon their niece, Cordelia, by the elderly Morton spinster sisters, is there resolution and accommodation. Cordelia's marriage to a local mill owner reenacts in class terms the religious disparity of the seventeenth-century marriage, but this time in a new spirit of harmony which, it is suggested, points toward a better future.

My Lady Ludlow (*Household Words*, June–September 1858), usually categorized as a novella, is one of a series of tales in *Round the Sofa* (1859).[19] These are linked together by the device of storytelling which takes place at the weekly gatherings arranged by Margaret Dawson, a crippled Edinburgh spinster, at which each guest in turn entertains the assembled company with a tale. Of these tales – which incorporate notable generic diversity – *My Lady Ludlow* is the loosest in structure, as well as the longest, consisting of the personal reminiscences of Margaret Dawson about her residence as a young woman with Lady Ludlow, an elderly aristocrat of the "old school" who holds sway over the local village and its inhabitants. The work charts the lives and experiences of various characters, and the developments in provincial society over several decades. It also includes an extended interpolated story (considered by some critics to be too long) about a tragic love affair in Revolutionary France, which, as well as offering the melodramatic elements of intrigue, revenge, and betrayal, reinforces the theme of social change which underpins the whole piece.

Complex in its multilayered narration, and voicing many of Gaskell's concerns – troubled child-parent relationships, unequal marriages, female loneliness and independence – the novella is, as Jenny Uglow comments, undeservedly "the least regarded" of Gaskell's shorter works.[20] Nostalgia and optimism combine in the recognition of the inevitable movement from a traditional hierarchical society to one in which the working classes will be educated, the landowning class will marry into the manufacturing or shopkeeping one, and the institutional power of the Established Church will be dissipated by contact with Dissent. The work also pays particular attention to the changing roles of women. Miss Galindo, the spinster who subverts the conventions of womanhood by becoming Lady Ludlow's clerk and negotiating with her male employees on equal terms ("She was amusingly conscious of her victory over [the lawyer's] contempt of a woman-clerk and his pre-conceived opinion of her unpractical eccentricity" [W, V, 12:173]) is a slightly comic figure. But she also signifies Gaskell's belief in the importance of developing female talents, and her conviction that a better future must include a shift in the hegemonies of gender, as well as of class and religion. This radical vision, together with a refusal to disregard the more discordant elements of human life and an acute observation of the complexities of its relationships, makes *My Lady Ludlow* paradigmatic of Gaskell's shorter pieces. Like this story, they deserve to be restored to their rightful prominence in her canon.

Notes

1 The new Pickering and Chatto edition of Gaskell's complete works (2005–6) makes all her known shorter pieces available for the first time.
2 The novellas are generally considered to be *The Moorland Cottage, Mr Harrison's Confessions, My Lady Ludlow,* and *Cousin Phillis. Cousin Phillis* is usually treated as a novel; *The Moorland Cottage,* while of interest in its foreshadowing of George Eliot's *The Mill on the Floss* (1859), seems designed for a slightly younger readership than most of Gaskell's works.
3 Charles Dickens to Elizabeth Gaskell, November 25, 1851, in *The Letters of Charles Dickens,* 12 vols., VI, ed. Graham Storey, Kathleen Tillotson, and Nina Burgis (Oxford: Clarendon Press, 1988), 545–6.
4 William Wetmore Story to Elizabeth Gaskell, *c.* September/October 1859, Harry Ransom Research Center, University of Texas at Austin.
5 Mat Hompes, "Mrs. E. C. Gaskell," *Gentleman's Magazine* 279 (August 1895), 124–38, 129–30.
6 Henry James, "The Art of Fiction" [1884], in Morris Shapira, ed., *Henry James: Selected Literary Criticism* (Harmondsworth: Penguin, 1968), 86.
7 Charles Dickens, "A Preliminary Word," *Household Words* 1 (March 30, 1850), 1.
8 Interestingly, Dickens suggested that Lizzie herself, and not her child, should die, because that would present a good moral lesson. Generally, he felt that there were too many deaths in Gaskell's short stories.
9 Elizabeth Gaskell, "Martha Preston," *Sartain's Union Magazine* 6 (February 1850), 133–8, 133.
10 *Ibid.,* 138.
11 Jenny Uglow, *Elizabeth Gaskell: A Habit of Stories* (London: Faber and Faber, 1993), 253.
12 In a letter of 1857, she claims to have forgotten its title (*L,* 169).
13 Laura Kranzler, introduction to Kranzler, ed., *Elizabeth Gaskell's Gothic Tales* (Harmondsworth: Penguin, 2000), xi; Alan Shelston, "The Supernatural in the Stories of Elizabeth Gaskell," in Valeria Tinkler-Villari and Peter Davidson, with Jane Stevenson, eds., *Exhibited by Candlelight: Sources and Development in the Gothic Tradition* (Amsterdam: Rodopi, 1995), 137–46; Jenny Uglow, ed., *Curious, If True: Strange Tales of Mrs Gaskell* (London: Virago Press, 1995).
14 Kranzler, introduction, xii.
15 Borrowing records of the Portico Library, Manchester, indicate that William Gaskell borrowed these texts; since books were not issued to women, it is very likely that these were for his wife's, as much as for his, consumption.
16 For a discussion of the publication of this work, see John Geoffrey Sharps, *Mrs Gaskell's Observation and Invention: A Study of her Non-Biographic Works* (Fontwell: Linden Press, 1970), Appendix 4. Tauchnitz issued it as a one-volume story in 1863.

17 Louise Henson, "Half Believing, Half Incredulous: Elizabeth Gaskell, Superstition and the Victorian Mind," *Nineteenth-Century Contexts* 24 (2002), 251–69, 259.

18 Charles Perrault (1628–1703) is best known for his *Tales of Mother Goose* (1697), which helped to establish the new literary genre of fairytale.

19 The others are "The Half Brothers," "An Accursed Race," "The Doom of the Griffiths," "Half a Lifetime Ago," and "The Poor Clare."

20 Uglow, *Elizabeth Gaskell*, 468.

9

PATSY STONEMAN

Gaskell, gender, and the family

"All else confusion"?: gender and social expectations

> Man for the field and woman for the hearth:
> Man for the sword and for the needle she:
> Man with the head and woman with the heart:
> Man to command and woman to obey;
> All else confusion.
> – Alfred, Lord Tennyson, *The Princess* (1847)

When Alfred, Lord Tennyson published *The Princess* in 1847, just as Elizabeth Gaskell was starting her writing career, it was to challenge attitudes like those expressed by the old king in these lines, and Tennyson was not alone in feeling that the doctrine known as "separate spheres" for men and women was ripe for change. Indeed, by 1865, the year of Gaskell's death, John Stuart Mill was able to present the first women's suffrage amendment in parliament. Nevertheless, Mill's speech, published in 1869 as *The Subjection of Women*, confirms that general assumptions about women's role had not changed: "[a]ll the moralities tell them that it is the duty of women, and all the current sentimentalities that it is their nature, to live for others; to make complete abnegation of themselves, and to have no life but in their affections."[1]

One book in this tradition, published in 1839, when Gaskell was the mother of two small daughters, was Sarah Lewis's *Woman's Mission*.[2] While Christian missionaries find their vocation among the heathen, Lewis argues, "woman's mission" is at home, exerting a beneficial influence on her menfolk. In particular, Lewis stresses the importance of mothers inculcating in their male children values of mutual respect, responsibility, and compassion before they pass beyond their mothers' influence into the public world. In the same year, however, women's lack of actual power under English law was demonstrated by the debate surrounding the first Infant Custody Act, and especially by the real-life story of Caroline Norton, who was denied access to her infant children when she offended her husband.[3] Nine years later, Anne Brontë's novel, *The Tenant of Wildfell Hall* (1848), gives us fictional confirmation that "woman's mission" can be a futile dream. Her heroine, Helen Huntingdon, marries a known profligate with the intention of reforming him through her feminine influence; instead, she is forced to flee the marital home to protect her infant son from her husband. During Gaskell's lifetime "woman's role" and the relation of men and women within their separate worlds were the subjects of endless prescription and debate, and it was among these shifting positions that she formed her opinions and began to write.

"Mrs." Gaskell: a dove in the public sphere

"Mrs. Gaskell," the title under which Gaskell's later novels were published, was her usual form of reference until quite recently. By contrast with the Brontës or George Eliot, "Mrs." Gaskell was self-evidently a wife and was also known as the mother of four daughters. For more than a century the title signifying her domestic status has colored readers' responses to her work. Most famously, in 1934 Lord David Cecil found that it "fitly symbolized" the difference between her and "her famous rivals" (Charlotte Brontë and George Eliot), who were "not ordinary women."

> Ugly, dynamic, childless, independent, contemptuous of the notion that women should be confined to that small area of family and social interests which was commonly regarded as the only proper province of their sex; fiercely resentful of the conventions that kept them within it – at every turn they flout the standards which were set up before the women of their day. In the placid dovecotes of Victorian womanhood, they were eagles.
>
> But we only have to look at a portrait of Mrs. Gaskell, soft-eyed, beneath her charming veil, to see that she was a dove.[4]

There is no doubt that the childless Brontë sisters felt more acutely than Gaskell the lack of purpose and opportunity in women's lives, and wrote more passionate appeals against it. Since Gaskell is sure that motherhood is one of the "greatest & highest duties" of a woman's life, her plans for unmarried women tend to involve them with other people's children rather than in intellectual or political careers (*PV*, 53). Gaskell is clear that even exceptional gifts, such as those of Charlotte Brontë, do not absolve a woman from domestic duties. Although "she must not shrink from the extra responsibility implied by the very fact of her possessing such talents," yet no other person "can take up the quiet regular duties of the daughter, the wife, or the mother, ... nor can she drop the domestic charges devolving on her as an individual, for the exercise of the most splendid talents that were ever bestowed" (*LCB*, II, 2:259).

What looks like acquiescence in Gaskell may, however, also be pragmatic negotiation. The well-traveled and urbane Gaskell knew more intimately than either the isolated Brontës or the modern reader the details of social expectation for women. For the modern reader, for instance, it comes as a surprise to find that Charlotte Brontë's first reviewers found her writing "coarse" and unfeminine, but Gaskell understands the small signals that occasioned this interpretation. The main aim of her *Life of Charlotte Brontë* (1857) was to restore Brontë's reputation by explaining this appearance of indelicacy, and her repeated emphasis on Brontë's dutiful attention to domestic and filial duties was motivated by a desire to reinstate Brontë in conventional regard. This emphasis can, however, give modern readers the impression that Gaskell herself is a conventional writer.

The best antidote to such a suspicion is to read Gaskell's letters. Fluent, unguarded, comical, and vivid, they leave us with an impression of a woman who was at the same time deeply involved with every aspect of domestic life and also humorously aware that her negotiations of it were sometimes less than orthodox. Writing to a friend, she explains that "[t]he difference between Miss Brontë and me is that she puts all her naughtiness into her books, and I put all my goodness" (*L*, 228). Far from feeling oppressed by the patriarchal family, she seems thoroughly to enjoy the challenges of her headlong life. Sometimes, though, she is near to being overwhelmed by its sheer busyness. She finds the balance of "home duties and individual life" a "puzzle," and is "sometimes coward enough to wish that we were back in the darkness where obedience was the only seen duty of women" – an admission suggesting that in general she relied on her own judgment (*L*, 106, 109). Her life was very varied: as well as the obvious tasks of providing food, clothing, and furnishing for the household, and caring for and teaching her daughters, there were innumerable duties which blur the boundaries between "private" and "public" existence – whether social work such as teaching in Sunday schools and relief work during the cotton famine, or cultural work such as placing her writing in journals and with publishers, and entertaining visiting artists, scientists, and other intellectuals.[5]

It is evident from Gaskell's letters that under favorable circumstances, Victorian women did have some freedom to act in the public world. Such freedom is not, however, a right; the financial and legal position of most women makes such freedom dependent on the complaisance of husbands and fathers. In this context Gaskell's Unitarian milieu is immensely important. Gaskell's father and husband were both ministers in the

Unitarian church, and her social and family life was enmeshed in Unitarian connections. Unitarians were the most radical of the many Dissenting groups in nineteenth-century England. Rejecting the idea of a divine Christ who suffered to redeem humanity from sins incurred by Adam, they adopted a more rational and optimistic position based on the belief that God created human beings with the capacity to govern themselves with both justice and compassion. Unitarians believed that women as well as men needed to be well educated, and Gaskell attended a seminary which provided her with what was, for the time, an excellent education.

"Education," moreover, in Unitarian circles, included far more than the acquisition of knowledge. Educators aimed crucially to establish independence of thought and a self-regulating morality in both men and women. As Coral Lansbury writes, "[t]o be born a woman in the Victorian era was to enter a world of social and cultural deprivation unknown to a man. But to be born a woman and a Unitarian was to be released from much of the prejudice and oppression enjoined upon other women."[6] This meant not only that Unitarian women had more freedom of action than many Victorian women, but also that their traditional role as mothers had a different importance. The family is the place where people are formed into social beings. Given the Unitarian emphasis on self-government based on careful early training, it follows that mothers, and all those who care for children, preside over the foundations of the polity.

Although Gaskell's first novel, *Mary Barton* (1848), has a "public" theme – class conflict in the new factories – she was moved to write it by two "private" events. The death of her only son, William, at a year old, gave her a generally sorrowing outlook on the world, and this was reinforced and generalized by the suffering in Manchester caused by bad harvests and unemployment.[7] In the novel her treatment of this "public" topic also begins with "private" life, describing a family outing in which the working-class men are careful to relieve their womenfolk of the burden of the children. Almost our first glimpse of John Barton is when he says to his neighbor, "and now, Mrs. Wilson, give me the baby" (*MB*, 1:5).

Cecil, more doctrinaire than the Victorians, could see no connection between "Mrs." Gaskell's domestic vision and her "industrial" theme: "it would have been impossible for her if she had tried, to have found a subject less suited to her talents," he wrote.[8] The Marxist critics Raymond Williams, Arnold Kettle, and John Lucas, who revived interest in Gaskell's works in the 1950s and 1960s, also assumed that Gaskell was naive in adopting a "novelistic" approach to her "social theme," using a story of personal relations as its framework.[9] More recent critics such as Catherine Gallagher, however, have shown that all the social writings of the period, not merely women's novels, were prominently concerned with the connection between public and private life.[10] Indeed, the urgencies of family need motivated some of the most "public" statements of the time; speeches by Chartist leaders such as Joseph Raynor Stephens and Richard Pilling repeatedly "conflated the right to vote with the right to care for self and family," just as, in *Mary Barton*, every radical speech made by John Barton and his friends contains reference to starving children.[11] In Barton's mind the death of his son Tom justifies his murder of Carson's son Harry.

Explaining and mitigating his actions for her middle-class readers, Gaskell compares such working-class reaction with that of Frankenstein's monster, "created" (as factory "hands" were "created" by factory owners) by a "father" whose obligation to his creature ends with the act of creation. Gaskell here appeals to the middle class to recognize its obligations to the workers, many of whom have been uprooted from a rural environment where the feudal assumptions of *noblesse oblige* still operate. Instead, the urban employers ignore the suffering of their workforce and punish them when they revolt, as if making "domestic rules for the pretty behaviour of children without caring to know that those children had been kept for days without food" (*MB*, 8:96). Modern readers are offended by the "paternalism" of such analogies which, by casting the workers as children, deny them adult agency. Gaskell's concept of parental responsibility, however, was not derived from the feudal model seen in Benjamin Disraeli's *Sybil* (1845), but from a more liberal ideal, based on her Unitarian beliefs.

"Appealing to reasonable men": control and sympathy in public affairs

Unitarians were particularly strong in the north of England where William Gaskell had his congregation; their energetic, self-reliant, and ambitious outlook made them particularly suited to the industrial opportunities of the north, and by the mid-nineteenth century, some of the most powerful figures in this newly industrial society were Unitarians. The danger Gaskell perceived was that a purely rational reliance on market mechanisms led the industrial entrepreneurs to ignore their human costs, and in her industrial novels her main aim was to evoke sympathy for the victims of the market. This approach has been seen as sentimental by Marxist critics who believe class struggle to be necessary; it was, however, central to the emerging liberal project of the nineteenth century.

Susan Johnston, in *Women and Domestic Experience in Victorian Political Fiction* (2001), argues that the liberal state (based on the idea of contracts between individuals, rather than despotic power) depends on individuals being able to balance their own rights against those of others. In

North and South (1855) the employer Mr. Thornton stands on the principle that the only connection between him and each of his workers is "that he has labour to sell and I capital to buy" (*NS*, I, 15:122). In this he is like Mr. Bradshaw in *Ruth* (1853), who feels that "all hope of there ever being any good men of business was ended" if "feelings, instead of maxims, were to be the guide" (*R*, 23:198). Thornton and Bradshaw invoke the idea of a contract governing their relations with employees, suppliers, and customers, and this in turn depends on the idea of the liberal individual as a "bearer of rights." Thornton resists the idea that he should intervene in the workers' welfare precisely on these grounds: "[b]ecause they labour ten hours a-day for us, I do not see that we have any right to impose leading-strings upon them for the rest of their time" (*NS*, I, 15:121). This recognition of workers as independent individuals logically requires recognition of each worker's implicit claim, that "I, too, am a man." This claim, however, is not meaningful in the abstract; it requires what Johnston calls "the exegesis of the other in terms of psychological depth." Her argument is that "[t]he profoundly political gesture made in Victorian fictions consists in precisely such exegesis." The domestic focus of Gaskell's industrial fiction thus appears as neither embarrassing nor irrelevant: "this explication of the other's claims to rights necessarily occurs in the context of the household, because the intimate space of the household is the domain of emotion, evaluation, and interior qualities – that is, the domain of the ends of life."[12]

In *Mary Barton* the worker George Wilson, on an errand of mercy for the starving Davenports, is contrasted with the Carsons, the mill owner's family, who are selfishly thoughtless, incapable of imaginative sympathy. While Carson speaks of an abstract "retrenchment," John Barton's argument is specific: "Han they ever seen a child o' their'n die for want o' food?" (*MB*, 6:74). Neither of these positions is inevitable or innate; Gaskell shows us each man in his home environment in order to suggest that the qualities which characterize them are produced within the family. Barton learned his habits of sympathy in imitation of "his mother's bravery," when, as "a little child," he had seen her "hide her daily morsel to share it among her children" (*MB*, 10:131). Harry Carson, on the other hand, has learned to be "proud of himself" for being handsome, well dressed, and gentlemanly: "his sisters were proud of him; his father and mother were proud of him: he could not set up his judgement against theirs" (*MB*, 6:77). The novel is mostly set within the Barton household, but the scenes in the Carson house are sufficient to suggest that the attitudes which animate the public clashes between workers and owners are grounded in domestic experience. Indeed, Johnston argues that the famous split in Victorian life between public and private values is an illusion, since "the household [is] the originary space in which the liberal self comes to be."[13]

If we accept this view, the notion of feminine influence takes a different complexion. So long as we perceive the "spheres" of men and women as separate, and founded on the different priorities of nurturance and competition, then the notion of influence is likely to be a weak one. A feminine influence that works by exerting pressure on an already established, and opposite, system of values is likely to be disregarded, since it carries no force but moral righteousness. If, however, we conceive the family as the space in which the character of boys as well as girls is formed, then the potential power of the woman, especially as mother, appears greater. Mothers – and all those who have the primary care of children – have a unique opportunity to shape future men and women. For this reason Gaskell's "industrial" novels, which move between private and public life, are not naive experiments with irrelevant or inappropriate sections; instead, they offer a radical critique of the ways in which separate spheres are created and maintained.

In middle-class homes the power of mothers is constrained by gender polarization. Most Victorian middle-class men were brought up to assume an extreme form of individualism which denied connection with other people except through the "cash nexus" – the monetary link between employer and employed – or through the hierarchical arrangement of the middle-class family. Their wives, following the prescription of separate spheres, tend to be affectionate but weak; Mrs. Carson, Mrs. Bradshaw, and Mrs. Hamley cosset and indulge their sons, but leave their education to their fathers. Several of Gaskell's short stories show in sensational terms the devastating effects of fathers who try to control their sons without cultivating personal bonds.

In *Ruth* Mr. Benson is nearly impoverished by embezzlement carried out by Richard Bradshaw, the son of a high-principled Dissenting manufacturer who is proud of his handling of his children. "If another's son turned out wild or bad, Mr. Bradshaw had little sympathy; it might have been prevented by a stricter rule ... Richard was an only son, and yet Mr. Bradshaw might venture to say, he had never had his own way in his life" (*R*, 19:211). The novel suggests that sons who are given neither responsibility for their own actions nor encouragement to imagine the feelings of others will act properly only when "strict rule" is in evidence. Richard uses the freedom outside his father's control to cheat his old friend, and in *Mary Barton* Harry Carson's fatal cartoon of the starving workmen is also the product of a mind in which freedom has not been shaped by responsibility.

By contrast, most of Gaskell's working-class men assume responsibility out of sympathy for those weaker than themselves. In *Mary Barton* it is John Barton and George Wilson who relieve the desperate Davenport family, performing small menial tasks "with the useful skill of a working-man" (*MB*, 6:69). Again, the link between private and public motivation is clear. Nicholas Higgins, in *North and South*, sees the strike as a responsible action because every striker has those who depend on him for nourishment and life. In this sense these men are feminized, and work together with their womenfolk rather than seeing the care of children as a "separate sphere." Within the existing channels of political communication, however, these feminized perceptions carry little weight. The Chartist petition in *Mary Barton* and the strike in *North and South* both fail to impress those who operate through control rather than sympathy.

North and South includes a whole chapter of debate on "Masters and Men," in which Thornton's mechanistic view of capital and labor is challenged by Margaret and her "feminine" father. Instead, they offer a "paternal" model which assumes temporary guidance rather than permanent authoritarian control. But Thornton's position is not changed by intellectual conviction. Rather, he needs to be motivated by personal contact with people about whom he has so far generalized; it is only when he sees one of his workers in his own home, with the orphan children he has adopted, that he realizes both the necessities and the generous qualities of the poor, and it is this which forces him to recognize the workers as independent and responsible people.

This *rapprochement*, however, would not have happened spontaneously; it needs the intervention of a woman who, belonging to a class which aligns her with neither masters nor men, could urge their contact from a position which was simply "feminine." Unlike Mrs. Bradshaw or Mrs. Hamley, Margaret's notion of the feminine role is energetic and self-reliant. Forced by necessity to take control within her own family, she is also forced to emerge from its protection, walking the streets and speaking directly to people of different classes. In her conversations with Thornton and Higgins, she might still seem to be exercising "influence" in a traditional way, but her intervention in the riot constitutes a startling excursion into the public sphere.

Barbara Leah Harman sees the riot scene as "a defining moment in the history of women's participation in public/political life," and clarifies this assertion by comparing it with the riot scene in Charlotte Brontë's *Shirley* (1849).[14] Brontë's heroines watch, invisibly, from a distance, knowing that "they would do no good by rushing down into the mêlée"; Margaret, however, risks social opprobrium by appearing in public in response to a complex motivation which includes a desire to protect the man she is coming to love, and a desire to prevent the workers from committing violence they will regret.[15] Interestingly, the mill-owner in *Shirley*, though temporarily exposed to feminine influence during an illness, reverts to his authoritarian ways on recovery, his wife taking upon herself the duty to act as his social conscience.[16] Thornton, on the other hand, is personally changed by his contact with Margaret and with Higgins.

As Thornton learns the value of "private" knowledge, so Margaret gains access to the public world as the owner of capital. She has not, however, been a popular heroine. It was easier for the feminist critics of the 1970s to endorse the rebellious but generalized assertions of Jane Eyre, that women "need exercise for their faculties, and a field for their efforts as much as their brothers do," than to consider the practicalities of where exactly that field of action might lie, within the existing state of society.[17] At the end of *North and South*, we are told that Margaret, left an orphan and an heiress, "took her life into her own hands." She does not, however, either immediately rejoice in her freedom or settle herself comfortably in the domestic sphere. Instead, she takes time to try "to settle that most difficult problem for women, how much was to be utterly merged in obedience to authority, and how much might be set apart for freedom in working" (*NS*, II, 24:416). This cautious, negotiating spirit is, perhaps, the characteristic position not of a rebellious daughter but of an anxious mother who, while keen to enlarge the daughter's sphere of action, at the same time recognizes the need to work within existing social patterns. It is an attitude of compromise, which is now beginning to be recognized as valuable for its realistic assessment of possibilities.

"A law unto herself": protection or independence for girls?

Gaskell took very seriously her own responsibility for the education of her daughters, and the touching anxiety with which she approached this task can be seen in the diary she kept to record the early progress of her eldest daughter, Marianne. In particular, we see the tension arising from her Unitarian desire to leave Marianne to make her own mistakes, and the recognition that in order to become a properly socialized being, the child must also learn to obey authority. Gaskell writes that at three years old, "[h]er little conscience ... is becoming very acute and well-judging" (*PV*, 65). The judicious balancing of freedom and guidance is intended to produce a child who is "a law unto herself," always a term of praise in Gaskell's work (*L*, 160). A very similar attitude can be seen in Leonard's early education in *Ruth* – a similarity that suggests that ideally there should be little difference in the treatment of boys and girls.

In her representations of existing society, however, Gaskell shows that boys and girls are liable to different faults, arising from their different education: boys have too much freedom, which leads to errors of judgment, aggression, and selfishness, while girls have too much protection, leading to ignorance, timidity, and abrogation of responsibility. In most matters Gaskell works to minimize these differences, aiming not only for more responsible men but also for more independent women. She implicitly deplores the conventional, infantilized women who, even when amiable, tend to be enfeebled or ineffective. Mrs. Hamley, in *Wives and Daughters* (1866), had "sunk into the condition of a chronic invalid" through sheer inactivity (*WD*, 4:41); Mrs. Bradshaw, in *Ruth*, "murmured faintly at her husband when his back was turned; but if his voice was heard ... she was mute" (*R*, 19:211). Such a mother does not provide a good role model for her daughters, and Jemima Bradshaw is scornful of her mother's "manner of proceeding, which savoured to her a little of deceit" (*R*, 19:211).

Jemima is emboldened by her observation of Ruth, with her self-governing morality, and when Ruth is accused, it is Jemima who springs to her defence: "I will not keep silence. I will bear witness to Ruth" (*R*, 26:338). In one story after another we see women summoning courage to act on their convictions. Mary Barton, Ruth Hilton, and Margaret Hale assert themselves in sensational circumstances – a sea chase, a cholera epidemic, and a riot, but even timid women like Mrs. Bradshaw in *Ruth* speak out in defense of their children.

In the area of sexuality, however, Gaskell remains tangled in the more general ideology of her time, struggling to reconcile on the one hand her rational wish to produce self-regulating adult women, and on the other an anxiety about a female "purity" which is conceived as so vulnerable that knowledge itself can damage it. The result is an inconsistent desire to educate girls to exercise independent judgment, while at the same time denying them information that would enable them to become "a law unto themselves" in sexual matters. This is an area where Unitarian principles seem under pressure from more widespread prescriptions.

"Conduct books" for women, recommending how they could best fulfill their domestic responsibilities, were common throughout the eighteenth century, consolidating an idea of the family as an essential unit of society with the wife as its moral center. In the nineteenth century the number of books directed at women and their conduct in the home greatly increased, while their direction subtly changed. In addition to moral rectitude came social propriety, giving rise to superficial patterns of behavior, particularly in the middle class, which assumed enormous importance as indicators of class status and social acceptability. By the 1840s middle-class women's lives were shaped by a mesh of social expectations which ranged from the duty to submit to husbands' sexual demands to the ability to interpret the social significance of minute differences of clothing.[18]

In some ways the ability to negotiate this complex system of appearances, which signalled acceptance or exclusion, was a source of power for Victorian women, and some feminist critics have argued that ladies like those in *Cranford* (1853) acquired significant "social capital" or status.[19] On the other hand, to live safely in this atmosphere of constant surveillance required an exhausting vigilance. In particular, mothers were responsible for the social education of daughters, whose virtue and marriageability would be judged by their conformity to these rules. Being too talkative or too reserved; walking alone, with a young man, or without a bonnet could be interpreted as a sign of dubious virtue, and once a girl's "character," or reputation, was questioned it was difficult to recover.

In this context the impulse to educate girls to be "a law unto themselves" is severely checked by the fear that such girls would be seen as "unmaidenly" (a favorite word of Gaskell's, very irritating to modern readers, which derives from this anxiety). Gaskell's dilemma is particularly evident in *Ruth*, where the heroine "was too young when her mother died to have received any cautions or words of advice, respecting *the* subject of a woman's life" (R, 3:44). The implication here is that if Ruth had had the necessary information, she would have been able to protect herself against Bellingham's seduction. The narrator, however, immediately recoils from the idea that such information should be given, doubting whether "wise parents ever directly speak" of this awesome topic (R, 3:44). Protection, rather than independence, is advocated.

In theory, Gaskell's position is that of Helen Huntingdon in *The Tenant of Wildfell Hall*, who argues for moderation: "I would not send a poor girl into the world, unarmed against her foes, and ignorant of the snares that beset her path: nor would I watch and guard her, till, deprived of self-respect and self-reliance, she lost the power, or the will to watch and guard herself."[20] In practice, however, she is always uneasy about how long protection should last. When Ruth in turn becomes a mother, we are told that "she fondly imagined" that she could guard her little boy "from every touch of corrupting sin by ever watchful and most tender care. And *her* mother had thought the same, most probably" (R, 15:161). Given Ruth's history, there is poignant irony in her reliance on protection whose continuance cannot be guaranteed. Yet Gaskell is very reluctant to end the necessary period of protection for girls where the dangers are sexual. Although she was sure of her moral rightness in writing the story of Ruth's seduction and unmarried motherhood, and upset that some of her readers thought it "an unfit subject for fiction," she nevertheless accepts that "[o]f course it is a prohibited book in *this*, as in many other households; not a book for young people, unless read with someone older (I mean to read it with MA some quiet time or other;)" (*L*, 220–1). At this time her daughter Marianne ("MA") was nineteen.

In *North and South* Margaret Hale is more mature than Ruth when she is left an orphan. Despite her strength of character, however, and her steady growth in maturity, the issue of sexuality is never satisfactorily confronted. When Fanny and the servants assume that Margaret has embraced Thornton because she is in love with him, it oppresses her as "an ugly dream of insolent words" (*NS*, I, 22:185). Despite appearances being against her, she finds it "insulting" when Mrs. Thornton assumes that the young man with whom she is seen walking at dusk is her lover, and even after this warning, she continues to deny any consciousness even of the appearance of impropriety (*NS*, II, 13:315). It seems, in fact, to be con- sciousness of sexuality itself which makes Margaret uncomfortable, rather than impropriety. When Mr. Lennox proposes to her at the beginning of the novel, Margaret "felt guilty and ashamed of having grown so much into a woman as to be thought of in marriage," and at the end, despite all the growing up she has done, she is still overcome "with beautiful shame" on coming to an understanding with Thornton (*NS*, I, 4:32–3; II, 27:436).

Interestingly, the problem of sexual knowledge seems to be one peculiar to middle-class girls. In *Mary Barton* Mary's Aunt Esther becomes a prostitute after being seduced in circumstances very like Ruth's, and although her story is told with harrowing appeals to sympathy, there is no suggestion that she did not know what she was agreeing to when she went off with her young soldier. Moreover, although Esther is desperate to save Mary from a similar fate, Mary seems to have assessed the threat from Harry Carson without help from her elders: "if I had loved you before, I don't think I should have loved you now you have told me you meant to ruin me; for that's the plain English of not meaning to marry me" (*MB*, 11:160). In *Sylvia's Lovers* (1863) the heroine is a country girl, and described as "no prude"; she accepts stolen kisses as a harmless pleasure and feels no shame at avowing her love for Charley Kinraid. *Sylvia's Lovers* is Gaskell's only extended and serious exploration of marriage in terms of passion and prudence. When Sylvia is tricked into a marriage with her cousin Philip Hepburn from which she cannot then escape, she is first choked with indignation at being kept from her lover, and then disillu- sioned by Kinraid's rapid consolation with another woman. Her life seems ruined: she has been "cheated by men as she trusted, and . . . has no help for it" (*SL*, 39:444). The story fades out in varieties of regret and remorse, leaving the reader disturbed and uncomfortable, but its focus is on interpersonal responsibility rather than "unmaidenly" shame.

Although critics have been scathing about Gaskell's reliance on a romance plot, in fact only three of her seven most developed tales end in marriage (*Mary Barton*, *North and South*, and *Wives and Daughters*); the others (*Cranford*, *Ruth*, *Sylvia's Lovers*, and *Cousin Phillis*) have less usual plots, and three of these describe less conventional households. Ruth lives with a bachelor Dissenting minister, his sister, and a female servant; Cranford is populated by single ladies; and Sylvia is happiest with a small community of women – her mother, her daughter, and her former rival, Hester Rose. There are many examples in Gaskell's shorter fiction of people, often women, grouping together into unorthodox "families," often for the protection of children.[21] These unorthodox families demonstrate that Gaskell's concern with the raising of children does not depend on a conventional concept of the heterosexual family, but rather on functional cooperation.

Many of these unconventional groupings include a female servant, who is often highly valued for her practical skills and nurturing attitudes, and in *Cousin Phillis* (1864) it is Betty, the servant, who counteracts the infantilization of the young heroine in a story which gives us Gaskell's most detailed and subtle exploration of the harm done by overprotective parents.[22] Phillis Holman, though clever and well-grown, is kept a child by parents who believe they are treating her in the best possible way by instructing her in all kinds of knowledge from Greek poetry to making pastry, while ignoring the fact that she is growing into a woman – "a stately, gracious young woman, in the dress and with the simplicity of a child" (*CP*, I, 228). This means that when her affections are aroused by a young man, who subsequently deserts her, she has no relief from her suffering. Her parents first ignore the cause of her distress, and then blame the young man. It takes her courageous declaration "I loved him, father!" to announce her independent existence; it is, however, Betty who insists that instead of weakly languishing, she must "do something for [her]self" (*CP*, IV, 308, 316).

In *Wives and Daughters*, Gaskell's last novel, the uncomfortable tension between independence and protection for girls seems to relax, and yet this is the first full-length novel in which the education of daughters becomes the focus of attention. Part of its plot does, indeed, give us another example of the dangers of too little protection for girls. Cynthia Kirkpatrick, left to her own devices at an early age by a mother whose attention is engrossed by the need to earn her living, becomes enmeshed in obligations which threaten her "character" and from which she can envisage no escape. Perhaps more important, it becomes evident in her conversation that her education has given her no settled convictions or sense of morality to guide her decisions. Motivated by expediency, she is not fit to be "a law unto herself," and her salvation lies in recognizing who, among her friends, will be a reliable guide to right action.

Mr. Preston, who puts Cynthia in such a difficult position, is one of a number of young men in Gaskell's novels who fascinate by their physical presence and tales of daring exploits. Will Wilson in *Mary Barton*, Charley Kinraid in *Sylvia's Lovers*, and Mr. Preston in *Wives and Daughters* offer a glamorous kind of masculinity which attracts young women because of its adventurous distance from their own lives. Wilson and Kinraid battle with the sea and its monsters; Preston subdues a spirited horse. *Wives and Daughters* offers a semi-comic commentary on such derring-do in the way in which Cynthia is rescued from her difficulties. Although the novel begins with an invocation of fairytales, this distressed damsel is rescued not by Prince Charming, but by her stepsister Molly, abetted by a strong-minded aristocrat (Lady Harriet) and a timid old maid (Miss Phoebe Browning), who are whimsically compared with Don Quixote and Sancho Panza.[23] Although the novel ends with Molly's marriage to Roger Hamley, its "hero" is Molly herself.

Like Mary Barton and Ruth Hilton, Molly Gibson loses her mother at an early age; unlike them, however, she is carefully looked after by a female servant and has a lively and humorous relationship with her father. Although Mr. Gibson shares Reverend Holman's wish to keep his daughter a child, is "startled to find that his little one was growing fast into a woman," and reacts to a young man's infatuation with alarm, the situation is treated with some humor (*WD*, 3:32; 5:55). From what we learn of Molly we as readers are ready to believe that his exaggerated protection of her – rushing her away to stay with neighbors, and remarrying in haste to provide her with a chaperone – is unnecessary, since his generally sensible treatment of Molly has already led her to become "a law unto herself," easily capable of dealing with a lovestruck apprentice.

Later in the novel, we see how Molly not only becomes the receptacle of other people's secrets, each with a sexual element (Osborne Hamley's secret marriage and Cynthia's secret engagement), but also deals with the threatening Preston entirely alone and on her own initiative, refusing to divulge the situation to her father and taking responsibility for whatever mistakes she may have made. The chapter title, "Molly Gibson to the Rescue" (chapter forty-four), may have a comical flavor, but her courageous actions, speaking the truth and refusing to be diverted from her intentions, make her a heroine fit for Unitarian principles. The implication of her heroism is that parents who provide rational and affective security during childhood are still likely to underestimate the independent potential of their daughters. The novel suggests that Molly would have been much better left to her own devices than "protected" by the second Mrs. Gibson.

Conclusion

Elizabeth Gaskell is not an obvious feminist, but gender issues prove central to her social vision. Her novels offer a thorough critique of the kind of masculine autonomy that deprives powerful middle-class men of the capacity to relate to other people – either their employees or their families. The corollary of this is the induced weakness of the "do-nothing lady" who, in John Barton's words, goes to bed "without having done a good turn to any one of God's creatures but herself" (*MB*, 1:8).

In her industrial novels Gaskell admires the warmth and sympathy of working-class life in which men as well as women adopt nurturing roles. In both *Mary Barton* and *North and South*, the heroines are forced by circumstances to take responsibility not only for themselves but also for the lives of others, and this is shown to strengthen and improve their characters. In *Mary Barton*, however, the burden of the nurturing role is left to the men; Mary sinks into a private sphere when her task is done, whereas Margaret thinks seriously about how to pursue her actions in the public sphere.

Although Gaskell's later novels appear to abandon "social" themes, in fact we can see a steady sharpening of focus on the upbringing of the young, especially girls, and the importance of the family (including "families" of unorthodox kinds) in shaping future citizens who will be both "a law unto themselves" and sympathetic to others. This change of focus has been seen as a diversion from social to merely domestic issues, but in the light of contemporary concerns about the formation of the liberal individual, Gaskell's novels appear not only shrewd, observant, and sympathetic, but as in the forefront of Victorian investigations into the nature of social responsibilities.[24]

More importantly, perhaps, the novels still have much to teach us about the dangers of gender polarization. The feminist perception that "the personal is political" has largely been understood in terms of women's oppression; domestic power structures have been redefined as "political" in the cause of women's emancipation. Gaskell's apparently more conservative approach shows us, however, that the personal is political in a more expanded sense, since it is in our infancy that we acquire the values which determine actions in the public world. Those who have the care of children need to produce sympathetic and responsible adults. If they do not, we shall continue to find in the "private" sphere what Virginia Woolf called "the egg of the very same worm" which, in the public world, hatches into a damaging autocracy.[25]

Notes

1 John Stuart Mill, *The Subjection of Women* [1869], in Mill, *On Liberty and other Essays*, ed. John Gray (Oxford: World's Classics, 1988), 486.
2 Sarah Lewis, *Woman's Mission* (London: J. W. Parker, 1839).
3 See Lyn Pykett, "Women Writing Woman: Nineteenth-Century Representations of Gender and Sexuality," in Joanne Shattock, ed., *Women and Literature in Britain 1800–1900* (Cambridge: Cambridge University Press, 2001), 78–98, 84–5.
4 Lord David Cecil, *Early Victorian Novelists: Essays in Revaluation* (London: Constable, 1934), 97–8.
5 See Jenny Uglow, *Elizabeth Gaskell: A Habit of Stories* (London: Faber and Faber, 1993).
6 Coral Lansbury, *Elizabeth Gaskell: The Novel of Social Crisis* (London: Paul Elek, 1975), 11.
7 Uglow, *Elizabeth Gaskell*, 153, 181.
8 Cecil, *Early Victorian Novelists*, 235.
9 Raymond Williams, *Culture and Society 1780–1950* (London: Chatto and Windus, 1958); Arnold Kettle, "The Early Victorian Social-Problem Novel," in Boris Ford, ed., *From Dickens to Hardy* (Harmondsworth: Penguin, 1958), 169–87; John Lucas, "Mrs Gaskell and Brotherhood," in David Howard et al., eds., *Tradition and Tolerance in Nineteenth-Century Fiction* (London: Routledge & Kegan Paul, 1966), 141–205.
10 Catherine Gallagher, *The Industrial Reformation of English Fiction: Social Discourse and Narrative Form 1832–1867* (Chicago: University of Chicago Press, 1985).
11 Lisa Surridge, "Working-Class Masculinities in *Mary Barton*," *Victorian Literature and Culture* 28 (2000), 331–43, 334.
12 Susan Johnston, *Women and Domestic Experience in Victorian Political Fiction* (Westport, CT: Greenwood Press, 2001), 132.
13 *Ibid.*, 10.
14 Barbara Leah Harman, *The Feminine Political Novel in Victorian England* (Charlottesville: University of Virginia Press, 1998), ix.
15 Charlotte Brontë, *Shirley* [1849], ed. Herbert Rosengarten and Margaret Smith (Oxford: World's Classics, 1998), 19:345. Harman makes a striking comparison of the two scenes in *The Feminine Political Novel*, 63.
16 See Catherine Barnes Stevenson, "Romance and the Self-Made Man: Gaskell Rewrites Brontë," *Victorian Newsletter* 91 (1997), 10–16.
17 Charlotte Brontë, *Jane Eyre* [1847], ed. Margaret Smith (Oxford: World's Classics, 2000), I, 12:109.
18 See Elizabeth Langland, *Nobody's Angels: Middle-Class Women and Domestic Ideology in Victorian Culture* (Ithaca: Cornell University Press, 1995), ch. 2.

19 Langland, *Nobody's Angels*, 121.
20 Anne Brontë, *The Tenant of Wildfell Hall* [1848], ed. Herbert Rosengarten (Oxford: World's Classics, 1993), I, 3:31.
21 See "Libbie Marsh's Three Eras," "Lizzie Leigh," "The Well of Pen-Morfa," "Half a Lifetime Ago," and "My Lady Ludlow."
22 Examples of these unconventional groupings include "The Old Nurse's Story," "The Manchester Marriage," "The Grey Woman" and "A Dark Night's Work"; Sally is also important in *Ruth*.
23 See WD, 49:557.
24 For an argument about the diversion from social themes in the late novels, see, for instance, Ruth B. Yeazell, "Why Political Novels Have Heroines: *Sybil, Mary Barton* and *Felix Holt*," *Novel* 18 (1985), 126–44.
25 Virginia Woolf, *Three Guineas* [1938] (Harmondsworth: Penguin, 1977), 61.

10

NANCY HENRY

Elizabeth Gaskell and social transformation

"What can you or I do? We are less than drops in the ocean, as far as our influence can go to re-model a nation."
– Elizabeth Gaskell, "The Moorland Cottage" (1850)

In Elizabeth Gaskell's story "The Moorland Cottage" (1850), Frank Buxton despairs of his power to change what he perceives to be the corruption of a "nation whose god is money" (*MC*, 7:61). Rather than working for change at home, he prefers the complete break, the fresh start of emigration to a "newer and purer state of society" in Canada or Australia (*MC*, 7:62). But his fiancée, Maggie Browne, assures him that if he stays, he will soon see "some heroic action meeting with a nation's sympathy, and you will rejoice and be proud of your country" (*MC*, 7:61). Heroic action, Maggie implies, has the power to redeem a corrupt society by example, by inspiring the average citizens – the mere "drops in the ocean" – to exert their influence for the better, and perhaps over time, to remodel a nation.

Gaskell's fiction is preoccupied with questions of social transformation. Her work as a whole contrasts two models of change: abrupt and violent on the one hand, slow and continual on the other. Violent change includes various degrees of resistance to tyranny, from the French Revolution, which is integral to "My French Master" (1853) and "My Lady Ludlow" (1858), to Frederick Hale's mutiny in *North and South* (1855), and the resistance to the press gangs in *Sylvia's Lovers* (1863). Gradual change includes the passing away of generations, families, even of "races," and Darwinian evolution, the language of which became available for application to social change during Gaskell's career.[1] Gaskell tracks gradual change in "Morton Hall" (1853), "Traits and Stories of the Huguenots" (1853), *Cranford* (1853), "An Accursed Race" (1855), "A Dark Night's Work" (1863), and *Wives and Daughters* (1866).

Since Gaskell is concerned with the effects of social transformation on individual people, as well as with the ability of people to effect social change, her fiction offers instances of both dramatic and quiet heroism.[2] Jem Wilson's saving the fire victims in *Mary Barton* (1848), Ruth Hilton's nursing the fever patients in *Ruth* (1853), Margaret Hale's attempt to save Mr. Thornton from the mob in *North and South*, and Philip Hepburn's rescue of Charley Kinraid and of Bella in *Sylvia's Lovers* are examples of the more dramatic kind of heroism. The quiet endurance of Mr. and Miss Benson in *Ruth* and of Hester Rose in *Sylvia's Lovers* are examples of true Christian behavior that gently influences others. These two forms of heroism are related. As Maggie Browne's comment in "The Moorland Cottage" suggests, the heroic act that meets with national sympathy could initiate the process of slow change and the remodeling of a nation.

For Gaskell, fiction might stir a nation's sympathies, and play several roles in documenting and encouraging the transformation of society. It could preserve a past that had disappeared or was disappearing. It could interpret the causes and consequences of change. It could also be an instrument of change by highlighting social problems and extending the sympathies of readers to the lives of those outside their experience. This chapter will consider the ways in which Gaskell's fiction evokes sympathy both for those swept up in violent forms of social transformation and for those struggling to adapt to more gradual but nonetheless powerful forces of change. In her short fiction and novels, she represents the fields of battle between sexes, classes, and nations. She contextualizes her romance and domestic plots in terms of the larger social processes of technological and scientific innovation. And she addresses fundamental philosophical questions: when does violent resistance to tyranny become justified? Do the changes in English society constitute progress?

The coexistence of revolutionary and evolutionary change in Gaskell's writing raises questions about her political sympathies. As one might conclude from the balancing of workers' and manufacturers' views in *North and South*, Gaskell was sympathetic to seemingly opposing perspectives. Political ambiguities and tensions characterize her life and writing. Her fiction combines elements of that conservative fear of revolution so ingrained in nineteenth-century English society and a commitment to liberal reform.

The complexity of her attitudes to change may be seen in the matter of emigration to the British colonies as a solution to poverty, disgrace, or discontent with society at home. The argument for emigration is offered in *Mary Barton* when Jem and Mary emigrate from England to Canada to escape the stigma attaching to Jem's trial for murder and the possibility that Mary would suffer if the identity of the true murderer came to light. As Jem reflects, "I could live it down if I stayed in England; but then what would not Mary have to bear?" (*MB*, 36:442). The argument against emigration is offered by Maggie in "The Moorland Cottage," who tells Frank that it would be "braver to stay, and endure much depression and anxiety of mind, for the sake of the good those always can do who see evils clearly" (*MC*, 7:61). Similarly, Gaskell aims to change society's attitudes toward "fallen women" at home in *Ruth*, yet she encouraged emigration for an actual seduced woman as her only hope of salvation. Charles Dickens was active in emigration schemes for fallen women, and in 1850 Gaskell wrote to him about a seduced girl whom she wanted to help emigrate to Australia so that she might start over with "as free and unbranded a character as she can" (*L*, 99). The incident is assumed to be an influence on "Lizzie Leigh" (1850), on Esther in *Mary Barton*, and on *Ruth*, though none of the seduced characters emigrates.

Gaskell had Unitarian and humanitarian views about social justice; she sympathized with Christian socialists and with the working poor. Yet she was unsure of her place on the political spectrum. In 1848 she wrote to Catherine Winkworth, "I never can ascertain what I am in politics; and veer about from extreme Right, – no, I don't think I ever go as far as the extreme Left" (*L*, 60–1). She often felt that she did not know enough about an issue to pronounce on it. In 1851 she wrote to her daughter Marianne, who had taken a stance in favor of free trade, urging her to read widely and deeply on the subject: "Seriously, dear, you must not become a *partizan* in politics or in anything else" (*L*, 148). She cautioned her not to confirm the popular view that women should not "meddle in politics": "Have as many and as large and varied interests as you can; but do not again give a decided opinion on a subject on which you can at present know nothing" (*L*, 148). This principle is one that Gaskell tried to practice, as is evident in letters, in which we see her striving to learn more about complex subjects, and in her fiction, in which open-mindedness, tolerance, and sympathy are stressed as qualities leading to social progress.

In her 1859 novel *Adam Bede*, George Eliot (Marian Evans) wrote about the need for realistic representations of "common, coarse people": "It is so needful we should remember their existence, else we may happen to leave them quite out of our religion and philosophy."[3] Unlike Eliot, Gaskell is not known for statements about her aesthetic practice or the moral relevance of realistic representations. Even before Eliot, however, she appreciated that extending one's imagination to the lives and minds of those in danger of being forgotten might be a moral as well as aesthetic exercise. She sought to bring working-class men to the attention of readers in order that their woes might not "pass unregarded by all but the sufferers" (*MB*, xxxvi). She began her writing career by using fiction to arouse sympathy and understanding, much as Harriet Beecher Stowe was to do in *Uncle*

Tom's Cabin (1852), though *Mary Barton*'s social agenda was more diffuse and lacked the clear goal of Stowe's novel: the abolition of slavery.

In "The Moorland Cottage" Maggie imagines a sympathetic identification that is analogous to that of the author, telling Frank that she sometimes wishes that she might be "transmigrated" into an American slave owner, "just that I might understand how he must suffer, and be sorely puzzled, and pray and long to be freed from his odious wealth, til at last he grew hardened of its nature" (*MC*, 7:62). Here Gaskell turns "transmigration" into a metaphor for imagination, for trying to think like someone whose behavior seems unfathomable. For her, such imaginative sympathy was Christian, since comprehension might prepare the ground for forgiveness and improvement. Yet the hope for peaceful change did not mean that oppression should be tolerated, whether from slave owners, factory owners, or ship captains. As Maggie's comments illustrate, slavery was a test case among humanists and Christians for the length to which understanding, followed by sympathy, might stretch.

Violent change

I should like some of the readers of Macmillan to remember the name of the late Colonel Robert Gould Shaw as the name of one who gave up his life for what he believed to be right – deliberately risked and cheerfully laid down, a prosperous, happy, beloved, and loving life.
– Elizabeth Gaskell, "Robert Gould Shaw" (1863)

It is important to remember that the French Revolution and the Revolutionary and Napoleonic wars with France (1793–1815) had shaped English identity in the first half of the nineteenth century. Gaskell was five years old when the Battle of Waterloo ended the Napoleonic wars in 1815. After that, although conflicts were ongoing in the colonies and India, Britain would engage in no major European war until the Crimean War (1854–5). The urgent sense of self-defense and of fighting for a just cause seemed to belong to the previous generation and to take on a mythic quality. The effects of British military activity abroad were remote, and the interest they held related to their impact on the economy at home. At the end of *Ruth*, for example, Gaskell refers to "some proud rejoicing of the nation," especially in her fictional town of Eccleston, because "by the national triumph of arms, it was supposed that a new market for the staple manufacture of the place would be opened" (*R*, 33:423). The conflict remains vague, but its economic consequences are celebrated.[4] In "The Sexton's Hero" (1847) her narrator disparages military heroism as unchristian because it is achieved by injuring others, yet another character, Jeremy, concludes that if military men

" 'sacrificed self to do what they sincerely believed to be right, I do not think I could deny them the title of hero' " (*MC*, 101–2). In *Mary Barton* John Barton does not consider the consequences of his crime any more than does "the soldier, who discharges his musket, picture to himself the desolation of the wife, and the pitiful cries of the helpless little ones" (*MB*, 35:432). Gaskell's distaste for violence is evident throughout her work, and yet the justness of the cause at times led her to praise military heroism.

In the late 1850s Gaskell began to take an interest in America. While in Rome in 1857, she met the American Charles Eliot Norton, and the two soon began a prolific correspondence and friendship. In 1859 she published *Lois the Witch*, set during the seventeenth-century Salem witchcraft trials. And when the American Civil War (1861–5) began, she recognized its importance. Reflexively antislavery, and therefore pro-Union, she wrote to Norton in 1861, "I had always faith in the Northerners; but now I believe I completely understand as well as sympathize" (*L*, 665). But she also deplored the effect of the Union blockade that prevented Southern cotton from reaching English mills and caused unemployment and financial hardship for manufacturers and workers in Manchester and elsewhere. She told the publisher George Smith in 1862, "I wish North & South would make friends, & let us have cotton, & then our poor people would get work" (*L*, 698). Still, her sympathy for those fighting the war was strong, and she strove to understand the conflict.

In 1863 Gaskell wrote a eulogy for the Union army colonel Robert Gould Shaw, the white commander of the Massachusetts 54th, the first regiment of black soldiers from a free state to fight in the American Civil War. When the Massachusetts 54th stormed Fort Wagner in South Carolina on July 18, 1863, Shaw was killed along with half of his regiment. Gaskell felt a personal connection to Shaw because in 1858 in Paris she had met his mother, Sarah Gould Shaw, who wrote about her family's desire to confront their country's "great national sin."[5] Written for an American audience in *Macmillan's Magazine*, Gaskell's brief article presents young Shaw as a hero, one of those who "laid down their lives for no party object, for no mere political feeling; but to see if their lives might avail, if ever so little, to set the captive free."[6] He exemplified what Maggie Browne called "some heroic action meeting with a nation's sympathy," inspiring others to stand up for a moral and a national cause.

In her memorial Gaskell makes Shaw's life and death symbolic and dramatic, and she tries to convey the full force of that drama:

> The regiment was marched up in column by wings, the first being under the command of Colonel Shaw. When about 1,000 yards from the fort, the enemy

opened upon them with shot, shell and canister. They pressed through this storm, and cheered and shouted as they advanced. When within a hundred yards from the fort, the musketry from it opened with such terrible effect that the first battalion hesitated – only for an instant. Colonel Shaw sprang forward, and, waving his sword, cried, "Forward, my brave boys," and with another cheer and shout, they pushed through the ditch, gained the parapet on the right, and were soon hand to hand with the enemy.[7]

This description shows Gaskell's desire to take readers into the scene of battle. On the outcome of the Civil War was staked the abolition of slavery in North America, one of the most profound social transformations of Gaskell's life. As reform had failed to bring about the change, violence was required, and she wanted readers to appreciate the historical consequences of the battles, whether won or lost. She took poetic license with facts that could not be known to her through direct experience, and in this way made remote events colorful and compelling. When fictionalizing violent moments leading to social change, she recognized that reading about those moments and heroes might contribute to slow and peaceful transformation through the understanding of history and the ability to imagine the experiences of others.

Historical fiction gave Gaskell the opportunity to look back and identify transformative events – the English Civil War in "Morton Hall" for example – and to track their influence on individual lives. Written in 1863, the same year that she published her appreciation of Shaw, her historical novel, *Sylvia's Lovers*, is set during the Revolutionary Wars with France. Compare her account of the storming of Fort Wagner to her description of the Battle of Acre (May 7, 1799) in *Sylvia's Lovers*:

led by Sir Sidney, they went under the shelter of English guns to the fatal breach, so often assailed, so gallantly defended, but never so fiercely contested as on this burning afternoon. The ruins of the massive wall that here and there had been broken down by the French were used by them as stepping stones to get on a level with the besieged, and so to escape the heavy stones which the latter hurled down; nay, even the dead bodies of the morning's comrades were made into ghastly stairs. (*SL*, 38:428)

Just as her focus on the contemporary battle tightened on Shaw, so this historical scene gradually telescopes in on Kinraid, who had fallen "under a stray musket-shot, and lay helpless and exposed upon the ground undiscerned by his men" (*SL*, 38:429). Gaskell's motives for narrating the battles at Fort Wagner and Acre are similar: to visualize and personalize world-changing events of the past and present.

Sylvia's Lovers explores various forms of heroism and sacrifice in historical perspective. Gaskell makes clear that Sir Sidney Smith is the hero who helped defeat Napoleon, turn the tide of the war, and affect the fate of nations. Kinraid is a whaling "specksioneer" who, having been "pressed" into service against his will, becomes an eager soldier on behalf of his country. Philip Hepburn is a quieter but no less dramatic hero. He saves Kinraid's life, risking his own to atone for his selfish failure to tell Sylvia that her lover Kinraid was captured by the press gang, not drowned as she believed. Sylvia's father, Daniel Robson, who had been a British soldier in the American War of Independence, leads the resistance against the press gang and is punished – sacrificed to the nation's rules of law and order. Like Jem Wilson in *Mary Barton* and Frederick Hale in *North and South*, Robson is trapped in an impersonal justice system looking to make an example of him. Unlike Wilson and Hale, but like Lois Barclay in *Lois the Witch*, he is put to death. His story becomes part of Gaskell's questioning of the value and consequences of violence.

Gradual change

We have our prejudices in England. Or, if that assertion offends any of my readers, I will modify it: we have had our prejudices in England.
– Elizabeth Gaskell, "An Accursed Race" (1855)

Momentous events such as the Crimean War and the American Civil War led Gaskell to think about the personal dimensions of broader social transformations and to situate her characters in actual historical events. In addition to violent scenes and heroic actions precipitating change, she observes the slower social transformations, which involve states of mind as well as habits of living. In "The Well of Pen-Morfa" (1850), she explains, "I could tell you of a great deal which is peculiar and wild in these true Welsh people who are what I suppose we English were a century ago."[8] In *The Life of Charlotte Brontë* (1857), she writes of the Yorkshire people:

[I]t would be wrong, and in my opinion faithless, to conclude that such and such forms of society and modes of living were not best for the period when they prevailed, although the abuses they may have led into, and the gradual progress of the world, have made it well that such ways and manners should pass away for ever. (*LCB*, I, 2:19)

These examples suggest her awareness of gradual social changes among various groups (the Welsh, Cagots, Yorkshiremen) and the importance of recording what has been lost. Capturing slow change over generations requires an approach quite different from the representation of mobs and battles. It is the gentle irony and the accumulation of episodes, as in *Cranford*, for which Gaskell is perhaps best known.

In the short precursor to *Cranford*, "The Last Generation in England," published in the American *Sartain's Union Magazine* (1849), Gaskell gives an explicit statement of a purpose for writing that would be only implicit in *Cranford*: "to put upon record some of the details of country town life, either observed by myself, or handed down to me by older relations; for even in small towns, scarcely removed from villages, the phases of society are rapidly changing; and much will appear strange, which yet occurred only in the generation immediately preceding ours" (C, 161).

One quality she thought lost was individuality: "Certainly there was more individuality of character in those days than now" (C, 163). The "history of English domestic life" she described in "The Last Generation" was a template for her later fiction, in which she developed the individuality of character so that social transformations might be seen as they affected the lives of those who lived through them (C, 161).

In *Sylvia's Lovers* the narrator is ironic about modern self-consciousness in contrast to sixty or seventy years ago when "few knew what manner of men they were, compared to the numbers now who are fully conscious of their virtues, qualities, failings, and weaknesses, and who go about comparing others with themselves ... with a vivid self-consciousness that more than anything else deprives characters of freshness and originality" (*SL*, 7:74). Freshness and originality of character were more important to Gaskell than introspection and self-consciousness. This was a tenet of her fiction, as she wrote to the novelist Herbert Grey, who sought her advice in 1859: "But certainly – whether introspection be morbid or not, ... [i]t is a weakening of the art which has crept in of late years" (*L*, 541). From Ruth to Miss Matty to Sylvia, we see Gaskell's attempt to appreciate those who act, while the morbidly introspective, like Mr. Hale or Osborne Hamley, are ineffectual.

Her observations about the loss of individuality and originality in modern society seem to echo the famous lines from Alfred, Lord Tennyson's *In Memoriam* referring to Nature: "So careful of the type she seems/So careless of the single life."[9] Disregard for the individual occurred not only in nature but also in the process of industrialization and the factory system. The grinding, mechanized work seemed to depersonalize, even dehumanize, the labourers – making "mere machines of ignorant men" – as she put it in *Mary Barton* (*MB*, 37:457).

Gaskell is rightly recognized for recording the ongoing transformation of England from an agrarian to a manufacturing economy. Her own move to Manchester in 1832 after marrying William Gaskell provided the experiential basis for her observations of working-class life in *Mary Barton*. The persistence of the rural past alongside the technological future is a theme in *Cranford*, in which the small town is "distant only twenty miles on a railroad" from the industrial city she calls Drumble (*C*, 1:1). The railway itself brings changes, including the death of Captain Brown, who saves a child from danger and is killed by an oncoming train. In *Cousin Phillis* the construction of the "little branch line between Eltham and Hornby" intrudes on the quiet life of Hope Farm (*CP*, I, 219). The infiltration of new technology, ideas, and people imperceptibly erodes the happiness of Phillis and her family.

The construction of railways was just one of the developments registered in Gaskell's fiction as transforming the landscape, economy, and everyday lives of English people. The decline of the landholding and rise of the capitalist class brought a change in values and a self-serving commercial attitude. In "The Moorland Cottage" Mr. Buxton, disillusioned by a tenant who has cheated him out of some profits, announces, "I'll not believe in gratitude again. There perhaps was such a thing once; but now-a-days the more you do for a person, the surer they are to turn against you, and cheat you" (*MC*, 7:68). In the upward mobility of families like the Carsons in *Mary Barton*, the old sense of responsibility toward the poor is lost. Men like Mr. Bradshaw in *Ruth* exemplify the hypocrisy and corruption that power without a tradition of responsibility might bring. In *Wives and Daughters* Gaskell looks back to an earlier period and contrasts the decline of Squire Hamley's feudal values with the rise of the insufficiently deferential Mr. Preston and the relatively newly landed Whig, Lord Hollingford.

And yet despite her cynicism about the rise of men such as Carson, Bradshaw, and Preston, Gaskell could not regret the transformation of the social order, especially as the change in England, as opposed to France and elsewhere in Europe after 1848, was gradual, rather than abrupt and violent. As with so many Victorian realist novelists, the conflict resulting from the desire to retain past ways even while new developments are sweeping them away is a constant theme in her work. It is foregrounded in *North and South*, in which the differences implied by the opposition in the title, like those in Jane Austen's *Pride and Prejudice* (1813), are multiple and overlapping rather than simple and binary.

New capitalists

> A thousand things you would not understand: investments, and leases, and value of land.
> – Elizabeth Gaskell, *North and South* (1855)

The nineteenth-century social transformation known as "industrialization" raised questions about what constituted progress. Technology was improving; markets were opening; finance was becoming more sophisticated; many grew rich. Yet the working classes suffered, first through loss of jobs to machines and later through unregulated factory conditions and the fluctuations of trade. Early in the nineteenth century, workers' responses included the Luddite movement, which advocated the destruction of machines that eliminated jobs. The Chartist movement of the 1840s was more rational, and sought political representation for workers. Remnants of resentment against machines persisted, as Gaskell suggests in *Mary Barton* when a Chartist supporter wants the government to "make th' masters to break th' machines. There's never been good times sin' spinning-jennies came up" (*MB*, 8:99). When Chartist demonstrations turned violent, Victorians were reminded of Luddite violence and of the threat of political revolution.

Among the literary responses to the social consequences of industrial change were the "condition-of-England" novels, including *Mary Barton* and *North and South*. Such novels represented the division of England, in words used by Benjamin Disraeli in *Sybil* (1845), into "two nations," rich and poor. They addressed the social problems arising from industrialization, urbanization, and unregulated laissez-faire capitalism, primarily in the north of England. They pointed to the need for reforms out of humanitarian concern, but also out of fear, ominously forecasting violence from a class of workers increasingly desperate, angry and organized.

When Charlotte Brontë read *Mary Barton*, she worried that it had anticipated her examination of manufacturer/worker conflicts in *Shirley* (1849), which is set during the Napoleonic wars abroad and Luddite rebellions at home.[10] Brontë had been alarmed by a Chartist demonstration, as well as by violent revolutions in Europe. She condemned challenges to authority and came to believe that "insurrections and battles are the acute diseases of nations" (*LCB*, II, 2:265). She had limited sympathy with workers' struggles, which *Shirley* views almost exclusively from the perspective of the mill owners.[11] Gaskell "disliked a good deal in the plot of *Shirley*" (*L*, 116). Discussing the novel in *The Life of Charlotte Brontë*, she refers to "those terrible times of insecurity to life and property on the one hand, and of bitter starvation and blind ignorant despair on the other" (I, 6:85), typically sympathizing with both property owner and worker.

Despite Gaskell's objection to the plot and her political differences with Brontë, *North and South* has much in common with *Shirley*. Both novels represent the hope of reconciliation between industrial capitalists and workers through the conversion of the capitalist. Both emphasize the influence of women in bringing about this reform. But the women's power goes beyond influence; both Shirley Keeldar and Margaret Hale inherit property and capital, becoming investors in new businesses (and new businessmen) as well as in social reform.

The forward-looking northern industrialists are a source of excitement and of moral concern for Shirley and Margaret. Margaret is attracted by the Milton men who "seemed to defy the old limits of possibility," admiring "their forgetfulness of themselves and the present, in their anticipated triumphs over all inanimate matter at some future time which none of them should live to see" (*NS*, I, 20:163–4). Even for the sophisticated Mr. Lennox, the Milton men are irresistible for their "energy, their power, their indomitable courage in struggling and fighting" (*NS*, II, 24:416). Margaret must remind him "how selfish and material were too many of the ends they proposed to themselves as the result of all their mighty, untiring endeavour" (*NS*, II, 24:416). Despite this selfishness, in the end, Thornton is redeemed by his consideration for others.

Thornton's father committed suicide over failed investments that turned his wife and son into aggressive capitalists. On the brink of bankruptcy himself, Thornton rejects a speculative opportunity because it would risk "ruining many for [his] own paltry aggrandisement" (*NS*, II, 25:424). Instead of rationalizing that his success would provide jobs for many, Thornton rejects the chance for gain on moral grounds. The speculative venture pays off without him, but he is consoled by having kept clear of mere gambling (*NS*, II, 25:428). Like *Shirley*'s Robert Moore, who resolves to "take more workmen; give better wages; lay wiser and more liberal plans; do some good; be less selfish," Thornton plans to build a new dining hall and provide educational opportunities for his workers.[12] Speaking of such "experiments," he concludes, "I am not sure of the consequences that may result from them. But I am sure they ought to be tried" (*NS*, II, 26:431). Gaskell's idealized man of the future, like Brontë's, embraces the social transformations of capitalism, justifying its laissez-faire philosophy, but possessing the humanistic sensibility to improve the lives of his workers.

To accompany this man of the future, Gaskell again follows Brontë in imagining the women of the future. Shirley, who owns the land on which Moore's mill stands, lends him £5,000, as he reminds her: "you well know who came to my rescue; from what hand I received the loan which saved me."[13] Shirley is Moore's landlord and chief investor. Her neighbors suspect that she is "involved in business speculations" with him and had "lost her money, and was constrained to mortgage her land," but really she has merely offered him a loan, sparing him ruin.[14] Similarly, Margaret emerges as Thornton's savior when she inherits the land on which his mill stands, making her his landlord. She proposes, "[I]f you would take some money of mine, eighteen thousand and fifty-seven pounds, lying just at this moment unused in the bank, and bringing me in only two and a half per cent. – you could pay me much better interest, and might go on working Marlborough

Mills" (*NS*, II, 27:435). Investment of the female character's capital thus becomes a means of compromise and reconciliation between his business interests and her genteel values. When Margaret inherits her money, she is "so entirely ignorant of all forms of business" that she depends completely on Lennox, who fails in wooing her (*NS*, II, 24:413). Later, in proposing to Thornton, her language becomes capitalistic ("bringing me only two and a half per cent"), while his takes on a moral tone ("my own paltry aggrandisement"), echoing Margaret's ongoing criticisms of capitalist values in the novel.

Gaskell's approval of women with the knowledge and the means to act is another way of suggesting a social transformation in which better-informed, more powerful women gradually emerge, while the victimized and the decorous continue to exist. In the preface to *Mary Barton*, Gaskell claimed, "I know nothing of Political Economy, or the theories of trade" (*MB*, xxxvi). Yet *Mary Barton* and later *North and South* reflect her understanding of trade and labor relations. Gaskell's work illustrates that those who are naive in money matters are at risk in the modern economy. Miss Matty in *Cranford* knows nothing of the bank shares she has inherited from her sister, which become worthless when the bank fails. Mr. Benson, the kindly minister in *Ruth*, is defrauded of his insurance company shares by the profligate Richard Bradshaw. In contrast to these victims, Margaret's investment in Thornton's mill, as much as her conjoined marriage and business proposal, marks her as a new kind of woman who desires both marriage and a good return on that money lying "unused in the bank."

Superstition and science

> I admire the patience of Mr Darwin's research ... His book will help to overthrow many old & cumbrous superstitions, even if it establish but few truths in their place.
>
> – Charles Eliot Norton to Elizabeth Gaskell (1859)

In 1850 Gaskell wrote that she believed the success of *Mary Barton* might be related to the timing of its publication and to the "great social revolutions" of 1848, which "directed people's attention to the social evils, and the strange contrasts which exist in old nations" (*L*, 115). Her fiction emphasizes some of those "strange contrasts" by showing that progress through education would never come equally or evenly in English society. In *North and South* Margaret returns to her beloved Helstone, somewhat idealized in contrast to the colorless, industrialized Milton Northern, and is confronted with one of the "savage country superstitions": an account of a cat having been roasted alive because its screams were thought to compel "the powers of darkness to fulfil the wishes of the executioner" (*NS*, II, 21:390). It is as unpicturesque a portrait of rural life as Boucher's family is of city life, but all the more shocking because the novel has led us to associate the southern countryside with sweetness and light, not darkness and brutality.

The coexistence within one nation of the progressive and the backward, the savage and the civilized, was a reality that complicated every Victorian model for social change. Gaskell assumes that attitudes in England are more advanced than elsewhere, but she reminds her readers of England's history of superstition and prejudice. Referring to the seventeenth-century Salem colonists in *Lois the Witch*, she writes, "We can afford to smile at them now; but our English ancestors entertained superstitions of much the same character at the same period, and with less excuse."[15] The advent of technology would do little to eliminate the entrenched beliefs of the past. For this, progressive thinkers looked to the growing authority of science.

After the new capitalist Thornton, Gaskell represented the new man of science, Roger Hamley, whose inclinations and actions led him to pursue new forms of knowledge that would help to educate the English out of their superstitious ways, and lead the nation into a modern world in which understanding kept pace with technology and the production of knowledge kept pace with the generation of capital. Gaskell, a distant relative of Charles Darwin, was aware of his scientific researches and of the impact of *On the Origin of Species* (1859). The struggle between old and new beliefs, their coexistence and contentions, is the background for her last novel, *Wives and Daughters*.

At the end of the unfinished novel, Mrs. Gibson has a moment of misunderstanding with her second husband:

> "It is such a pity!" said she, "that I was born when I was. I should so have liked to belong to this generation."

> "That's sometimes my own feeling," said he. "So many new views seem to be opened in science, that I should like, if it were possible, to live till their reality was ascertained, and one saw what they led to." (*WD*, 60:681)

Mrs. Gibson has another social change in mind: "in this generation there are so many more rich young men than there were when I was a girl" (*WD*, 60:681). The exchange reveals differences not only in the characters of the mismatched couple but in the very kinds of social transformation that the novel represents. Mr. Gibson, a country doctor, maintains an interest in scientific discovery at a distance. His second wife, on the fringes of aristocratic society, keeps up an interest in fashion and the lives of the fashionable. In their different ways, both are attentive to equally important and significantly gendered transformations. The narrator occasionally makes connections between such technological and social changes, as when she observes that "before railways were, and before their consequences, the excursion-trains, ... to go to a charity-ball ... was a very allowable and favourite piece of dissipation to all the kindly old maids who thronged the country towns of England" (WD, 26:294). Transportation affected entertainment, just as technological advances in the means of production contributed to there being "many more rich young men." *Wives and Daughters* is notably free of violent change, except in the old squire's recollections of the English defeat of Boney and the French, but the interdependence of different kinds of gradual change is frequently emphasized.

Mrs. Gibson rarely offers profound insights, but occasionally, as one of the wives invoked in the title, her comments touch on the novel's central themes. She remarks to her stepdaughter, "The future is hidden from us by infinite wisdom, Molly, or else I should like to know it; one would calculate one's behaviour at the present time so much better if one only knew what events were to come" (WD, 48:551). No one in *Wives and Daughters* knows what is to come. Yet the historical setting means that the author knows something of what succeeding generations will bring. Unlike George Eliot's narrator in *Middlemarch* (1872), the narrator rarely offers the wisdom of hindsight, and *Wives and Daughters* leaves us with a sense of openness about the future, with only hints of the gradual social transformations in store for the next generation of Gibsons and Hamleys.

Yet perhaps the open-endedness of Gaskell's last, unfinished novel has less to do with its incompleteness, or with the ignorance of its characters about the future, than with Gaskell's awareness that assessing and evaluating social change was an imprecise science at best. Her fiction shows us that even as technology and industrial capitalism were creating energy, innovation, and unprecedented new wealth, some people still lived in the direst poverty. Even as education and literacy spread, ignorance and superstition persisted. Roger Hamley's forays into Africa yielded the mere rudiments of a new body of knowledge. The unspecified discoveries he makes, which cause such a buzz among the landed men of science who have financed his expeditions, might do little to enlighten Englishmen about the people who lived in Africa, or eradicate the prejudices that Gaskell emphasizes among those interested in his specimens of the flora and fauna of unfamiliar regions. The enlightened Mr. Gibson, for example, makes several gratuitous comments about "black folk," such as that if Roger "shares my taste, their peculiarity of complexion will only make him appreciate white skins more" (WD, 35:411).

Roger's scientific career is clearly based on that of Darwin. But at the time Gaskell wrote the novel, it was too early to say how his theories might aid in the types of social transformation in which she was most interested, how they might, in the words of Charles Eliot Norton, "overthrow many old and cumbrous superstitions." Women like Molly and Cynthia would still have to confront, as her next-generation heroine Margaret Hale would in *North and South*, "that most difficult problem for women, how much was to be utterly merged in obedience to authority, and how much might be set apart for freedom in working" (*NS*, II, 55:416). Before deciding to give up Roger and marry the wealthy Mr. Henderson, Cynthia plans to become a governess in Moscow, "in a family owning whole provinces of land, and serfs by the hundred" (*WD*, 60:628). She prefers, at least for a moment, the idea of going back in time to the kind of feudal society for which Squire Hamley also yearns. Inevitably, however, in order to survive, both Squire Hamley and Cynthia must look forward and embrace the new – modern agriculture and a French daughter-in-law for him, London and the freedom of wealth for her.

Finally, Gaskell's contribution to the understanding and furthering of social transformation in her age came through her writing, and the sympathy it sought to extend from middle-class readers to their less enlightened and less fortunate fellow citizens. The woman who narrates the story about the scalded cat in *North and South* appalls Margaret because she does so with "such utter want of imagination and therefore of any sympathy with the suffering animal" (*NS*, II, 21:391). In her fiction Gaskell, like her contemporaries Eliot and Dickens, represented social change, but also furthered it in the direction she saw as progress by encouraging the possibility of sympathetic identification with individual characters who endure transformations that are difficult to predict and comprehend.

Notes

1 See Louise Henson, "History, Science, and Social Change: Elizabeth Gaskell's 'Evolutionary' Narratives," *Gaskell Society Journal* 17 (2003), 12–33.

2 See J. R. Watson, "Elizabeth Gaskell: Heroes and Heroines, and *Sylvia's Lovers*," *Gaskell Society Journal* 18 (2004), 81–94.

3 George Eliot, *Adam Bede* [1859], ed. Valentine Cunningham (Oxford: World's Classics, 1996), II, 17:178.

4 For the argument that this reference is to the first Opium War, see Nancy Henry, introduction to Elizabeth Gaskell, *Ruth*, ed. Nancy Henry (London: Everyman, 2001).

5 Elizabeth Gaskell, "Robert Gould Shaw," *Macmillan's Magazine* 9 (December 1863), 113–17, 114.

6 *Ibid.*, 115.

7 *Ibid.*

8 Elizabeth Gaskell, "The Well of Pen-Morfa," in Gaskell, *My Lady Ludlow and Other Stories*, ed. Edgar Wright (Oxford: World's Classics, 1989), 1:124.

9 Alfred, Lord Tennyson, *In Memoriam*, in *Tennyson's Poetry*, ed. Robert W. Hill, Jr. (New York: Norton, 1999), 55:7–8. *In Memoriam* also provides the epigraph for *Sylvia's Lovers*.

10 See Jenny Uglow, *Elizabeth Gaskell: A Habit of Stories* (London, Faber and Faber, 1993), 247.

11 On Brontë's conservative politics, see Philip Rogers, "Tory Brontë: *Shirley* and the 'Man,'" *Nineteenth-Century Literature* 58 (2003), 141–75, 145.

12 Charlotte Brontë, *Shirley* [1849], eds. Andrew and Judith Hook (London: Penguin, 1979), 37:594.

13 *Ibid.*, 16:288.

14 *Ibid.*, 28:467.

15 Elizabeth Gaskell, *Lois the Witch*, in Elizabeth Gaskell, *Cousin Phillis and Other Tales*, ed. Angus Easson (Oxford: World's Classics, 1981), 2:127.

II

JOHN CHAPPLE

Unitarian dissent

"However I told him what *I* did believe – (more I suppose what would be called Arian than Humanitarian)."

– Elizabeth Gaskell to Charles Eliot Norton (1861)

In 325 the Council of Nicaea declared that God the Father, Son, and Holy Ghost exist as three equal persons in a divine unity. Dissenting Protestants ejected from the Church of England in 1662 for refusing to accept the authority of bishops retained this orthodox Trinitarian doctrine, but in the next century some followed Arius (*c*.256–336) in the belief that Christ was divine but inferior to God the Father. Others came to believe that Christ was only human, and were insultingly labeled Socinians after two sixteenth-century heretics. Although most anti-Trinitarians held that Christ was a divinely inspired guide and teacher, they were not regarded as Christians, even by other Dissenters. Between 1689 and 1813 denial of the Trinity was technically against the law of England. Unitarian polemics against other legal and political disabilities, and frequent support for French Revolutionary principles, caused many to be ostracized as dangerous radicals. In 1791 "Church and King" mobs destroyed the house, library, and papers in Birmingham of Joseph Priestley (1733–1804), famous scientist and leading Unitarian minister, and rioted in Manchester, not long before Elizabeth Gaskell's father arrived to teach in a new college there.[1]

Calvinism

I fancy I can't care for doctrine so much as most people, it never hurts me much, except *high* Calvinism.

– Elizabeth Gaskell to Edward Hale (1857)

Jean Calvin (1509–64) was a Reformation Protestant who taught that God had foreordained everlasting hell for all but the "chosen few." Priestley led those who rejected this severe doctrine outright. He read the Bible selectively, discarding everything he regarded as contrary to human reason, a God-given faculty. He condemned beliefs in "original sin" inherited from Adam and Eve and in Christ's "atonement" for human sins as grievous superstitions, preaching instead a chain of cause and necessary consequence through which a benevolent God ensured that we could work out our own salvation on this earth. For Unitarians, the search for truth was a supreme value, consistent with Enlightenment ideals of freedom of rational thought and inquiry, liberty of conscience, tolerance, and self-improvement.

Elizabeth Gaskell stands squarely in this tradition. Although Unitarianism as such is absent from her fiction, its humane perspectives are omnipresent. Criticism of social evils, compassion for suffering humanity, and hard-won trust in divine providence pervade the stories that became her most satisfying form of personal action. In her powerfully dramatic tale "The Heart of John Middleton" (1850), she writes as a fanatical Ranter or Primitive Methodist fired by stories of a vengeful Old Testament God, who ultimately follows the dying words of his virtuous wife and finds salvation. In *Ruth* (1853) the stern Calvinism of Mr. Bradshaw, whose wife seemed "thoroughly broken into submission," is defeated and Ruth allowed to redeem herself (*R*, 15:153). *Mary Barton* (1848) goes even further, allowing redemption even after death.[2]

Elizabeth Gaskell's family and background

Gaskell's father William Stevenson (1770–1829) was christened in Holy Trinity Episcopal parish church in Berwick-upon-Tweed. In 1787 he went to a Dissenting academy at Daventry that prepared ministers who could not in conscience subscribe to the Thirty-Nine Articles of the Church of England, as demanded by the two English universities of Oxford and Cambridge. Although he failed to complete his five-year course, he received an education in natural sciences, "doctrine of the human mind," divinity and classics. Free discussion was encouraged; at this time the Enlightenment thrived in Dissenting academies and the universities of Edinburgh and Glasgow. In about 1793 he became classical tutor at Manchester New College, which was largely Unitarian but imposed no religious tests. John Dalton, Quaker and scientist, was a colleague. There, it is claimed, Stevenson became an Arian and ministered to a small Unitarian congregation at Dob Lane, a hotbed of political radicals. In 1796 he abandoned both chapel and college, publishing a plan to modernize education in *Remarks on the Very Inferior Utility of Classical Learning*. He might not have been Unitarian for more than a few years.

In 1797 he married Elizabeth Holland, from a Cheshire Unitarian family, in a Church of England ceremony as demanded by the law up to 1835.

While they were living in Midlothian, their son John was baptized in the established Presbyterian Church of Scotland in 1798. By 1809 the Stevensons had moved to Chelsea, where Elizabeth was born, her name being entered in a general register of Nonconformist births. After her mother died in 1811, Stevenson married again. His second wife was the sister of Anthony Todd Thomson, the doctor present at Elizabeth's birth in Chelsea and a major figure in the parish. The first child of this marriage was baptized by a Unitarian minister, William Turner, a relative, but the second was christened in Chelsea parish church.

Elizabeth, taken to Knutsford as a baby, was brought up by her mother's widowed sister Hannah. The extended Holland family of her aunt and mother were strong supporters of Knutsford's Old Dissenting Chapel, which had been Unitarian since 1740. Here began Gaskell's deep, ingrained knowledge of the Bible. Unlike Maggie Browne in "The Moorland Cottage" (1850) or Molly Gibson in *Wives and Daughters* (1866), Unitarian girls often received more than a home-based education. At the age of eleven she was sent to an excellent if conventional school for girls in Warwickshire run by the Byerley sisters, one of whom had married Todd Thomson. Although the Byerleys had Unitarian connections, they kept pews in the Anglican parish church. Her father's only surviving letter to Elizabeth, of July 1827, when she had left school, shows that he continued to supervise her secular education: "I hope you [are] again applying to your Latin and Italian."[3]

Unitarianism in the early nineteenth century

Dissenting academies produced a learned, intellectual, and conscientious ministry. Thomas Belsham (1750–1829) resigned as principal of Daventry in 1789 when he realized that he had moved from Trinitarian orthodoxy to totally Humanitarian beliefs. An aggressive controversialist, in his later years he emphasized the "divine religion of Jesus ... which at once irradiates the understanding and convinces the judgment, which captivates and rules the heart."[4] Another forceful minister, Robert Aspland (1782–1845), established the British and Foreign Unitarian Association in London in 1825. By then "new Dissent," in the form of ardent Methodism, was numerically superior. There were hardly more than two hundred Unitarian congregations in England and Wales, though their social and cultural influence was out of all proportion to their size. Great wealth was gained by families like the L(l)oyds in banking, the Courtaulds in silk, the Strutts, Fieldens and Gregs in textiles, and the Flowers in brewing.[5]

William Gaskell (1805–84) came from a prosperous Unitarian manufacturing family in Warrington. After a Glasgow M.A. he went on to

Manchester New College, which had moved to York, as a ministerial candidate. Belsham then took him under his wing, and in 1828 Gaskell was appointed junior minister at Cross Street Chapel, Manchester, in preference to the charismatic James Martineau (1805–1900). A few days later Gaskell baptized the first child of Mary and Henry Green, a Glasgow contemporary who had been chosen as minister of Knutsford's Dissenting Chapel in 1827. Close, continuous friendship with the Green family reinforced Elizabeth's connection with the religion of her upbringing.

Unitarianism united

The union and energy of Unitarians will be the reformation of England, and the reformation of England will be the regeneration of the world.
– William Johnson Fox

A second meeting of Aspland's Unitarian Association was deliberately held outside London in 1830, at Cross Street Chapel in Manchester. The *Report of the Proceedings* lists scores of names, which formed the largely elite circles of Gaskell's early married life, interlocking personal and business relationships based on wealth and education as well as religion. Unitarian networks and affinities extended to America. Henry Ware, Jnr., professor in the Harvard Divinity School, spoke for the American Unitarian Association. A resolution recommended the philanthropic city missions of Joseph Tuckerman, minister of the poor in Boston. Cross Street Chapel soon began to employ a missioner to give practical help to families who could not afford even the few pence a week needed for its schools. He reported on a monthly basis to a committee of which J. G. Robberds (1789–1854), the senior minister, and William Gaskell were important members. *Mary Barton* contains passages lifted directly from the printed reports.

Unitarians had always been prominent in establishing bible, literary and philosophical (scientific) societies, charity schools for girls as well as boys, mechanics' institutes and the like. Repeal of most legal disabilities between 1828 and 1833 meant that they could compete for places in parliament and local government. Unitarian authors and politicians, lawyers and doctors, councillors and administrators flourished. Tolerant, progressive, and liberal, they cooperated with other faiths in good works. William Gaskell's doctor brother Samuel, who toiled in a Manchester emergency hospital during a cholera epidemic in 1832, must have valued the work of Irish Catholic priests with the sick and dying. But there were some rude setbacks. William Turner's peaceful joint-secretaryship of the ecumenical Auxiliary Bible Society in Newcastle for nearly twenty years was disrupted in 1831. Placards proclaiming his "Soul-destroying Heresy" were posted by fervent Evangelicals all over the town, just a few months after Elizabeth Stevenson had visited him there.

Unitarians were much involved in printing, publishing, and book selling. Turner established a Unitarian Tract Society when it became legal to do so, reprinting selected American items. "Character," Caleb Stetson wrote, anticipating George Eliot, "is formed by a long series of acts, insignificant perhaps in themselves, but, as units in the sum of moral existence, and germs of deep-rooted habit, they will influence our whole future destiny."[6] Turner also published a sermon by that eloquent and mystical American divine William Ellery Channing (1780–1842), entitled *The Superior Tendency of Unitarianism to Form an Elevated Religious Character* (1827). William Johnson Fox thought that Channing had a power "better fitted, and more uniformly directed, to the excitement of feeling" than either Priestley or Belsham.[7]

Unitarianism divided

Socinianism Moonlight – Methodism &c A Stove! O for some Sun that shall unite Light & Warmth!
  – Samuel Taylor Coleridge, *Notebooks*

With his rich bass voice and irresistible rhetorical flow, William Johnson Fox (1786–1864) was the keynote speaker at the grand Manchester display of unity in 1830, when Priestleyan rationalism was still dominant. However, his obituary of the unimaginative Belsham in the same year concludes in Romantic eulogy: "Doctrines now ... present themselves to the mind, not as hard propositions, but as living principles. The chaos has become a harmonized world, and that world becomes surrounded with an atmosphere; beams of light play through it; sounds of melody vibrate in it; the beauty of colour is generated by it; man inhabits it, and becomes a living soul."[8] Percy Bysshe Shelley's *Prometheus Unbound* (1820) and William Wordsworth's "Tintern Abbey" (1798) echo behind his words. Fox even maintained that Unitarian Christianity assumed "its perfect form" in the preaching of Channing.[9]

Some ministers, especially the combative Martineau, now began to appeal to imagination, the soul's natural piety, and the known devotion of other sects rather than the clear-eyed rationalism of the Priestley tradition. This tended to undermine ministers like William Gaskell and the indefatigable educationist John Relly Beard, who defended more traditional doctrines and practices in their weekly newspaper, *The Unitarian Herald*, though Channing's fervor appealed to all parties. Gaskell's early experience of Romantic poetry and Edward Bulwer's mystical novel *Eugene Aram*

(1832) made her receptive to this more emotional form of Unitarianism which was in tune with the new spirit of the age. But she did not warm to Martineau himself.[10]

Fox transformed the Unitarian *Monthly Repository* into a campaigning literary journal. In 1832 he called for "streets, alleys, workshops, and jails, to complete the scenery of the poetry of poverty." In 1834 he declared, "Man has crippled female intellect, and thereby enfeebled his own."[11] His early feminist contributors rejected current domestic ideology: family as well as state needed democratic reform.[12] Ironically, within a few years Fox had spun Byronically out of the Unitarian orbit. His relationship with the young composer Eliza Flower was perhaps platonic, but in 1833 he imprudently advocated divorce on grounds of incompatibility. Separated from his wife, Fox, together with his children and Eliza Flower, went to live elsewhere. In later decades strong progressive influences were brought to bear on Gaskell by his daughter Eliza Bridell-Fox, Anna Jameson, Mary Howitt, Bessie Parkes, Barbara Bodichon, and others. Gaskell also read feminist novels by Geraldine Jewsbury, Frederika Bremer, and George Sand, but never adopted out-and-out radical ideas. Her close friend, the Unitarian lawyer William Shaen, teased her for being "'too much of a woman' in always wanting to obey somebody" (*L*, 280).

A Unitarian courtship and marriage

Let the pretty creatures amuse themselves. Let every Jack have his Jill. I suppose I shall have mine sometime if Miss Blank will consent.
　　　　　　　　　　　– Edward Herford, *Diary*

Unitarians were far from puritanical; social intercourse was generally easy, inclusive, and polite. Gaskell's brilliant early letters to Harriet Carr are not devotional. They are packed with gossip, fun, and chatter about races, reviews, fêtes, bazaars, suppers, and balls, where unmarried young women could see and be seen – diversions condemned as sinful by strict Evangelicals, Anglican as well as Dissenting. Unitarian clerical families were discreetly cheerful, too. Turner's daughter Mary (1786–1869) had married J. G. Robberds of Cross Street Chapel, and in the private houses of his affluent congregation Elizabeth Stevenson enjoyed excellent suppers, games, charades, and dances. It was at the Robberds's home that she was courted by William Gaskell.

On Thursday, August 30, 1832, William and Elizabeth were married in Knutsford parish church. Their honeymoon saw them bowling westward along the North Wales coast road in a coach with two bugles blowing between sparkling sea and rich-tinted hills, off to stay with a Holland uncle in beautiful country near Tremadog. For a time they could joyously defer Turner's advice to his daughter Mary in 1812: "You have perused the strong and often coarse, though too often well-founded, strictures of Mrs [Mary] Wollstonecraft. I need not, therefore, say anything to you on the *general* rights and obligations of Husband and Wife: you are neither of you, I trust, disposed to be jealous of each other's rights, or grudging in the discharge of mutual obligations" (*PV*, 115). Unitarian women were intelligent, active, and strong-minded, but most believed that husbands had the right to take the lead in a marriage. Fortunately, Elizabeth could boast that William would never have "*commanded*" her (*L*, 109).

Early married life

> How all a woman's life, at least so it seems to me now, ought to have a reference to the period when she will be fulfilling one of her greatest & highest duties, those of a mother.
>
> – Elizabeth Gaskell, *Diary*

The married life that started so splendidly was soon touched with tragedy. In summer 1833 Elizabeth's first child, a daughter, was stillborn. Infant deaths were common, and the diary she kept between 1835 and 1838 when her second child, Marianne, was an infant was understandably resigned: "Do with her Oh Lord as seemeth best unto thee, for thou art a God of Love & will not causelessly afflict" (*PV*, 63). Does the Unitarian optimism of the second clause seem a little forced? William, loving but more reserved in expressing his feelings, attempted to moderate her fears. (Neither parent then knew that tragedy would strike again: they lost two baby sons in the 1840s.) Her painful self-scrutiny was in an older mode: "Oh my Father, help me to regulate my impatient temper better" (*PV*, 70). This awareness of human fallibility is offset by the ideals of love, trust, and truthtelling she expresses. Neither parent worried that Marianne was backward in walking and talking, but eventually a school would be desirable, "to perfect her habits of obedience, to give her an idea of conquering difficulties by perseverance" (*PV*, 67). Gender differences did arise, briefly: "She is a sweet little creature in general; full of good feeling. She would give rather too freely towards the poor ... William says he fears I excite her sensibilities too much; I hope not, for I should dread it as much as he can do" (*PV*, 68).

The Gaskells educated their daughters at home with the help of tutors, then sent them on to small Unitarian boarding schools. A "young lady" life was discouraged, despite the difficulty of finding equally cultivated young Unitarian men to marry. When in 1858 Gaskell made friends with Charles

Bosanquet, from an Evangelical Church of England family, she found that he "had some unknown horror of Unitarians," and she later suspected that religious bigotry prevented her daughters from finding marriage partners (*L*, 647). Unitarians remained marginalized for denying the full divinity of Christ, a judgment that William Gaskell opposed with earnest eloquence: "We have been refused the Christian name; we have been stigmatized as blasphemers, enemies of the cross of Christ, and deniers of the Lord who bought us ... They profess to take Jesus as their heaven-inspired Guide and Teacher; so do we."[13]

Certain that eternal salvation did not depend on correctness of belief, William Gaskell worked on charitable committees with all kinds of people. Like his wife, he avoided political speeches, public meetings, and "noisy obtrusive ways" of doing good, publishing his *Temperance Rhymes* anonymously in 1839 (*L*, 187). Unitarian ministers were intellectually open-minded. Biological evolution they thought consistent with God's plan for human progress. In a fine funeral sermon of 1859 for J. A. Nicholls, Gaskell also drew an analogy from the scientific theory that no particle of matter is ever annihilated. For him, both science and theology promised "a new and higher condition of being."[14]

Manchester Unitarianism

Mr Gaskell has promised as soon as the *formal* bridal calls are made, to go with me and introduce me to most of the families under his care, as their minister's wife, and one who intends to try to be their useful friend. My dear colleague too has promised her assistance and advice with regard to my duties.
– Elizabeth Gaskell to William Turner (1832)

Cross Street Chapel's ministers were paid good salaries and expected to take a lead in civic life. In his public capacity William Gaskell wore a dress-suit like older-fashioned Unitarian divines. Robberds, who found the Church of Scotland minister in Dunkeld Cathedral "blithering," shabbily dressed, and sporting "a dirty snuffy silk or cotton handkerchief," could not help contrasting his appearance with that of his slim, elegant colleague Gaskell – "Dissenters as we are," he wrote huffily to his wife.[15] Even so, Robberds preached that religion was more than churchgoing or strong devotional impulses. It should be carried into everyday life. The rich were only stewards of their wealth.

Mary Robberds was the "dear colleague" who was to advise Gaskell how to become a "useful friend" of chapel families in the early days (*FL*, 21). Mary's daughter explains what this came to mean for Gaskell in practice: "She steadily and consistently objected to her time being considered as belonging in any way to her husband's congregation for the purposes of congregational visiting [and ...] leadership in congregational work."[16] However, Gaskell was willing to help the chapel's schools. When teaching some of the girls in her own home conflicted with the opportunity in 1853 to meet the famous actress Fanny Kemble at a dinner, she wrote to Mary Green: "I find I 'cannot serve two masters,' but must just stop at home – and now that's decided" (*FL*, 80).

Her social conscience was randomly exercised, but always practical and discriminating. She would not write for Fanny Mayne's Evangelical *True Briton* because it "much would do harm in a set of people where R. Catholics & protestants are so closely mixed together [Manchester]" (*FL*, 107). She asked her much-loved sister-in-law Mrs. Anne Robson, with her husband, a Unitarian pillar of the Warrington Antislavery Society, not to send on the black lecturer Sarah Parker Remond: both Gaskells disapproved of antislavery feelings being stirred in England, because no "definite, distinct, practical *course of action*" seemed feasible (*L*, 530). Like Charles Dickens, they disdained "telescopic philanthropy."[17] She enlisted Dickens's aid on behalf of a teenage prostitute in prison, "with a wild wistful look in her eyes, as if searching for the kindness she has never known" (*L*, 99). She admired Florence Nightingale for her "utter unselfishness in serving and ministering" at large but deplored her "want of love for individuals" (*L*, 320). Compare her letter of 1855 to Maria James: "I had to be at the school, 2 miles from here at 9, – till 12; then on to see a family of nine children who have just lost their mother in a confinement" (*FL*, 121). She then writes at length about rescuing a little girl left with a deranged father.

Doctrine and devotion

> I quite agree with you in feeling more devotional in Church than in Chapel; and I wish our Puritan ancestors had not left out so much that they might have kept in of the beautiful and impressive Church service.
> – Elizabeth Gaskell to Marianne Gaskell (1854)

One school suggested for Marianne was turned down without hesitation. It was "so common – the very worst style of dogmatic hard Unitarianism, utilitarian to the backbone" (*L*, 136). Gaskell loved the poetry of George Herbert and Wordsworth, and read and quoted from Dante's Italian and the French of Saint Francis de Sales in *North and South* (1855). She found High Anglican services spiritually nourishing as well as beautiful, apart from their references to God the Father, Son, and Holy Ghost. "The one thing I *am* clear and sure about is this that Jesus Christ was not equal to His father; that, however divine a being he was *not* God," she told Marianne, stressing Unitarian dogma in this instance (*L*, 860); but her private devotions were informed by the pious Anglican reticence of John Keble's "Evening" hymn from *The Christian Year* (1827) and the humble trust of John Henry Newman's "Lead, kindly Light" from *Lyra Apostolica* (1836).[18] Even fideism ("We do not reason – we believe") and the inward, poetic spirituality of the time are seen in *North and South*, where Margaret Hale in distress spent hours upon the beach, "soothed without knowing how or why" by "the eternal psalm" of the waves (*NS*, II, 24:414).

She steered her own course through a mesh of cross-currents. Unitarian ministry at Cross Street became too inflexible for her: "So his colleague Mr Ham goes (and we women Gaskells are none of us sorry, – oh! for some really spiritual devotional preaching instead of controversy about doctrines, – about whh I am more & more certain *we can never be certain* in this world)" (*L*, 537). Ham's young successor in 1859, James Drummond, was "so tender as well as so earnest in his religious feelings" that she felt like his mother in private life and a disciple when he was in the pulpit (*FL*, 217). No doubt she was creating a suitably docile female persona for her correspondent, an American Unitarian minister, but her preferences are clear. When her young daughter Florence became engaged in 1863 to a Cambridge academic, Charles Crompton ("not exactly a Unitarian, nor exactly Broad Church"), she found him religious-minded but lacking in poetry and imagination (*L*, 706). He was not "what one calls *spiritual*" (*L*, 706). It is true that she clung to her children, but her attitude to male authority was ever fluctuating, often ironic, never simple.

Non-Unitarian connections

When Manchester New College returned from York in 1840, Francis Newman, an extreme freethinker, became professor of classics, a post he held until 1846. To Gaskell he seemed entirely holy, modest, and openhearted. And when in 1863 he returned to Manchester to give a talk on antislavery, her husband, too, was "*admiring* almost to enthusiasm, which as you know," Susanna Winkworth wrote to her sister Catherine, "is saying much in Mr. Gaskell's case."[19] Both sisters had studied German with William Gaskell. Susanna, introduced by Gaskell to the liberal theologian Karl J. von Bunsen, became Unitarian for a time and was an influential translator of German mystical writings in the 1850s. Catherine, who remained an Anglican and yet a very special friend of Gaskell, was a superb translator of German hymns.

After the national success of *Mary Barton* in 1848, friendships outside Manchester multiplied remarkably. Gaskell distributed the publications of the Christian Socialists F. D. Maurice, J. M. Ludlow, and Charles Kingsley as widely as she could; though Anglicans, they regarded her stories as those of a natural ally. She began to move in very superior Anglican circles. In May 1853 she went "with the Dean of Hereford, and the Dean of Salisbury (for a good Unitarian Ly Coltman knows a mighty number of Deans) to see Mr Nashs reformatory schools" (*L*, 858). She visited the home of a revisionist historian of Christianity, Henry Hart Milman, Dean of St Paul's Cathedral. A stay in the Close at Winchester with Mrs. Catherine Lyall, widow of the Dean of Canterbury, made her "inclined to resent any disturbance of the vested interest of the dignified clergy by whom I was surrounded" (*FL*, 217–18). She jokes about the incongruity, but Manchester Unitarians, some of whom actively disliked her, seem lost in her wake. Although William Gaskell and others must have supported her, the first volume of *Ruth* was burned by two men in his congregation and another forbade his wife to read it.

At Oxford, "that sweet City with its dreaming spires," she met Matthew Arnold, the son of an old friend and the new professor of poetry at the university.[20] She made many non-Manchester friends among the clerical Fellows during 1857. She already knew the professor of ecclesiastical history, Arthur Stanley, and his mother Catherine through Cheshire connections. Like other advanced thinkers, Stanley supported Benjamin Jowett, Regius Professor of Greek, who was under continuous fire for subjecting the Bible to "Higher Criticism." Gaskell noted that one of his persecutors was the principal of King's College London who had "turned out Mr Fred Maurice from his professorship there on acct of his heresy about the eternal duration of punishment" back in 1853 (*L*, 609). Her private, up-to-date partisanship coexisted with a nostalgic longing for custom and ceremony. In Magdalen Chapel, she rejoiced, there was "so beautiful a service that we must needs go and attend the evening service (an hour later) in New College Chapel" (*L*, 481).

In the 1850s she often visited Paris, relishing the diverse, sophisticated Continental society she met at the *salonnière* Madame Mohl's. In 1857 she went on to Rome for a long stay, taking her daughters Marianne and Meta, both in their early twenties, and Catherine Winkworth. They attended spectacular Holy Week ceremonies in the Vatican, with tickets provided by Monsignor George Talbot, a papal chamberlain. They hoped to hear Father Henry Manning, formerly an Anglican archdeacon, preach (famous preachers were a Victorian diversion). His tally of converts ran into hundreds, but he and other Catholics in Rome, especially Aubrey de Vere, failed in their attempts to convert the Gaskells, according to Catherine Winkworth. We do not know the details, as no more than a few unimportant notes by Gaskell, an inveterate letter-writer, have survived. Afterward, she ached with yearning for Italy – for its bewitching scenes and the company of Anglo-American expatriates rather than for Italians and Catholicism. Like Ellinor in "A Dark Night's Work" (1863), she seems to have renewed her artistic youth in Rome.

In 1850 Pius IX had reestablished the Roman Catholic hierarchy in England, appointing Nicholas Wiseman Cardinal Archbishop of Westminster. "Papal aggression" was furiously condemned. Robberds rather cleverly preached against "the spirit of popery" in all churches. Charlotte Brontë, in London the following year, sent a venomous description of Wiseman to her father in Haworth. In comparison, Gaskell treated the Roman Catholicism of Frederick Hale and his Spanish wife in *North and South* with delicacy, and in 1860 (a year in which John Relly Beard branded Romanism "the abomination of desolation") she wrote sympathetically to the Knutsford minister's wife, Mary Green, about her son John Philip, a Roman Catholic convert.[21] When news came that Marianne, in Rome with friends during 1862, had fallen under Manning's "evil influence," it was a great shock (L, 682). Gaskell deplored Marianne's susceptibility and supported her husband, whose position as a senior Unitarian minister must have been a factor. But it is to William that she attributes an "*extreme dislike & abhorrence of R. C-ism*" (L, 687). And after this she displayed tolerance more than once in her fiction, most notably in her warm-hearted treatment of Osborne Hamley and his Roman Catholic wife in *Wives and Daughters*.

Conclusion

> I did feel as if I had some thing to say about it that I *must* say, and you know I
> can tell stories better than any other way of expressing myself.
> – Elizabeth Gaskell to Mary Green (1853)

Gaskell's conscience drove her to publish works that seriously upset the complacent and uncaring, even if they were important members of her husband's congregation. Unitarian in a deeper sense, she laid bare social and moral evils and yet showed that reconciliation and redemption could spring out of human suffering. Her practical charity and sense of duty in times of distress made her work to the point of breakdown in Manchester, but she increasingly traveled in Britain and abroad, deliberately searching out very different cultures and beliefs. As she had written to Catherine Winkworth, "I am myself and nobody else, and can't be bound by another's rules" (*L*, 64). She found the beauty of Anglican liturgy particularly appealing, and responded to the language and spirituality of many authors, whether they were Unitarians or not. She cultivated but did not completely agree with more radical young friends. A residual conventionality combined with her impulsive, mercurial nature to make her condemn other people's behavior too easily, most obviously in her biography of Brontë.

Yet her fiction is often animated by humor. The invasion of "good, orthodox, aristocratic, and agricultural Hanbury" by "Baptism, Bakers, Bread, and Birmingham" is gently satirized in *My Lady Ludlow* (1858); the Established Church is said to regard Dissenters "almost as if they were rhinoceroses."[22] More seriously, in *North and South* Mr. Hale's conscience impels him to leave his Anglican vicarage to become a Dissenter in a northern city, leading up to a tableau of typically Unitarian tolerance: "Margaret the Churchwoman, her father the Dissenter, Higgins the Infidel, knelt down together. It did them no harm" (*NS*, II, 3:233). Similarly, Farmer Holman, the Independent preacher in *Cousin Phillis* (1864), is shown chanting a psalm in the fields, just like the Lutherans in "Six Weeks at Heppenheim" (1862) who sing their harvest hymn in the vineyard. Against such heartfelt evocations of harmony and community, we must set Gaskell's idiosyncratic liking for terror and the supernatural. She could not resist inventing a grandmother witch for "The Poor Clare" (1856) in this exploration of madness, revenge, and the uncanny. In her historical novella *Lois the Witch* (1859), she plumbed savage depths of evil, hysteria, and irrational superstition in 1690s Salem. She was unusually receptive, with an interest, like Robert Browning's Bishop Blougram, "on the dangerous edge of things," so alien to both the science of her day and the Enlightenment lucidity of her Unitarian inheritance.[23] "I am not," she once declared to Henry Bright with her usual verve, "(*Unitarianly*) orthodox!" (*L*, 784–5).

Notes

1 See R. K. Webb, "The Gaskells as Unitarians," in Joanne Shattock, ed., *Dickens and Other Victorians: Essays in Honour of Philip Collins* (New York: St. Martin's Press, 1988), 144–71, 144–6; J. A. V. Chapple, *Elizabeth Gaskell: The Early Years* (Manchester: Manchester University Press, 1997), 32–3, 46.

2 See Michael Wheeler, "Elizabeth Gaskell and Unitarianism," *Gaskell Society Journal* 6 (1992), 32–9.

3 William Stevenson to Elizabeth Stevenson, July 2, 1827, quoted in Chapple, *Elizabeth Gaskell*, 287.

4 [William Johnson Fox], "On the Character and Writings of the Rev. T. Belsham," *Monthly Repository and Review* 38 ns. (February 1830), 73–88; (March 1830), 162–72; (April 1830), 244–53, 80–1.

5 See R. K. Webb, "The Background: English Unitarianism in the Nineteenth Century," in Leonard Smith, ed., *Unitarian to the Core: Unitarian College Manchester, 1854–2004* (Lancaster: Carnegie Publishing, 2004), 11–13.

6 Caleb Stetson, *On Piety at Home* (Newcastle: J. Marshall, 1832), 5.

7 [Fox], "On the Character," 251.

8 *Ibid.*

9 *Ibid.*

10 On changes in Unitarian thinking, see Angus Easson, *Elizabeth Gaskell* (London: Routledge & Kegan Paul, 1979), 8–12, 22, and Webb, "The Gaskells as Unitarians," 146–51. On Gaskell's response to Bulwer, see Chapple, *Elizabeth Gaskell*, 389.

11 W. J. Fox, quoted in Richard and Edward Garnett, *The Life of W. J. Fox* (London: John Lane, 1910), 112.

12 See Kathryn Gleadle, *The Early Feminists: Radical Unitarians and the Emergence of the Women's Rights Movement, 1831–51* (Basingstoke: Palgrave Macmillan, 1998), 5–7, 29–57, 112–13.

13 William Gaskell, *Protestant Practices Inconsistent with Protestant Principles* (London: H. Hunter; Manchester: Johnson and Rawson, 1836), 13.

14 See William Gaskell, *Christian Views of Life and Death* (London: E. T. Whitfield; Manchester: Johnson and Rawson, 1859), 9, 13.

15 John Gooch Robberds, quoted in Chapple, *Elizabeth Gaskell*, 410.

16 Mary Jane Herford, quoted in Chapple, *Elizabeth Gaskell*, 425.

17 Charles Dickens, *Bleak House* [1853], ed. Nicola Bradbury (Harmondsworth: Penguin, 1996), ch. 4.

18 See *L*, 863; *FL*, 221, 300, 184; *NS*, II, 16:348.

19 Susanna Winkworth to Catherine Winkworth, June 4, 1863, in Susanna Winkworth and M. J. Shaen, eds., *Letters and Memorials of Catherine Winkworth*, 2 vols. (Clifton: E. Austen, 1883–6), 2:391–2. Information provided by Peter Skrine.

20 Matthew Arnold, "Thyrsis," in *Arnold: Poems*, selected by Kenneth Allott (Harmondsworth: Penguin, 1954), l. 19.

21 John Beard, *The Confessional: A View of Romanism* (London: Simpkin, Marshall, 1860), ii–iv. For Gaskell's letter to Mary Green, see *FL*, 209–11.

22 Elizabeth Gaskell, *My Lady Ludlow*, ed. Charlotte Mitchell, in *The Works of Elizabeth Gaskell*, 10 vols. (London: Pickering and Chatto, 2005), III, 14:282, 290; 10:239.

23 Robert Browning, "Bishop Blougram's Apology," in *Robert Browning's Poetry*, ed. James F. Loucks (New York: Norton, 1979), l. 395.

12

SUSAN HAMILTON

Gaskell then and now

Writing to an unknown correspondent in 1862, Gaskell insisted that "I do not think I ever cared for literary fame; nor do I think it *is* a thing that ought to be cared for. It comes and it goes" (*L*, 694). The story of Gaskell's rise and fall in literary status is well known. That literary status has alternately gathered strength and dissipated in the near 150 years since her sudden death in 1865 from heart failure aged fifty-five, at the peak of her writing career: she was feted during her lifetime but fell into obscurity after her death. Yet, although the narrative arc of Gaskell's reputation is well charted, it nonetheless bears closer scrutiny.

In the months immediately following her death, Gaskell's contemporaries cared a great deal about her fame. Newspaper obituaries and periodical press summations of her writing laid the groundwork for a reputation that was later chased into the shadows by modernism's onslaught on the Victorians, and remained remarkably unchanged until revisited in the 1960s and 1970s by materialist and feminist critics. Gaskell's reputation has since regained lost ground, and been given nuance and complexity – as much the result of shifting critical investments in literary studies as of the fact that literary reputation itself is now the subject of critical inquiry. Gaskell's reputation continues to have its champions and detractors. But most distinctive in the push and pull defining Gaskell's critical fortunes has been the way that her reputation has been shaped until very recently by a robust critical impulse to define her writing achievements by a single book. Whether the book is *Cranford* (1853) or *North and South* (1855), *Cousin Phillis* (1864), or *Mary Barton* (1848), an urge to identify Gaskell's writing achievement almost exclusively with a single title has yielded a critical reputation deeply riven into opposed streams of writing: the "social problem" novels *Mary Barton*, *Ruth* (1853), and *North and South*, on the one hand, and the novels of provincial life, *Cranford*, *Cousin Phillis*, and *Wives and Daughters* (1866), on the other, with near-complete oblivion for most of her short stories.[1]

The jostling over which book exemplified Gaskell's strengths began immediately after her death. Just days later, Henry Fothergill Chorley, writing in the *Athenaeum* on November 18, 1865, offered the first of many positive but tempered rankings of Gaskell. He considers her "if not the most popular, with small question, the most powerful and finished female novelist of an epoch singularly rich in female novelists" (*CH*, 508). Chorley favors *Wives and Daughters*, "that excellent, quiet story ... involving no 'mission'" (*CH*, 508). The choice of best book is perhaps unduly swayed by Gaskell's still very recent death. Nevertheless, Chorley's embrace of *Wives and Daughters* comes alongside his care to identify and marginalize the novels ranged against that text in his estimation. The "mission" novel *Ruth* is "based on a mistake" and *North and South* is a novel compromised by its origins in "the author's intense but prejudiced desire to right what is wrong" (*CH*, 508). The evaluative streaming of Gaskell's fiction has begun.

The *Saturday Review* on that same day, November 18, 1865, began its review of Gaskell's career confident that she "had written herself into a well-deserved popularity" at the time of her death (*CH*, 509). But the need for careful moderation in praise is soon established. Gaskell is held up as a writer who

> without being unique, or in any sense extraordinarily original in her range of subjects or in her method of treatment, sometimes not rising above a level which has been reached by many other English story-tellers ... sometimes one-sided in social views, sometimes indiscreet in following her personal impulses too blindly, ... has yet achieved a success which will live long after her.
>
> (*CH*, 509)

The *Saturday Review* flatly refuses to endorse the works representing one-sidedness (*Mary Barton* and *North and South*) and indiscretion (*The Life of Charlotte Brontë*, 1857) for posterity, opting for *Cranford* as "the most perfect of Mrs. Gaskell's creations" (*CH*, 509).

In the same way, David Masson, in *Macmillan's Magazine* in the month after her death, writes with warmth that the "world of English letters has just lost one of its foremost authors" (*CH*, 514). He continues, however, with mild praise, which suggests that her writing challenges the urge to rank it highly. Masson determines to rest his praise on the very quality that generates veneration, but also, somehow, reservation: "Other novelists have written books as clever, and many have written books as innocent; but there are few, indeed, who have written works which grown-up men read with delight, and children might read without injury" (*CH*, 517). The innocence of Gaskell's work is lauded; its political strivings downplayed. This intricate praise (itself based on comments about Gaskell made by

George Sand passed along by Richard Monckton Milnes immediately after her death) continues as Masson suggests that it "is impossible to determine now the exact position which Mrs. Gaskell will hold ultimately amongst English writers of our day" (*CH*, 517). "It will be a high one," Masson ventures with confidence, only immediately to temper his approbation by observing, "Miss Austen's popularity has survived that of many writers of her time, whose merits were perhaps greater in themselves" (*CH*, 517).

Here Masson, like Chorley and the *Saturday Review* before him, is stymied by Gaskell's popularity at the time of her death. It is Gaskell's celebrity, the way in which *Mary Barton* claimed such signal success and, more recently, *Wives and Daughters* "acquired almost at once a singular popularity," that discommodes the critical impulse (*CH*, 517). The drive to bind that celebrity to the "right" text appears overwhelmingly pressing. Masson opts finally for *Cranford* and *North and South* as the novels that "will be read when we all are dead and buried," even though he thinks that other novels by other writers "excel them in innate power" (*CH*, 517). The puzzle that is Gaskell's celebrity remains confounding in its effects on critical summations.

Gaskell's celebrity and the quiet charm of the preferred fictions are contradictions that these reviewers find difficult to hold in tension. Masson notes that the celebrity attending *Mary Barton* also brought trouble for Gaskell, a critical disfavor that returned with the publication of the contentious *Ruth* and *The Life of Charlotte Brontë*. There is a sense here that the narrative arc of Gaskell's fame is somehow incoherent, with a meteoric rise failing to be followed by greater and surer successes. The popular but unprovocative provincial novels seem one way out of an ostensible critical impasse. Certainly, the urge to eulogize Gaskell as a woman writer seemed to preclude the possibility of placing her politics at the front and center of any critical assessment. Masson's review, which begins by noting the unseemliness of invading Gaskell's privacy, prefers to focus on the "quiet" provincial novels, the "perfection and completeness," the "gentle sadness" of Gaskell's writing, as the only fitting testimony to a popular woman writer. As Linda K. Hughes and Michael Lund argue in *Victorian Publishing and Mrs. Gaskell's Work*, Victorian assessments of Gaskell's career followed Masson's lead in their overall tendency to commend the "quiet," nostalgic achievements of *Cranford*, *Cousin Phillis*, and *Wives and Daughters*, and to characterize Gaskell's strengths as emotional rather than intellectual.[2]

Only a few of the northern papers preferred to highlight Gaskell's overtly political or "social condition" novels in their assessments of her career in the months following her death. The *Unitarian Herald*, with which William

Gaskell was associated, insisted on a link between Gaskell's personal life and her literary celebrity, documenting home visiting, work with prison philanthropist Thomas Wright, and her tutoring of working girls in geography and English history, as the basis of "that sympathetic insight into the character of our northern manufacturing poor, which has been one of the strongest elements of her literary success" (*CH*, 507). Hughes and Lund stress that the *Unitarian Herald* chose to elaborate on Gaskell's unconventional domesticity. She "steadily and consistently objected to her time being considered as belonging in any way to her husband's congregation for the purposes of congregational visiting, and to being looked to for that leadership in congregational work which is too often expected of 'the minister's wife.'"[3] The *Manchester Guardian*, too, claimed Gaskell for the north and so, implicitly for a nineteenth-century reader, for provocative politics. Endorsing *Mary Barton* and *North and South* over her other works, the *Manchester Guardian* finds the social problem novel to be as "representative of its writer as of special phases in modern society," and lauds Gaskell as a "writer fresh, untrammelled, uninfluenced by, the 'spirit of the age'" (*CH*, 484, 485). Writing against the grain already so visible in the eulogies after Gaskell's death, the newspaper not only favors the industrial novels that other periodicals sidestep, but deliberately skirts the charming provincial stories so central to other assessments. *Wives and Daughters*, for the *Manchester Guardian*, is "a less characteristic work" (*CH*, 485). Even in these dissenting assessments, however, the privileging of Gaskell's social problem fiction comes at the expense of a woman writer's conscious political intent. The newspaper insists that Gaskell wrote with "purity of purpose," shielding her posthumous reputation from accusations of bias (*CH*, 486). The *Unitarian Herald* likewise indicated that Gaskell's insight into the Manchester working class was "unconsciously" acquired (*CH*, 507).

Nearly a decade later, William Minto's comments in the *Fortnightly Review* testify to the grip that these initial critical assessments had on Gaskell's reputation, as they repeatedly created and then favored a separate "provincial" stream of writing. Minto was "one of [Gaskell's] most thoughtful critics," as Kathleen Tillotson described him in 1954.[4] His appraisal of Gaskell's writing stands out in the decade after her death for granting so central a place to the "social problem" fiction in her reputation. His September 1878 article revisits critical responses to *Mary Barton* in the wake of a reprinting of W. R. Greg's powerful critique of that novel's political message. Minto is full of praise for Gaskell's imaginative powers, and aims to rebut Greg's contention that the novelist held a prejudiced "brief" for the working men of Manchester, countering that Gaskell's "brief," if she had one, was much larger. "To promote a better under-standing between different sections of society," writes Minto, "to remove prejudices, to enlarge the limits of tolerance and charity, to dispel the ignorance of ways of life different from our own ... may be said to have been the central purpose of all Mrs. Gaskell's earlier novels" (CH, 558). But what is also significant about Minto's comments is his simultaneous delimiting of the importance he gives to the "social problem" novels even as he grants it in his assessment. Picking up on the deflection of overt political purpose in the northern newspapers, Minto suggests that if Gaskell had a central purpose in writing, she also "does not seem to have been conscious of any moral intention, but to have simply obeyed her strong descriptive instinct" (CH, 560). She is a writer "whose works touch the heart rather than the imagination or the philosophical intellect" (CH, 561).

Minto's judicious critical response to Greg ends with the now char-acteristic putting of Gaskell in her womanly place, here smoothly done. Celebrated as she was in her day, and as popular as she remains, Gaskell's ranking ten years after her death is among "those who are comparatively unambitious in their efforts, and who, having a just measure of their own powers, succeed perfectly in what they undertake" (CH, 562). Gaskell's virtues are decidedly feminine ones: unconscious artistry and moderation. Her achievement is to have perfected her art "within a definite field, without straining to get beyond it" (CH, 563). Like many a reviewer before him who had relegated Gaskell to the lower echelons of reputable nine-teenth-century writers, Minto now adds to her unassuming status the virtue of Gaskell's apparent complicity in her second-rate ranking. She never intended, "strained," to go higher.

In her own day, as we see in these reviews, the debate on the "woman question" that dominated the periodical and serial presses raised the question of what a woman could write about, and whether or not she should write at all. Should a woman, to adapt Minto's terms, write beyond the "definite field" assigned her by Victorian culture? Masson had observed that Gaskell's private life "differed from those of most women who write novels, in being calmer and less eventful. Neither necessity, nor the unsatisfied solitude of a single life, nor, as I fancy, an irresistible impulse, threw her into the paths of literature. She wrote, as the birds sing, because she liked to write" (CH, 514). The need to make sense of a woman's writing career, either as compensation for an absent domestic life or, as in Mrs. Gaskell's case, as no more than the effortless expression of a natural gift for storytelling, is profound. But what is also voiced in these reviews is a perceived tension between Gaskell's celebrity and the consistency of her writing, as if the "pull" between literary reputation and domesticity would naturally have an unbalancing effect.

The gendered terms of appraisals such as Masson's reach an apotheosis in David Cecil's influential reading of her work in *Early Victorian Novelists: Essays in Revaluation* (1934). I will reprise these terms at some length because, like Chorley, Masson, and Minto before him, Cecil's evaluation of Gaskell's work laid down the terms that shaped critical responses to her work for decades to come. It is tempting to read Cecil's appraisal as exceptional, so uncompromising is its resolve to respond to her work solely through the terms of the most traditional of gender scripts. But I would argue that whereas the clarity of Cecil's script is exceptional, the conclusions of his critical practice are not. We can draw a direct line linking Cecil to the writers who, immediately after her death, sought to make sense of the popular and esteemed woman writer. More than any one review, Cecil's revaluation of Gaskell settled her in a vision of limpid domesticity that proved intractable for decades. His resounding and unassailable answer to all the critical conundrums that Gaskell's writing presents is domesticity.

By 1934 the solution to the problem that Gaskell's reputable celebrity presented to her critics was fully solved by her femininity. Her celebrity and status (as carefully circumscribed as ever) come to rest precisely on that which seems most to jar against them: her domesticity. For Cecil, it is Gaskell's domesticity and womanhood that won her the place she held in English literary history. His appraisal is significant for its unflinching embrace of the determining effects of femininity on Gaskell's literary status. In Cecil's much-repeated opening dictum, "[t]he outstanding fact about Mrs. Gaskell is her femininity."[5] From here, the gender script is rolled out, yard after yard, without hesitation. Gaskell is a "dove" where other women writers such as Charlotte Brontë and George Eliot are eagles. She is "all a woman was expected to be; gentle, domestic, tactful, unintellectual, prone to tears, easily shocked" (198). She is "not a powerful writer" (200), "not sophisticated" (206), and her "charm at once exquisite and natural, homely and delicate [is] the charm of an untaught voice ... of a child's unconscious grace of movement" (208).

There are times when Cecil flirts dangerously with derision. If Gaskell is not a powerful writer in his estimation, Cecil also denies her the power of the limited domestic world in which he so firmly fixes her. "[E]ven such violent emotions as ladies in vicarages did feel," Cecil explains, "are beyond Mrs. Gaskell's imaginative range" (200). Extolling Gaskell's "freshness of outlook," Cecil lingers over her "mental palate, fed always, as it were, on the fruit and frothing milk of her nursery days" (207). She "utters the most time-honoured reflections with the unselfconscious, unhesitating interest of one to whom they have never occurred before"(207). Rescuing himself just before the point of brute attack, Cecil is quick to pull back, however, observing that "we, caught by the youthful infection of her spirit, listen to it as if for the first time too" (207). Here Gaskell's talent for "refreshment" has as its beneficiary the sophisticated world-weary critic of the 1930s, long weaned from his nursery milk; but the link to the cognoscenti of the London press, who took one-sided pleasure in Gaskell's ability to whisk them away from the urban intensity of an industrial world to the muted delights of provincial town life, is clear.

The litmus test of Gaskell's limitations is, in Cecil's view, her inability to present a masculine world. Granted that her world is "narrow," Gaskell compounds her limitations by her inability to "draw a full-length portrait of a man," even such men as inhabit the small worlds she reigns over (209). This limitation, true for almost all women novelists by Cecil's account, is "glaringly true" (209) for Mrs. Gaskell. The "submissive, super-feminine character of the Victorian woman impeded her view of them, even in so far as they did come within her line of vision" (210). Such limitations are paired with few strengths, and even those do not denote a conscious artist at work, but a consummate housewife. Gaskell's style, "less obviously faulty than that of her contemporaries," is not the consequence of artistic integrity. Rather, "her tidy feminine mind would have been ashamed to let her inspiration appear before the world in so careless and ill-fitting a dress." In any case, "it is not, of course, a great style" (230).

Cecil concludes with the expected favoring of the domestic and pastoral line in Gaskell's oeuvre. What are "imperishable," Cecil writes, are *Sylvia's Lovers* (1863), *Cranford*, *Cousin Phillis*, and *Wives and Daughters*. Within that list, *Sylvia's Lovers* (hardly discussed at all in the forty-four pages devoted to Gaskell) and *Cousin Phillis* "are not great, in any sense of the word." *Cranford* and *Wives and Daughters* are "not exactly great either. But they express a stronger side of Mrs. Gaskell's talent. And they have their place among the classic English domestic novels" (240). It is hard not to conclude that Cecil has revaluated Gaskell right out of literary history.

I have excerpted Cecil's remarks at such length not to belabor their gendered terms, but to ensure that the critical weight of the remarks is well registered. His comments have left an indelible mark, if only because of the gargantuan task left to critics who seek to dispel them. The first reappraisals of Gaskell's work necessarily ranged themselves against him, however discreetly. Those reconsiderations gained ground in the 1950s with the appearance of such studies as Aina Rubenius's *The Woman Question in Mrs Gaskell's Life and Works* (1950), Annette Hopkins's *Elizabeth Gaskell: Her Life and Works* (1952), Kathleen Tillotson's *Novels of the Eighteen-Forties* (1954), and Arnold Kettle's "The Early Victorian Social-Problem Novel" (1958).[6] Hopkins's book sought to secure Gaskell's reputation through a study of the influences of French fiction on her narrative forms, a view of Gaskell as worldly and sophisticated that Cecil would not recognize. Kettle's chapter, "The Early Victorian Social-Problem Novel," claims the centrality of Gaskell's industrial novels not just to her reputation, but to the formation of early Victorian culture. Tillotson's influential book went even further, claiming Gaskell as the exemplary writer of social-problem fiction. Where Cecil echoed many of Gaskell's contemporary critics in seeing her social problem novels as ill-conceived "writing outside her range," Tillotson lauded Gaskell's writing strategies as those of an astute political writer who knows how to gain an audience for her ideas. Commenting on the opening chapters of *Mary Barton*, "the outstanding example – outstanding in merit as in contemporary fame," Tillotson praises Gaskell's slowness and reassurance as choices.[7] The reassessment is certain, but the split between domestic and social problem novels, so decided at her death, remains in such studies. Significantly, Cecil's book was reissued in 1958, when the reappraisals had gained ground. Cecil offered a new preface with the reissue, but no new critical judgments. A second substantial surge of interest in Gaskell marked the centenary of her death. Alongside the monumental edition of her letters by Arthur Pollard and J. A. V. Chapple, Edgar Wright's *Mrs. Gaskell: The Basis for Reassessment* (1965) sought to establish Gaskell as a major novelist of a period fast coming back into critical fashion.[8]

It was the early feminist attention of the 1970s and 1980s that brought Gaskell back into focus, by vigorously revisiting the problem of domesticity that has haunted her critical reputation since her death. With a set of critical investments that reframes Gaskell's writing in ways that Cecil could not imagine, feminist critics in this period found Gaskell *in her entirety* a politically and ideologically compelling figure. Their feminist critical practice eschewed the narrowly formalist practice, which had hardened Gaskell's minor status on the basis of perceived ideological ambivalence and aesthetic disarray. Studies such as Jenni Calder's *Women and Marriage in Victorian Fiction* (1976), Elaine Showalter's *A Literature of Their Own* (1977), and Nina Auerbach's *Communities of Women* (1978), took up the gendered scripts that Cecil read as self-evident and natural, and turned them to critical account.[9] Showalter's landmark feminist study, in particular her chapter "The Double Critical Standard and the Feminine Novel," catalogues the range of strengths and weaknesses attributed to women writers by nineteenth-century reviewers. Her list, "sentiment, refinement, tact, observation ... [but no] originality, intellectual training, abstract intelligence ... [or] knowledge of male character," establishes that Cecil never got beyond the gendered critical standards of the 1860s, exposing the gender biases of a long trail of reviewers of women's fiction, Gaskell's included, that masqueraded as objective critical assessment.[10] These feminist studies also point to an important shift in Gaskell's reputation. Where contemporary and early twentieth-century summations compared Gaskell to other writers primarily for the purposes of an aesthetic ranking that was implicitly political, these studies used comparative methods to explore Victorian culture. Gaskell matters in these studies because of what she tells us about larger cultural processes in which she participated, both as writer and as celebrity.

Critical response of the 1970s and 1980s follows the lead of this early feminist criticism, but registers also the influence of cultural studies as it explores Gaskell's work for its purchase on the woman question, Victorian celebrity, publishing history, working-class autodidacts, and Chartism, among other concerns. Further, the cultural-studies critical practice now prevalent turns to Gaskell for the very ambivalences that once banished her from the great formalist canon. Given the tendency in cultural studies not to focus on the single author, Gaskell is at this time often one element in a larger field of inquiry.[11] Where she is the focus of a single study, critics offer important revisions of her place in Victorian culture, and point to new directions for critical engagement with her.[12] The work of Hilary Schor and Deirdre d'Albertis, for example, is particularly important for the ways in which it takes up the question of "personality" through a careful study of Gaskell's relation to publicity. These works reconceptualize what it means for an author to circulate as a celebrity.

Most significantly, the massive expansion in Gaskell scholarship has brought new editions of many of Gaskell's texts aimed at enlarging the audience for her work, and making possible new critical engagements. In the past ten years popular publishing houses such as Wordsworth's have brought cheap editions of Gaskell's work to a new public. Prominent academic publishing houses have also repackaged the novels, commissioning new introductions and offering new ways of reading Gaskell's texts, from the densely theoretical to the more traditional offering of contextual information for reading.[13] Gaskell's work once again circulates in a range of editions (from cheap to majestic), as it did when the stunning critical success of *Mary Barton* meant that four editions of the novel were available simultaneously.

Any shortfall in the lists of established houses is remedied by electronic publishing. Mitsuharu Matsuoka, webmaster of the invaluable Gaskell Web, oversees an impressively large e-text archive of Gaskell's published work. Although the archive is editorially uneven, with links to relevant scholarly articles available for some entries but not others, its greatest contribution is in making available editions of the many short stories Gaskell wrote that have not attracted publishing house interest. The stories are presented with a minimum of editorial framing. Most appear without a headnote of any kind, though some begin with a short quotation from A. A. Ward's notes from the 1906 Knutsford edition of Gaskell's works and others make use of a brief note from Jenny Uglow's 1993 biography.[14] The Gaskell e-text archive performs admirable service, making difficult-to-find material readily accessible. But it does not entirely escape all the disadvantages of electronic publishing. Material is presented with little or no editorial framework or is erratically ornamented with notes, photographs, and drawings, including the George Du Maurier sketches that accompanied original publications and amateur photographs of story settings such as Sawley, Pendle Hill, and the well of Pen-Morfa.

Complementing the increased availability of good editions of Gaskell's primary texts, the reissue of Chapple and Pollard's *The Letters of Mrs Gaskell* (1997) and the publication of Chapple and Alan Shelston's *Further Letters of Mrs Gaskell* (2003) make available Gaskell's vibrant, chatty, and quick-witted letters. New biographies – Uglow's authoritative *Elizabeth Gaskell: A Habit of Stories* (1993), Chapple and Anita Wilson's *Private Voices: The Diaries of Elizabeth Cleghorn Gaskell and Sophia Isaac Holland* (1996), Anna Unsworth's *Elizabeth Gaskell: An Independent Woman* (1996), and Chapple's *Elizabeth Gaskell: The Early Years* (1997), also ensure that materials are ready to hand for readers whose interests are as much biographical as they are critical.

Further evidence of the substantial increase in scholarly activity around Gaskell is the publication of a crucial new bibliographical work, Nancy S. Weyant's *Elizabeth Gaskell: An Annotated Bibliography of English-Language Sources, 1976–1991* (1994) and its companion volume, *Elizabeth Gaskell: An Annotated Guide to English Language Sources, 1992–2001* (2004).[15] The first lists 339 sources including twenty-eight Masters theses and senior honours theses, supplementing Robert L. Selig's *Elizabeth Gaskell: A Reference Guide* (1977) and Jeffrey Egan Welch's *Elizabeth Gaskell: An Annotated Bibliography, 1929–1975* (1977).[16] It is the first Gaskell bibliography to make use of computer-database developments in bibliographic studies such as OCLC and RLIN, as well as traditional resources such as *Humanities Index*, *Women's Studies Abstracts*, and the *Comprehensive Bibliography of Victorian Studies*. The companion volume adds hundreds more scholarly items on Gaskell's writing. Weyant excludes book reviews and has developed a "quantitative criterion" in her selection process, which further excludes all sources that mention Gaskell merely in passing or which offer only a short two- or three-page consideration of her work. The articles summarized in Weyant's bibliography attest to the growing importance of Gaskell's short stories, the neglected *Sylvia's Lovers*, and some of her travel writing. In most of her contemporaries' accounts, Gaskell's prolific short stories are almost entirely sidestepped. They were then inconsequential, a critical assessment that has remained true until relatively recently.

Weyant's bibliography also reveals that the boom in the Gaskell industry has been considerably fueled by the Gaskell Society, whose journal has substantially reshaped Gaskell as a figure for study. Combining popular and academic concerns, the Gaskell Society is one of the engines pushing forward the rehabilitation of Gaskell's reputation. Formed in September 1985 after a literary lunch celebrating the 175th anniversary of Gaskell's birth, the Knutsford-based society has branches in America, Italy, and Japan. It also produces an annual scholarly journal, the *Gaskell Society Journal*, and a newsletter with information on society meetings; organizes visits to places associated with Gaskell and her fiction; and hosts an annual conference. The impact of the society and its journal on Gaskell's reputation for popular and academic audiences is difficult to underestimate. Nearly half of the past ten years' academic work on Gaskell has been published in the society's journal.

The question of celebrity, producing as well as safe-guarding Gaskell's reputation as a writer of cultural significance, has also largely fallen to the Gaskell Society and its large web presence. Its success here has been staggering. The society initiated the BBC's 1999 production of *Wives and Daughters*, the success of which led to the BBC's production of *North and South* in 2004. Gaskell joins Jane Austen, George Eliot, and Anthony Trollope as writers to whose books the BBC turns to extend its heritage drama line-up. In joining such company, Gaskell participates in the larger phenomenon of the heritage drama, a genre understood to fulfill a palliative function for a late twentieth- and early twenty-first century British society alarmed by intensified class division and increasing globalization. Madeleine Dobie explores the ways in which the post-heritage genre uses the past to explore current controversial issues.[17] She focuses specifically on the conjunction of the post-heritage drama and the work of pre-twentieth-century women writers, arguing that films of such novels combine a niche-marketing pitch to a feminist-identified audience (in their gestures to social and political concerns of feminism) with an appeal to a broader audience (through their evocation of signature romantic-comedy or date-movie elements). A film adaptation such as *North and South*, marketed as a "passionate love story" set against "the backdrop of Victorian England's industrial north," shows the ways in which Gaskell's novel provides a new canvas on which to draw current preoccupations with class and gender.[18]

The society, working with the Manchester Historical Buildings Trust and the English Heritage Society, is also behind the recent successful push to have Gaskell's last Manchester home, 84 Plymouth Grove, recognized as a literary heritage site. Gaskell has also recently played a part in the city of Manchester's bid to become a United Nations World Heritage Site as the world's first industrialized city. As this activity suggests, Gaskell's canonization on the web has not been a formal or aesthetic one. Where Gaskell's literary output raised critical questions of categorization, labeling, and perhaps of worth for academic readers, her emerging status as a twenty-first-century "celebrity" author, with BBC productions of *Wives and Daughters* and *North and South*, a radio production of *Cranford*, and a central place in Cheshire's tourism industry, suggests that the ambivalence and equivocation that long dogged her critical reception does not shape her "public," nonacademic reputation.

Interestingly, if the web were the primary guardian of Gaskell's reputation, her critical stature would acquire new asymmetries to rival the deeply gendered asymmetries of her contemporaries' approach to her work. Complementing Professor Matsuoka's Gaskell information page, which provides e-texts of Gaskell's work, links to *Gaskell Society Journal* articles, a discussion list, and a range of basic research tools, the Gaskell Society acts as the chief caretaker of Gaskell on the web. This "web Gaskell" is very much the woman settled in her Plymouth Grove home, connected irrevocably to Knutsford, writing masterpieces deserving the greater acclaim that television adaptations can provide, and feted with annual conferences. The other "web Gaskell" is shaped by the claims of tourism (for Manchester, for Knutsford, for Lancashire), and by the claims of the heritage industry, and the BBC. She is as divided a figure as ever she was in 1865. The city of Manchester focuses exclusively on Gaskell as the author of *Mary Barton* in the interests of making vivid the role of "the poor uneducated factory-workers of Manchester" in the shaping of that city (*MB*, xxxv). In its efforts to promote Lancashire as a "place of inspiration for many of our greatest novelists," Lancashire Tourism turns to Gaskell, too.[19] The small Lancashire town of Carnforth presents a Gaskell "escaping the unhealthy atmosphere of the city" as often as she can by fleeing to Silverdale.[20] Unsurprisingly, Lancashire Tourism claims *Cranford*, not *Mary Barton*, for itself, suggesting that Gaskell based the novel on "the nearby town of Carnforth, a charming market town not far from Silverdale."[21] The divisions are etched once more.

In the epilogue to their study, Hughes and Lund quote Anne Thackeray Ritchie's preface to an 1891 edition of *Cranford*: "It remains for readers of this later time to see how nobly she held her own among the masters of her craft."[22] The question of whether or not Gaskell "holds her own" still partially animates the scholarly debate of her work. We are still entangled in the inheritance of a critical tradition founded on the eulogies and critical reviews that appeared immediately after Gaskell's death, and which saw her work as formally and aesthetically incoherent and ideologically over-determined. Yet years of Gaskell criticism demonstrate beyond any question that past and present assessments of Gaskell are important for what they tell us about Gaskell and Victorian culture and the history of literary-critical practice. Gaskell now "holds her own" in new places, for new audiences, and in different ways. Heritage-granting bodies, television production studios, academic conferences, and tourism industries, produce different Gaskells – often domestic, as often industrial. The constant reconsideration of Gaskell's status, begun in 1865 by the writers of her obituaries and those who reviewed her literary career, continues with different questions and different scripts.

Notes

1 For a recent attempt to tie Gaskell's reputation to a single text, in this case *North and South*, see Malcolm Pittock, "The Dove Ascending: The Case for Elizabeth Gaskell," *English Studies* 6 (2000), 531–47.

2 Linda K. Hughes and Michael Lund, *Victorian Publishing and Mrs. Gaskell's Work* (Charlottesville: University of Virginia Press, 1999), 158–9.

3 *Ibid.*, 159.

4 Kathleen Tillotson, *Novels of the Eighteen-Forties* (London: Clarendon Press, 1954), 208.

5 Lord David Cecil, *Early Victorian Novelists: Essays in Revaluation* (London: Constable, 1934), 197. Further references will be made parenthetically in the text.

6 Aina Rubenius, *The Woman Question in Mrs Gaskell's Life and Works* (Nendeln: Kraus, 1950); Annette Hopkins, *Elizabeth Gaskell: Her Life and Works* (London: J. Lehmann, 1952); Tillotson, *Novels of the Eighteen-Forties*; and Arthur Kettle, "The Early Victorian Social-Problem Novel," in Boris Ford, ed., *From Dickens to Hardy*, Pelican Guide to English Literature, 6 vols. (Harmondsworth: Penguin, 1958).

7 Tillotson, *Novels of the Eighteen-Forties*, 202.

8 Edgar Wright, *Mrs. Gaskell: The Basis for Reassessment* (Oxford: Oxford University Press, 1965).

9 Jenni Calder, *Women and Marriage in Victorian Fiction* (Oxford: Oxford University Press, 1976); Elaine Showalter, *A Literature of Their Own* (Princeton: Princeton University Press, 1977); and Nina Auerbach, *Communities of Women* (Cambridge, MA: Harvard University Press, 1978).

10 Showalter, *A Literature of Their Own*, 90.

11 See Christine L. Krueger, *The Reader's Repentance: Women Preachers, Women Writers, and Nineteenth-Century Social Discourse* (Chicago: University of

Chicago Press, 1992); Amanda Anderson, *Tainted Souls and Painted Faces: The Rhetoric of Fallenness in Victorian Culture* (Ithaca: Cornell University Press, 1993); Elizabeth Langland, *Nobody's Angels: Middle-class Women and Domestic Ideology in Victorian Culture* (Ithaca: Cornell University Press, 1995); Elsie B. Michie, *Outside the Pale: Cultural Exclusion, Gender Difference, and the Victorian Woman Writer* (Ithaca: Cornell University Press, 1995); and Mary Poovey, *Making a Social Body: British Cultural Formation, 1830–1864* (Chicago: University of Chicago Press, 1995).

12 Hilary Schor, *Scheherezade in the Marketplace: Elizabeth Gaskell and the Victorian Novel* (New York: Oxford University Press, 1992); Deirdre d'Albertis, *Dissembling Fictions: Elizabeth Gaskell and the Victorian Social Text* (New York: St. Martin's Press, 1997).

13 Shirley Foster usefully compares the Oxford, Penguin, and Everyman editions in "Gaskell in Paper," *Gaskell Society Journal* 11 (1997), 96–102. http://www. Lang.nagoya-u.ac.jp/~matsuoka/EG-Foster-Paper.html.

14 Jenny Uglow, *Elizabeth Gaskell: A Habit of Stories* (London: Faber and Faber, 1993).

15 Nancy S. Weyant, *Elizabeth Gaskell: An Annotated Bibliography of English Language Sources, 1976–1991* (Metuchen, NJ: Scarecrow, 1994), and *Elizabeth Gaskell: An Annotated Guide to English Language Sources, 1992–2001* (Metuchen NJ: Scarecrow, 2004).

16 Robert L. Selig, *Elizabeth Gaskell: A Reference Guide* (Boston: G. K. Hall, 1977), and Jeffrey Egan Welch, *Elizabeth Gaskell: An Annotated Bibliography, 1929–1975* (New York: Garland, 1977).

17 Madelaine Dobie, "Gender and the Heritage Genre," in S. R. Pucci and J. Thompson, eds., *Jane Austen and Co.: Remaking the Past in Contemporary Culture* (Albany: State University of New York Press, 2003), 247–59.

18 See the webpage for the BBC production of *North and South* at http://www.bbc.co.uk/drama/northandsouth

19 See http://www.visitlancashire.com/site/living_legends/famous_lancastrians/literary_connections

20 *Ibid*.

21 *Ibid*.

22 Hughes and Lund, *Victorian Publishing*, 164.

GUIDE TO FURTHER READING

NATALIE ROSE

Primary sources

Chapple, J. A. V. and Arthur Pollard, eds. *The Letters of Mrs. Gaskell.* [1966] Manchester: Mandolin, 1997.
Chapple, John and Alan Shelston, eds. *Further Letters of Mrs. Gaskell.* Manchester: Manchester University Press, 2003.
Chapple, J. A. V. and Anita Wilson, eds. *Private Voices: The Diaries of Elizabeth Gaskell and Sophia Holland.* Keele: Keele University Press, 1996.
Easson, Angus, ed. *Elizabeth Gaskell: The Critical Heritage.* London: Routledge, 1991.
The Works of Elizabeth Gaskell. General ed. Joanne Shattock. Vols. I–III, V, VII. London: Pickering and Chatto, 2005.

Biography

Chapple, John. *Elizabeth Gaskell: A Portrait in Letters.* Manchester: Manchester University Press, 1980.
  Elizabeth Gaskell: The Early Years. Manchester: Manchester University Press, 1997.
Foster, Shirley. *Elizabeth Gaskell: A Literary Life.* Houndmills: Palgrave Macmillan, 2002.
Handley, Graham. *An Elizabeth Gaskell Chronology.* Houndmills: Palgrave Macmillan, 2005.
Uglow, Jenny. *Elizabeth Gaskell: A Habit of Stories.* London: Faber and Faber, 1993.
Unsworth, Anna. *Elizabeth Gaskell: An Independent Woman.* London: Minerva, 1996.

Bibliography

Selig, Robert L. *Elizabeth Gaskell: A Reference Guide.* Boston: G. K. Hall, 1977.
Welch, Jeffrey Egan. *Elizabeth Gaskell: An Annotated Bibliography, 1929–1975.* New York: Garland, 1977.
Weyant, Nancy S. *Elizabeth Gaskell: An Annotated Bibliography of English Language Sources, 1976–1991.* Metuchen, NJ: Scarecrow, 1994.

Elizabeth Gaskell: An Annotated Guide to English Language Sources, 1992–2001. Metuchen, NJ: Scarecrow, 2004.

Selected criticism

Anderson, Amanda. *Tainted Souls and Painted Faces: The Rhetoric of Fallenness in Victorian Culture.* Ithaca: Cornell University Press, 1993. 108–40.

Auerbach, Nina. *Communities of Women: An Idea in Fiction.* Cambridge, MA: Harvard University Press, 1978. 78–97.

Bigelow, Gordon. *Famine, Fiction, and the Rise of Economics in Victorian Britain and Ireland.* Cambridge: Cambridge University Press, 2003. 144–81.

Billington, Josie. "Watching a Writer Write: Manuscript Revisions in Mrs. Gaskell's *Wives and Daughters* and Why They Matter." *Real Voices: On Reading.* Ed. Philip Davis. New York: St. Martin's Press, 1997. 224–35.

Bodenheimer, Rosemarie. "Private Grief and Public Acts in *Mary Barton*." *Dickens Studies Annual* 9 (1981). 195–216.

   The Politics of Story in Victorian Social Fiction. Ithaca: Cornell University Press, 1988. 53–68.

Boiko, Karen. "Reading and (Re)Writing Class: Elizabeth Gaskell's *Wives and Daughters*." *Victorian Literature and Culture* 33 (2005). 85–106.

Bonaparte, Felicia. *The Gypsy-Bachelor of Manchester: The Life of Mrs. Gaskell's Demon.* Charlottesville: University of Virginia Press, 1992.

Brown, Pearl L. "From Elizabeth Gaskell's *Mary Barton* to her *North and South*: Progress or Decline for Women?" *Victorian Literature and Culture* 28 (2000). 345–58.

Chapman, Alison, ed. *Elizabeth Gaskell:* Mary Barton *and* North and South. Icon Critical Guides. Duxford, Cambridge: Icon, 1999.

Childers, Joseph. *Novel Possibilities: Fiction and the Formation of Early Victorian Culture.* Philadelphia: University of Pennsylvania Press, 1995. 158–78.

Colby, Robin. *Some Appointed Work To Do: Women and Vocation in the Fiction of Elizabeth Gaskell.* Westport, CT: Greenwood Press, 1995.

D'Albertis, Deirdre. *Dissembling Fictions: Elizabeth Gaskell and the Victorian Social Text.* New York: St. Martin's Press, 1997.

David, Deirdre. *Fictions of Resolution in Three Victorian Novels:* North and South, Our Mutual Friend, *and* Daniel Deronda. New York: Columbia University Press, 1981. 1–49.

Davis, Deanna L. "Feminist Critics and Literary Mothers: Daughters Reading Elizabeth Gaskell." *Signs* 17 (1992). 507–32.

Dickerson, Vanessa D. *Victorian Ghosts in the Noontide: Women Writers and the Supernatural.* Columbia: University of Missouri Press, 1996. 103–36.

Dodsworth, Martin. Introduction to *North and South.* Harmondsworth: Penguin, 1970.

Dolin, Tim. "*Cranford* and the Victorian Collection." *Victorian Studies* 36 (1993). 179–206.

Eagleton, Terry. "*Sylvia's Lovers* and Legality." *Essays in Criticism* 26 (1976). 17–27.

Easson, Angus. *Elizabeth Gaskell.* London: Routledge, 1979.

Elliott, Dorice Williams. "The Female Visitor and the Marriage of Classes in Gaskell's *North and South*." *Nineteenth-Century Literature* 49 (1994). 21–49.

Ellison, David. "Glazed Expression: *Mary Barton*, Ghosts and Glass." *Studies in the Novel* 36 (2004). 484–508.

Felber, Lynette. "Gaskell's Industrial Idylls: Ideology and Formal Incongruence in *Mary Barton* and *North and South*." *Clio* 18 (1988). 55–72.

Flint, Kate. *Elizabeth Gaskell*. Plymouth: Northcote House, 1995.

Frawley, Maria. "Elizabeth Gaskell's Ethnographic Imagination in *The Life of Charlotte Brontë*." *Biography* 21 (1998). 175–94.

Foster, Shirley. "Violence and Disorder in Elizabeth Gaskell's Short Stories." *Gaskell Society Journal* 19 (2005). 14–24.

Gallagher, Catherine. *The Industrial Reformation of English Fiction: Social Discourse and Narrative Form, 1832–1867*. Chicago: University of Chicago Press, 1985. 62–87.

Gavin, Adrienne. "Language Among the Amazons: Conjuring the Creativity in *Cranford*." *Dickens Studies Annual* 23 (1994). 205–25.

Gillooly, Eileen. "Humor as Daughterly Defense in *Cranford*." *ELH* 59 (1992). 883–910.

Guest, Harriet. "The Deep Romance of Manchester: Gaskell's *Mary Barton*." *The Regional Novel in Britain and Ireland, 1800–1990*. Ed. K. D. M. Snell. Cambridge: Cambridge University Press, 1998. 78–98.

Guy, Josephine. *The Victorian Social-Problem Novel: The Market, The Individual, and Communal Life*. New York: St. Martin's Press, 1996. 137–73.

Hardy, Barbara. "*Cousin Phillis*: The Art of the Novella." *Gaskell Society Journal* 19 (2005). 25–33.

Harman, Barbara Leah. *The Feminine Political Novel in Victorian England*. Charlottesville: University of Virginia Press, 1998. 46–75.

Harsh, Constance D. *Subversive Heroines: Feminist Resolutions of Social Crisis in the Condition-of-England Novel*. Ann Arbor: University of Michigan Press, 1994.

Henson, Louise. "History, Science and Social Change: Elizabeth Gaskell's 'Evolutionary' Narratives." *Gaskell Society Journal* 17 (2003). 12–33.

Homans, Margaret. *Bearing the Word: Language and Female Experience in Nineteenth-Century Women's Writing*. Chicago: University of Chicago Press, 1986. 223–76.

Hughes, Linda K. and Michael Lund. *Victorian Publishing and Mrs. Gaskell's Work*. Charlottesville: University of Virginia Press, 1999.

Ingham, Patricia. *The Language of Gender and Class: Transformation in the Victorian Novel*. London: Routledge, 1996. 55–77; 166–84.

Jaffe, Audrey. "Under Cover of Sympathy: *Ressentiment* in Gaskell's *Ruth*." *Victorian Literature and Culture* 21 (1993). 51–65.

Jenkins, Ruth Y. *Reclaiming Myths of Power: Women Writers and the Victorian Spiritual Crisis*. Lewisburg, PA: Bucknell University Press, 1995. 93–116.

Johnston, Susan. *Women and Domestic Experience in Victorian Political Fiction*. Westport, CT: Greenwood Press, 2001. 83–102; 103–34.

Knezevic, Borislav. "An Ethnography of the Provincial: The Social Ethnography of Gentility in Elizabeth Gaskell's *Cranford*." *Victorian Studies* 41 (1998). 405–26.

Krueger, Christine L. *The Reader's Repentance: Women Preachers, Women Writers, and Nineteenth-Century Social Discourse*. Chicago: University of Chicago Press, 1992. 157–233.

" 'Speaking Like a Woman': How to Have the Last Word on *Sylvia's Lovers*." *Famous Last Words: Changes in Gender and Narrative Closure*. Ed. Alison Booth. Charlottesville: University of Virginia Press, 1993. 135–53.

"The 'Female Paternalist' as Historian: Gaskell's 'My Lady Ludlow.' " *Rewriting the Victorians: Theory, History, and the Politics of Gender*. Ed. Linda M. Shires. London: Routledge, 1992. 166–83.

Kucich, John. "Transgression and Sexual Difference in Elizabeth Gaskell's Novels." *Texas Studies in Language and Literature* 32 (1990). 187–213.

Kuhlman, Mary H. "A Survey of Gaskell Scholarship, or Things Written Recently about Gaskell." *Gaskell Society Journal* 13 (1999). 14–35.

Langland, Elizabeth. *Nobody's Angels: Middle-Class Women and Domestic Ideology in Victorian Culture*. Ithaca: Cornell University Press, 1995. 113–47.

Lansbury, Coral. *Elizabeth Gaskell: The Novel of Social Crisis*. New York: Barnes and Noble, 1975.

Litvack, Leon. "Outposts of Empire: Scientific Discovery and Colonial Displacement in Gaskell's *Wives and Daughters*." *Review of English Studies* 55 (2004). 727–58.

Lucas, John. "Mrs Gaskell and Brotherhood." *Tradition and Tolerance in Nineteenth-Century Fiction*. Ed. David Howard et al. London: Routledge & Kegan Paul, 1966. 141–205.

Malton, Sara A. "Illicit Inscriptions: Reframing Forgery in Elizabeth Gaskell's *Ruth*." *Victorian Literature and Culture* 33 (2005). 293–310.

Masters, Joellen. " 'Nothing More' and 'Nothing Definite': First Wives in Elizabeth Gaskell's *Wives and Daughters*." *Journal of Narrative Theory* 34 (2004). 1–26.

Matus, Jill L. *Unstable Bodies: Victorian Representations of Sexuality and Maternity*. Manchester: Manchester University Press, 1995. 56–88; 113–31.

Michie, Elsie B. *Outside the Pale: Cultural Exclusion, Gender Difference, and the Victorian Woman Writer*. Ithaca: Cornell University Press, 1993. 78–141.

Miller, Andrew. "The Fragments and Small Opportunities of *Cranford*." *Genre* 25 (1992). 91–111.

"Subjectivity Ltd: The Discourse of Liability in the Joint Stock Companies Act of 1856 and Gaskell's *Cranford*." *ELH* 61 (1994). 139–57.

Morris, Pam. *Imaging Inclusive Society in Nineteenth-Century Novels: The Code of Sincerity in the Public Sphere*. Baltimore: Johns Hopkins University Press, 2004. 137–62.

Mossman, Mark. "Speech, Behavior, and the Function of Utopia: Restraint and Resistance in Elizabeth Gaskell's *Cranford*." *Nineteenth-Century Feminisms* 5 (2001). 78–87.

Mulvihill, James. "Economies of Living in Elizabeth Gaskell's *Cranford*." *Nineteenth-Century Literature* 50 (1995). 337–56.

Nash, Julie. " 'Ruled by a Powerful and Decided Nature': Servants and Labor Relations in Gaskell's 'Condition of England Novels.' " *Nineteenth-Century Feminisms* 6 (2002). 19–40.

Nestor, Pauline. *Female Friendships and Communities: Charlotte Brontë, George Eliot, Elizabeth Gaskell*. Oxford: Clarendon Press, 1985. 28–82.

Nord, Deborah Epstein. *Walking the Victorian Streets: Women, Representation, and the City.* Ithaca: Cornell University Press, 1995. 137–78.

O'Farrell, Mary Ann. *Telling Complexions: The Nineteenth-Century English Novel and the Blush.* Durham, NC: Duke University Press, 1997. 58–81.

Parker, Pamela Corpron. "Fictional Philanthropy in Elizabeth Gaskell's *Mary Barton* and *North and South.*" *Victorian Literature and Culture* 25 (1997). 321–31.

"Constructing Female Public Identity: Gaskell on Brontë." *Literature and the Renewal of the Public Sphere.* Ed. Susan VanZanten Gallagher and M. D. Walhout. Basingstoke: Macmillan, 2000. 68–82.

Pettitt, Clare. "Cousin Holman's Dresser: Science, Social Change, and the Pathological Female in Gaskell's *Cousin Phillis.*" *Nineteenth-Century Literature* 52 (1998). 471–89.

Poovey, Mary. "Disraeli, Gaskell, and the Condition of England." *The Columbia History of the British Novel.* Ed. John Richetti. New York: Columbia University Press, 1994. 508–32.

Price, Leah, "The Life of Charlotte Brontë and the Death of Miss Eyre." *SEL* 35 (1995). 757–68.

Pryke, Jo. "The Treatment of Political Economy in *North and South.*" *Gaskell Society Journal* 4 (1990). 28–39.

Reddy, Maureen T. "Gaskell's 'The Grey Woman': A Feminist Palimpsest." *Journal of Narrative Technique* 15 (1985). 183–93.

"Men, Women, and Manners in *Wives and Daughters.*" *Reading and Writing Women's Lives: A Study of the Novel of Manners.* Ed. Bege K. Bowers and Barbara Brothers. Ann Arbor: UMI Research Press, 1990. 68–85.

Ricks, Christopher. *Essays in Appreciation.* Oxford: Clarendon Press, 1996. 118–45.

Rogers, Philip. "The Education of Cousin Phillis." *Nineteenth-Century Literature* 50 (1995). 27–50.

Sanders, Andrew. "Varieties of Religious Experience in *Sylvia's Lovers.*" *Gaskell Society Journal* 6 (1992). 15–24.

Schaffer, Talia. "Craft, Authorial Anxiety, and 'The Cranford Papers.'" *Victorian Periodicals Review* 38 (2005). 222–39.

Schor, Hilary. *Scheherezade in the Marketplace: Elizabeth Gaskell and the Victorian Novel.* New York: Oxford University Press, 1992.

Shaw, Marion. "*Sylvia's Lovers*, Then and Now." *Gaskell Society Journal* 18 (2004). 37–49.

Spencer, Jane. *Elizabeth Gaskell.* Basingstoke: Macmillan, 1993.

Starr, Elizabeth. "'A Great Engine for Good': The Industry of Fiction in Elizabeth Gaskell's *Mary Barton* and *North and South.*" *Studies in the Novel* 34 (2002). 385–402.

Stevenson, Catherine Barnes. "'What Must Not Be Said': *North and South* and the Problem of Women's Work." *Victorian Literature and Culture* 19 (1991). 67–84.

Stone, Donald. *The Romantic Impulse in Victorian Fiction.* Cambridge, MA: Harvard University Press, 1980. 133–72.

Stone, Marjorie. "Bakhtinian Polyphony in *Mary Barton*: Class, Gender, and the Textual Voice." *Dickens Studies Annual* 20 (1991). 175–200.

Stoneman, Patsy. *Elizabeth Gaskell.* Brighton: Harvester, 1987.

Surridge, Lisa. "Working-Class Masculinities in *Mary Barton*." *Victorian Literature and Culture* 28 (2000). 331–43.

Unsworth, Anna. "Some Social Themes in *Wives and Daughters*, I: Education, Science and Heredity." *Gaskell Society Journal* 4 (1990). 40–51.

"Some Social Themes in *Wives and Daughters*, II: The Social Values of the 1860s and 'Old England' Compared." *Gaskell Society Journal* 5 (1991). 51–61.

Watson, J.R. "Elizabeth Gaskell: Heroes and Heroines, and *Sylvia's Lovers*." *Gaskell Society Journal* 18 (2004). 81–94.

Wright, Edgar. *Mrs Gaskell: The Basis for Reassessment*. Oxford: Oxford University Press, 1965.

Wright, Julia M. " 'Growing Pains': Representing the Romantic in Gaskell's *Wives and Daughters*." *Nervous Reactions: Victorian Recollections of Romanticism*. Ed. Joel Faflak and Julia M. Wright. Albany: State University of New York Press, 2004. 163–85.

Wright, Terence. *Elizabeth Gaskell: "We Are Not Angels": Realism, Gender, Values*. Houndmills: Palgrave Macmillan, 1995.

Wynne, Deborah. "Hysteria Repeating Itself: Elizabeth Gaskell's 'Lois the Witch.' " *Women's Writing* 12 (2005). 85–97.

Yeazell, Ruth Bernard. "Why Political Novels Have Heroines: *Sybil*, *Mary Barton* and *Felix Holt*." *Novel* 18 (1985). 126–44.

Zlotnick, Susan. *Women, Writing, and the Industrial Revolution*. Baltimore: Johns Hopkins University Press, 1998. 62–122.

Internet resources

The Gaskell Society. http://gaskellsociety.users.btopenworld.com/index.html

The Gaskell Web. http://www.lang.nagoya-u.ac.jp/~matsuoka/gaskell.html

Index

Cambridge Companions To ...

AUTHORS

Edward Albee edited by Stephen J. Bottoms

Margaret Atwood edited by Coral Ann Howells

W. H. Auden edited by Stan Smith

Jane Austen edited by Edward Copeland and Juliet McMaster

Beckett edited by John Pilling

Aphra Behn edited by Derek Hughes and Janet Todd

Walter Benjamin edited by David S. Ferris

William Blake edited by Morris Eaves

Brecht edited by Peter Thomson and Glendyr Sacks

The Brontës edited by Heather Glen

Byron edited by Drummond Bone

Albert Camus edited by Edward J. Hughes

Willa Cather edited by Marilee Lindemann

Cervantes edited by Anthony J. Cascardi

Chaucer, second edition edited by Piero Boitani and Jill Mann

Chekhov edited by Vera Gottlieb and Paul Allain

Coleridge edited by Lucy Newlyn

Wilkie Collins edited by Jenny Bourne Taylor

Joseph Conrad edited by J. H. Stape

Dante second edition edited by Rachel Jacoff

Charles Dickens edited by John O. Jordan

Emily Dickinson edited by Wendy Martin

John Donne edited by Achsah Guibbory

Dostoevskii edited by W. J. Leatherbarrow

Theodore Dreiser edited by Leonard Cassuto and Claire Virginia Eby

John Dryden edited by Steven N. Zwicker

George Eliot edited by George Levine

T. S. Eliot edited by A. David Moody

Ralph Ellison edited by Ross Posnock

Ralph Waldo Emerson edited by Joel Porte and Saundra Morris

William Faulkner edited by Philip M. Weinstein

F. Scott Fitzgerald edited by Ruth Prigozy

Flaubert edited by Timothy Unwin

Brian Friel edited by Anthony Roche

Robert Frost edited by Robert Faggen

Elizabeth Gaskell edited by Jill L. Matus

Goethe edited by Lesley Sharpe

Thomas Hardy edited by Dale Kramer

Nathaniel Hawthorne edited by Richard Millington

Ernest Hemingway edited by Scott Donaldson

Homer edited by Robert Fowler

Ibsen edited by James McFarlane

Henry James edited by Jonathan Freedman

Samuel Johnson edited by Greg Clingham

Ben Jonson edited by Richard Harp and Stanley Stewart

James Joyce second edition edited by Derek Attridge

Kafka edited by Julian Preece

Keats edited by Susan J. Wolfson

Lacan edited by Jean-Michel Rabaté

D. H. Lawrence edited by Anne Fernihough

David Mamet edited by Christopher Bigsby

Thomas Mann edited by Ritchie Robertson

Christopher Marlowe edited by Patrick Cheney

Herman Melville edited by Robert S. Levine

Arthur Miller edited by Christopher Bigsby

Milton second edition edited by Dennis Danielson

Molière edited by David Bradby and Andrew Calder

Nabokov edited by Julian W. Connolly

Eugene O'Neill edited by Michael Manheim

Ovid edited by Philip Hardie

Harold Pinter edited by Peter Raby

Sylvia Plath edited by Jo Gill

Edgar Allan Poe edited by Kevin J. Hayes

Ezra Pound edited by Ira B. Nadel

Proust edited by Richard Bales

Pushkin edited by Andrew Kahn

Philip Roth edited by Timothy Parrish

Shakespeare edited by Margareta de Grazia and Stanley Wells

Shakespeare on Film edited by Russell Jackson

Shakespearean Comedy edited by Alexander Leggatt

Shakespeare on Stage edited by Stanley Wells and Sarah Stanton

Shakespeare's History Plays edited by Michael Hattaway

Shakespearean Tragedy edited by Claire McEachern

Shakespeare's Poetry edited by Patrick Cheney

George Bernard Shaw edited by Christopher Innes

Shelley edited by Timothy Morton

Mary Shelley edited by Esther Schor

Sam Shepard edited by Matthew C. Roudané

Spenser edited by Andrew Hadfield

Wallace Stevens edited by John N. Serio

Tom Stoppard edited by Katherine E. Kelly

Harriet Beecher Stowe edited by Cindy Weinstein

Jonathan Swift edited by Christopher Fox

Henry David Thoreau edited by Joel Myerson

Tolstoy edited by Donna Tussing Orwin

Mark Twain edited by Forrest G. Robinson

Virgil edited by Charles Martindale

Edith Wharton edited by Millicent Bell

Walt Whitman edited by Ezra Greenspan

Oscar Wilde edited by Peter Raby

Tennessee Williams edited by Matthew C. Roudané

Mary Wollstonecraft edited by Claudia L. Johnson

Virginia Woolf edited by Sue Roe and Susan Sellers

Wordsworth edited by Stephen Gill

W. B. Yeats edited by Marjorie Howes and John Kelly

TOPICS

The Actress edited by Maggie B. Gale and John Stokes

The African American Novel edited by Maryemma Graham

American Modernism edited by Walter Kalaidjian

American Realism and Naturalism edited by Donald Pizer

American Women Playwrights edited by Brenda Murphy

Australian Literature edited by Elizabeth Webby

British Romanticism edited by Stuart Curran

Canadian Literature edited by Eva-Marie Kröller

The Classic Russian Novel edited by Malcolm V. Jones and Robin Feuer Miller

Contemporary Irish Poetry edited by Matthew Campbell

Crime Fiction edited by Martin Priestman

The Eighteenth-Century Novel edited by John Richetti

Eighteenth-Century Poetry edited by John Sitter

English Literature, 1500–1600 edited by Arthur F. Kinney

English Literature, 1650–1740 edited by Steven N. Zwicker

English Literature, 1740–1830 edited by Thomas Keymer and Jon Mee

English Poetry, Donne to Marvell edited by Thomas N. Corns

English Renaissance Drama second edition edited by A. R. Braunmuller and Michael Hattaway

English Restoration Theatre edited by Deborah C. Payne Fisk

Feminist Literary Theory edited by Ellen Rooney

The French Novel: From 1800 to the Present edited by Timothy Unwin

Gothic Fiction edited by Jerrold E. Hogle

Greek and Roman Theatre edited by Marianne McDonald and J. Michael Walton

Greek Tragedy edited by P. E. Easterling

The Irish Novel edited by John Wilson Foster

The Italian Novel edited by Peter Bondanella and Andrea Ciccarelli

Jewish American Literature edited by Hana Wirth-Nesher and Michael P. Kramer

The Latin American Novel edited by Efraín Kristal

Literature of the First World War edited by Vincent Sherry

Medieval English Theatre edited by Richard Beadle

Medieval Romance edited by Roberta L. Krueger

Medieval Women's Writing edited by Carolyn Dinshaw and David Wallace

Modern American Culture edited by Christopher Bigsby

Modern British Women Playwrights edited by Elaine Aston and Janelle Reinelt